PREDATORS AND PARASITES

PREDATORS AND PARASITES

Persistent Agents of Transnational Harm and Great Power Authority

Oded Löwenheim

THE UNIVERSITY OF MICHIGAN PRESS
ANN ARBOR

Copyright © by the University of Michigan 2007
All rights reserved
Published in the United States of America by
The University of Michigan Press
Manufactured in the United States of America
⊚ Printed on acid-free paper

2010   2009   2008   2007   4   3   2   1

A CIP catalog record for this book is available from the British Library.

Library of Congress Cataloging-in-Publication Data

Löwenheim, Oded.
    Predators and parasites : persistent agents of transnational harm
and great power authority / Oded Löwenheim.
        p.   cm.
    Includes bibliographical references and index.
    ISBN-13: 978-0-472-09953-5 (cloth : alk. paper)
    ISBN-10: 0-472-09953-1 (cloth : alk. paper)
    ISBN-13: 978-0-472-06953-8 (pbk. : alk. paper)
    ISBN-10: 0-472-06953-5 (pbk. : alk. paper)
        1. International relations.   2. Great powers.   3. World politics.
    I. Title.

    JZ1310.L69   2007
    327.1'17—dc22   2006006239

Contents

Acknowledgments

Many good friends and colleagues helped and supported me during the writing of this book. To all these people I would like to express my thanks here.

First and foremost, I thank Robert Keohane, who in a seminar he once gave in Jerusalem encouraged me to think seriously about pirates and other delinquent transnational actors. It was he who first showed me that my subject was "kosher." I am greatly thankful to Jeremy Shine, former acquisition editor for political science at the University of Michigan Press, for his initial interest in this book. There are not enough words to describe how much I am indebted to Jim Reische, who took over for Jeremy at the University of Michigan Press. Jim was one of the most supportive and helpful persons I encountered throughout this project.

I owe a big intellectual debt to Jeremy Paltiel, from Carleton University, for long hours of discussions and brainstorming. It was he who suggested the title for this book, and his ideas and sharp perception of international politics helped me to crystallize my thinking about predators and parasites of authority in world politics. I have also benefited from discussions with many people from the Munk Centre for International Studies at the University of Toronto, where I spent two wonderful years as a Halbert post-doctoral fellow between 2001 and 2003. Ron Deibert, Michael Donnelly, Joshua Goldstein, Rick Halpern, Louis Pauli, Janice Stein, and David Welch always were willing to hear me and were happy to give good advice or insightful comments. The vibrant intellectual atmosphere at the Munk Centre and the seminars in which I presented some of my ideas were crucial for the "construction" of this book.

And speaking of construction, it is a great pleasure to thank Alexander Wendt for his support and help throughout the years. Although I have not met him, I consider him one of my most important teachers in international relations. His writings and our e-mail correspondences stimulated me to think thoroughly about my thesis and to critically and rigorously examine every argument. Alex's theories in general and his comments on this book in particular provided me with one of the rarest things in academia—hope. Richard Mansbach's penetrating comments on the book, as well as his common sense and experience, also strengthened me along the way. I will always cherish Dick's friendly, straightforward, and honest approach. Kal Holsti read parts of the book too, and his support was also of great help.

Oren Barak, my friend and colleague at the Hebrew University, kept my spirits up during the last two years. Oren read large parts of the book, introduced me to the writings of Foucault, and found the weakest points in the book, and I always knew that I could count on him for intelligent criticism. Other friends from Jerusalem contributed much as well. Amir Lupovici made me contemplate the social construction of rationality. His encyclopedic knowledge of international relations theory was invaluable. Emanuel Adler was a friend and a source of wisdom. A single conversation with Emanuel can turn one's world upside down, and sometimes this was exactly what I needed. Tal Dingott-Alkopher's writings about rights in world politics also provided help and important insights. Avraham Sela shared his experience with me, and his frank comments on my ideas on Great Power authority helped me to return to reality from pure theoretical realms. Galia Press Barnathan, Yaacov Bar Siman-Tov, Uri Bialer, Raymond Cohen, Arie Kacowicz, Noam Kochavi, Korina Kagan, Sasson Sofer, and Yaacov Verzberger all gave very useful and helpful observations and helped to solve many problems along the way. Barak Mendelsohn, from Cornell University, also provided many thoughtful comments and raised very interesting ideas. I am also indebted to Gil Merom from Tel Aviv University for several important remarks in the early phases of this project. Benny Miller, from Haifa University, trained me in logical and scientific thinking and was always happy to assist in solving any intellectual puzzle.

Shlomo Grinner, Einat Vaddai, Lior Avni, and Gadi Heiman provided very useful research assistance. Mauricio Diamant helped me with reading Spanish. And without the excellent and intelligent linguistic and stylistic editing of Colette Stoeber this project would have remained in the original language it was written in: Bad English. My students at the

Hebrew University were my captive audience, and for their forbearance I can only be thankful.

Generous funding during the writing of the book was provided by the Halbert Exchange Program at the University of Toronto, the Leonard Davis Institute for International Studies at the Hebrew University of Jerusalem, and the Israel Foundations Trustees (Project #37/2004).

Finally, I wish to thank my family for their love. My wife, Idit, and my son, Oshri, were a constant source of joy and warmth. How lucky and blessed I am to have them. My father, Avigdor, taught me from childhood to love books, and it is thanks to him that I became a scholar. My mother, Marta, and my sister, Nava, were always caring and loving.

During the writing of this book my beloved cousin Eran Schwartz unexpectedly died. He was nineteen years old, a bright, sensitive, and intelligent young man. I would like to hope that he would have read this book. It is to his memory and honor that I dedicate this book.

Oded Löwenheim
Jerusalem, October 2005

Introduction

[A]t length the crisis of indignant Europe have [*sic*] resounded in the English parliament; the voice of outraged humanity has prevailed over false political considerations and vengeance is about to reach the pirates of the coast of Africa. The time is passed, when Algiers, rich in the spoils of her Christians, could say in the avarice of her heart, "I keep the sea under my laws, and the nations are my prey." She is about to be attacked in her walls, like the bird of prey in her nest.

When these lines appeared on September 14, 1816, in the *Courier,* the official organ of the British government, the British navy had already descended on Algiers in what was likely the second largest cannonade of a littoral target by a naval force during the Age of Sail. This attack was considerably costly: on top of significant financial outlays, the British lost 128 men and suffered 690 wounded. Yet only seventeen years earlier, Horatio Nelson, the nation's most popular sea hero of the time, exclaimed, "My blood boils that I cannot *chastise* these pirates. *They could not show themselves in the Mediterranean did not our country permit.* Never let us talk of the cruelty of the African slave trade while we permit such a horrid war" (quoted in Perkins and Douglas-Morris 1982, 23; emphasis added).

The Barbary pirates of Algiers, Tunis, and Tripoli are an important historical manifestation of what I dub in this book "persistent agents of transnational harm" (PATHs). My aim is to understand why Great Powers counter the practices of PATHs (not so obvious a question, as we shall see later) and to examine the variation and change in this Great Power response. I define a PATH as a private (nongovernmental) group, organization, or network that operates across state borders and deliberately causes or facilitates harm in the pursuit of its interests. Harm is understood in this book as material damage and injury to persons' bodies or property or economic costs resulting from such damage.[1] Harm can be propagated through the use of organized violence, but it can also arise from certain transborder flows (such as disposal of hazardous waste, air pollution, or the exportation of tobacco products) or a conscious violation of international prohibitions on various behaviors and practices. I argue, for instance, that "drug-induced deaths" are an example of the latter possibility.

The harmful agent is "persistent" in that it does not respect (in practice and/or in word) the state's superior right or legitimate *authority* to order it to cease harm. Consequently, the propagation of harm will cease only when the self-interests of the PATH favor it or when extrinsic considerations and factors compel it to change or abandon its practice (such as increasing material costs or diminishing rewards).

In this book I follow a Weberian logic, arguing that modern political authority is founded on the institutionalization of organized violence within states. I define "organized violence" as the systematic and purposive enactment of designated means of physical coercion and destruction. However, for authority as institutionalized organized violence to exist within individual states in the long run, some degree of self-restraint is required among states. This self-restraint, I argue, is based on three clusters of interrelated norms and rules that make up what I call the *institutions of transborder organized violence*. These are sovereignty, actorhood in the sphere of transborder violence, and the laws of war. Furthermore, contrary to the conventional wisdom of international relations (IR) theory, which contrasts anarchy and hierarchy and argues that in international politics the lack of central legal authority results in anarchy, I claim that these institutions of transborder violence in world politics *do* confer authority (as legitimized power) on certain states: the Great Powers. I believe that IR theory has too narrow a concept of anarchy and hierarchy and that we have to acknowledge the existence of other forms of authority not constituted on a single formal and central/pyramidical, or legal, authority. Sociologists and political theorists have long maintained that authority is a multifaceted phenomenon. In this book, I borrow concepts from sociology, international law, and political theory to present a theory of authority in world politics, and through the concept of authority I explain the variance in Great Power response toward persistent transnational harmful actors.

Accordingly, I argue that the policy of a Great Power toward PATHs depends not solely on the material consequences of the transnational harmful practice as such, but more significantly on the level of threat the Great Power perceives the PATHs to be to its authority. The further the harmful transnational agent is seen to undermine the existing international structures of authority and hierarchy, the harsher is the policy against it. I argue that Great Powers categorize PATHs as either destructive (predatory) or merely abusive/exploitive (parasitic) of their authority depending on their understanding of the threat the transnational actors pose to the institutions of transborder violence. In chapter 1 I explain how these institutions enable Great Power authority in world politics, and in chapter 2 I explore the differences between predatory and parasitic PATHs in this context.

I. The Rationale for the Book

What prompted me to write a book on Great Powers and PATHs was the idea that through this perspective we can fill a lacuna in systemic theory of world politics. Traditionally, systemic theory in IR literature has occupied itself almost solely with the interactions of the Great Powers with each other, overlooking how the relationship between Great Powers and smaller actors (state and nonstate) affects Great Power interaction and the structure of international politics.[2] Part of my argument is that under certain conditions PATHs can actually influence the Great Powers' *inter*-relations. My discussion of PATHs and the Great Powers is also closely related to the issue of the threat that weak and failed states pose for international security.[3] In the 1990s, much was written on whether the next threats to U.S. and Western security would emerge from rising Great Powers (namely, China) or from failed regional states that host (willingly or unwillingly) organized crime groups, terrorists, and other forms of actors that could be defined as PATHs (see, e.g., David 1989; Goldgeiger and McFaul 1992; Lake and Morgan 1997; Gholz, Press, and Sapolsky 1997; Mearsheimer 2001). The attacks of 9/11 brought this debate to the fore in U.S. policy. The American response to 9/11 was intended not only to fight the terrorists but to confront the structural conditions that give rise to and motivate this form of violence. State building in this context is perceived as no less important than the military aspects of the War on Terror.[4]

Thus, in light of the need to integrate nonstate actors and weak states into systemic IR theory, this book explores the effect that their connection with PATHs has on the Great Powers and consequent international responses. On the empirical level, I use the examples of Barbary piracy and the threat of al Qaeda's global terror to demonstrate how a polity's weakness or failure—or actual inexistence—enables PATHs to harm the Great Powers. The parallels—and the differences—between the pirate bases of the Barbary Coast and the Afghan stronghold of al Qaeda are very important to an understanding of the effects of state weakness or inexistence on the activity of the PATHs.

The Barbary city-states of Tunis, Tripoli, and Algiers, nominally under Ottoman suzerainty, were for hundreds of years magnets for various transnational adventurers, holy warriors, and aggrieved renegades who exploited the weakness of these polities in their raiding and plundering of European shipping and settlements. Even though the Europeans often tried to pacify the Barbary corsairs by sending the rulers of the Barbary polities tribute and presents and even by signing formal peace treaties with them (to the extent that they were elevated in European diplomatic language to "states," "powers," "kingdoms," and "regencies"), the pirates remained essentially unruly. The weakness of their nominal Ottoman sovereign meant that it could not (and usually did not want to) prevent corsairing from continuing. In fact, the Algerian corsair community was notorious for strangling to death deys (the official Ottoman rulers of the city) who tried to prevent the corsairs from preying on the seas. In addition, the status of the Barbary centers of transnational violence within the overall structure of the Ottoman Empire was never exactly clear. Eventually in 1816, due to overwhelming technological and naval power superiority, the British succeeded in significantly curbing Algerian piracy, and the 1830 French occupation abolished that piracy altogether. In other words, because of state weakness or even inexistence in the Barbary Coast, it was only Great Power intensive military intervention and territorial occupation that ended the harmful practice of the pirates. Although this intervention was possible earlier in history, we shall see that previous maritime European powers lacked the political will to pursue it, largely due to their perception of the corsairs as mere thieves or pests of a parasitic nature.

In the case of al Qaeda, one of the major reasons for the emergence of the terror network is state weakness in the Middle East, and weak or failed states such as Afghanistan, Sudan, Somalia, Yemen, and now post-Saddam Iraq serve the terrorists as bases, training fields, and recruiting grounds. In fact, Afghanistan's case was so unique in terms of state weakness that many experts considered al Qaeda as a terrorist group sponsoring the Taliban regime and not vice versa. However, the ability of individuals to inflict huge destruction due to globalization and the nature of modern technology significantly reduces the importance of weak or failed states to terrorism. In the nineteenth century, the Great Powers could stop piracy by destroying the territorial bases of the pirates; in the twenty-first century, the occupation or destruction of terrorist bases does not necessarily eliminate the threat. The ability of the terrorists to relocate a great deal of their coordination, recruitment, fund-raising, propaganda and other types of activity from territorial bases in weak states into cyberspace considerably hurts the ability of the Great Powers to stop terrorism through destruction of physical bases. In chapter 5 I critically examine the War on Terror in Afghanistan and argue that, beyond the pure military logic involved in the American-led campaign, questions of retributive justice and validation of hegemonic authority played a role that cannot be overlooked.

This empirical discussion leads me to the theoretical aspect of the connection between failed or weak states and PATHs. In this context, chapter 2 addresses Great Power punishment of such states for their cooperation with or nonconfrontation of PATHs. Because PATHs are often much more elusive targets than states, they are inherently less punishable. Consequently, Great Powers tend to shift their attention to states (or other types of polities in the past; see subsequent discussion) that they perceive are colluding with the PATHs or aggravating the authority predicament they pose by not confronting them. In this manner, I show how important the ability to punish is within the very concept of the Great Powers. Without an object to suffer the punishment of a challenged Great Power, the idea of power itself—and with it the very role identity of the Great Powers—becomes hazy. In a sense, pariah and weak (institutionally and also militarily) states such as Afghanistan are ideal role validators for Great Powers that cannot directly punish an elusive PATH network such as al Qaeda. Afghanistan and the Taliban were much more "real" and observable targets than al Qaeda, which could be said to be as much a brand name and an ideology as a recognizable terror group.

The phenomenon of PATHs is also significant in the theoretical discussion of transnational relations and the effect of these relations on the special status of the Great Powers in the international system. Although the literature on transnational relations is extensive, it has not conceptualized how persistent transnational *harmful* practices affect the position of the Great Powers as leaders of the international system. Thus, although Janice Thomson's (1994) seminal work on sovereignty and the exclusion of nonstate extraterritorial wielders of violence from the international system inspired this book to a great extent, I develop an aspect that Thomson left unexplored: the concept of Great Power authority and its relationship to sovereignty. Thomson only implicitly deals with the Great Powers as a special category of states. This book fills in this lacuna by connecting Thomson's and others' discussion of sovereignty as a constitutive institution of international society to a distinct understanding of Great Power authority. Through the phenomenon of PATHs I hope to show the socially constructed dimensions in the power of the Great Powers. Thomson's study shows how the principle of legitimate actorhood in transborder violence (i.e., who has the recognized right to authorize or participate in such violence) and sovereignty became one and the same in the modern era. Thus, her main focus is on norm emergence. But the reality of world politics after 9/11 reveals the importance of theorizing possible norm decay and the system preservation response of the Great Powers to such decay. Beyond the material threat embodied in terror such as bin Laden's and al Qaeda's, it is the presumption of such nonstate actors that they have a legitimate right to "punish" the Great Powers and the difficulty of disciplining them that makes them so alarming. Punishment, as I discuss in this book, is inherent to authority. But exacting punishment largely depends on the punished actor being sensitive to the costs inflicted by the punisher. This ability to punish might be hindered by the organizational structures, motivations, values, interests, or goals of a "species" of actor (e.g., hierarchical territorial states as opposed to "flat" transnational networks). Modern Great Power authority cannot allow the existence of nonstate actors that presume they have a legitimate right to punish states or that are able to elude the exaction of material costs. Thus, in order to better understand the threat that nonstate harmful actors pose to the Great Powers, I untie the mutual inclusiveness of sovereignty and actorhood and provide a three-legged conception of the institutions that enable Great Power authority (sovereignty, actorhood, laws of war). Through this analysis, I intend to highlight the social construction of the concept of power and to emphasize that power as we know it in international politics today is actually authority—or *legitimized* power within a cartel of states in which the Great Powers are gatekeepers. Thomson was interested in the reasons behind the construction of a cartel that excluded and delegitimized nonstate extraterritorial organized violence. This book shows how this "cartelization" of world politics by states was germane to the emergence of the Great Powers as a distinct class of states and why various kinds of harmful transnational practices are seen by the Great Powers as destructive or abusive of their authority. In this vein, the theoretical distinction between variants of PATHs (predatory and parasitic) presented here could be useful in leading to a clearer understanding of the policy of Great Powers toward these actors in real terms. This, I hope, will be achieved through a combination of theoretical arguments and detailed case studies.

This book also builds on Gerry Simpson's (2004) important study on sovereign inequality. But while he employs mainly legal concepts to understand the special nature and status of the Great Powers in world politics, my book sheds light on the *political* foundations of Great Power authority and examines this authority from the perspective of PATHs—an issue that Simpson has not elaborated enough.[5] Dealing with *nonstate* outsiders (as opposed to outsider states) to Great Power authority also helps to provide a wider perspective on notions of authority in world politics. This book then is about political, not necessarily legal, authority. However, I adhere to Alexander Wendt's (1999, 280) conception of international law as part of the meta-structure of international *politics*. Thus, I try to integrate Thomson's and Simpson's works, to add a new dimension to each of them, and to enlarge the empirical testing of the phenomenon of persistent transnational harm in world politics through detailed case studies.

II. The Uniqueness of PATHs

In contrast to PATHs, most forms of transnational actors do not challenge in principle the superior right of the state to govern them (including the state's right to administer the law upon them through coercion). Indeed, Rodney Hall and Thomas Biersteker argue that private authority, parallel to state authority, has emerged in recent decades in world politics to the extent that "[t]he state is no longer the sole, or in some instances the principal, source of authority, in either the domestic arena or in the international system" (2002, 5). But even if we concede to this viewpoint, an important question arises: Why are states, and especially the Great Powers, willing to tolerate, consent to, or delegate authority to certain private agents and actors and, at the same time, resist giving up their authority to other private actors? This book attempts to answer this question in the context of harmful practices of persistent nonstate groups.

The propagation of intentional harm or the conscious facilitation of illegal damages is an important consideration in the discussion of state versus private authority. Multinational companies might compete with states for market shares or bargain with them on various issue areas of allocation. They might even create transnational harm through air pollution or the selling of products that contribute to health hazards, for example. Epistemic communities, environmental networks, human rights coalitions, and many other transnational groups often pressure states to endorse or reject certain policies or to limit their intervention in various issue areas.[6] But such actors almost always avoid inflicting or causing illegal harm in the advancement of their goals. When faced with a state demand to cease harms to which they are responsible, they might bargain with the state, but if the state insists on its demand they eventually comply without the state having to resort to physical coercion or threaten with such coercion against them. In chapter 2, I denote such actors as "insiders to authority." On the other hand, the persistent propagation of harm in the *modern states system* (as opposed to the early modern system of the sixteenth and seventeenth centuries) distinguishes the transnational actors I study from other transnational networks and groups in that it reveals them as actors that reject the right of the state to govern them. Thus, I dub them "outsiders to authority." Even the modern private military companies (PMCs)—which could be said to be agents of transnational harm because of their active armed involvement in various domestic and international conflicts or their logistic services to the armed forces of states—are distinct from PATHs in the persistency factor. The harm propagated by PATHs—through designated violent means or conscious violations of certain prohibitions—cannot be stopped by states except through coercive means or through threatening or rewarding the self-interest of the transnational agents. In this context, Ian Hurd's distinction between "interested" and "self-interested" actors is very important.

> [W]e should avoid confusing the generic statement that individuals pursue "interests" in the sense of choosing means to achieve goals, with the particular assumption of "self-interestedness," referring to an instrumental attitude toward other actors and toward rules. Many diverse models of human behavior accept that actors pursue "interests," but they disagree on whether they are "self-interested" in this strong sense. The distinction is essential, because the controversy between self-interest and legitimacy comes in competing

accounts of how interests are formed, not in whether actors pursue goals. Without this difference, there is no behavior that could possibly contradict the self-interest hypothesis. (Hurd 1999, 387)

Unlike PATHs, which cease their harmful practice only when they are coerced through force or when their self-interest is at stake, PMCs are in effect law-abiding actors in most cases. They contract only with legitimate governments (those internationally acknowledged), follow the rules and regulations of their origin state (they are licensed by state governments), and are eventually accountable to international law because their contracting states and origin states *are* so accountable.[7] Furthermore, because they are multinational companies, PMCs' very existence is constituted by state law. Thus, when British and South African authorities decided to disband the PMC Executive Outcomes in December 1998 (one of the very few PMCs that actually engaged its workers in armed combat), the company went out of business. Indeed, some of its employees and operatives went to work for other PMCs, which remained licensed and legitimate firms. But Executive Outcomes could have retained its organizational existence by becoming a mercenary army—or a criminal group. That the company disbanded and most of its workers did not become illegal mercenaries points to the fact that it was not a *persistent* propagator of harm (again, note the previously mentioned distinction between interested actors and self-interested actors). Its interests were within the framework of the law. Therefore, Britain and South Africa could disband the company simply through legal means.[8] Criminal organizations or terrorist groups, on the other hand, cannot be disbanded by legal means and speech acts alone: the core practice of PATHs denies or ignores state authority, whereas the core practice of PMCs acknowledges it. And although either kind of actor can at times be involved in practices that acknowledge state authority or defy it (e.g., a criminal group that diversifies into legitimate business or a PMC that engages in unauthorized use of force), the decisive question is whether the core practice of the agent is congruent with structures of state authority.

The practice and sometimes also the rhetoric of PATHs suggest that they do not take existing institutions and structures of metapolitical authority for granted. Most other transnational actors, on the other hand, usually comply with state authority because they consider it to be legitimate and right;[9] they do not go through the process of calculating the costs and benefits of compliance for each interaction with the state or its laws. Even multinational corporations (MNCs)—supposedly the embodiment of economic self-interest—usually pay their taxes, not because they are coerced to do so or consider taxation to be an instrumental policy but because they consider it to be their *obligation* within the institution of property rights and the law.[10] Of course, tax evasion and other white-collar crime exist. Offshore financial centers proliferated in the 1990s and were used by various corporations to evade taxes. A spate of financial scandals erupted in the United States in the 1970s and in the early years of this century. However, financial crime is not the norm in the political economy; in fact, "much of mainstream economics is predicated on the assumption that economic agents act within the law."[11] Furthermore, if corporations and firms were purely self-interested in the sense of denying the legitimacy of others' rights and in viewing others as purely instrumental (both the state and other economic actors), they would exploit *every* opportunity to make illicit revenues.

However, modern political and economic activity depends on and is constituted by the institution of property rights, which is guaranteed by the state and thus provides the state with a moral value and purpose. In fact, as Michael Walzer argues, taxes are a form of redistribution that redraws the line between politics and economics, "and they do so in ways that strengthen the sphere of politics" (1984, 122). Property rights entail not only positive prerogatives and claims to some material or intellectual objects but also recognition of the entitlements of other right holders as well as those of the *enforcer* of rights. This requires treating other right holders and even the enforcer of rights as actors with moral endowments, not merely as objects or instruments. The result is an avoidance of certain acts and behaviors toward others, even when opportunity knocks at the door.

PATHs, on the other hand, do not comply with authority when the latter is present, nor are they accountable to the state. This aspect in the issue of PATHs, neglected in literature on transnational relations, has become more crucial since the twenty-first-century materialization of "mega-terrorism." Although some work on the current War on Terror seems to characterize groups like al Qaeda in such terms,[12] a comprehensive theoretical conceptualization of Great Powers and PATHs is still missing, as is a historical and comparative perspective on the phenomenon. The purpose of this book therefore is to illuminate, through a theoretical and empirical examination of Great Power policy toward PATHs, the normative and institutional superstructures that, I believe, constitute world politics. More specifically, this book seeks to join the developing literature that deals with the issue of authority and hierarchy in world politics and the unique status of the Great Powers within the international hierarchy (e.g., Hurd 1999; Cronin 2001; Lake 2003; Simpson 2004). This book endorses the view that Great Powers serve as gatekeepers and authors of norms in a cartel of sovereign states and that PATHs challenge this cartel from the outside. In this context, I seek to explain why Great Powers perceive different PATHs as posing varying degrees of challenge to this cartel and to Great Power leadership within it.

III. The Case Studies and the Methodology of the Book

As mentioned previously, my methodology will be comparative and historical. Throughout history, Great Power response toward PATHs has varied considerably. In 1816, the British intensively employed their navy to eliminate the piracies of the Barbary corsairs. But this came after more than two centuries of British tolerance—at times even cooperation—with the pirates. This British, and more generally international, tolerance or acceptance of the depredations of the North African Barbary pirates was one of the major reasons why the corsairs could comfortably establish themselves in an unprecedented institutionalized system of ransom and sea predation. That system included formalized ransom negotiations (through permanent European representation at the Barbary ports), the issuing of special passports to ships belonging to nations that paid the corsair city-states annual tribute, and the periodic renegotiation of "peace" treaties with the pirates (which were in effect nothing more than tribute agreements). According to one recent study, this institutionalized system of piracy was responsible for the enslavement of more than one million Europeans during two and a half centuries, the killing of tens of thousands of others, and the creation of an atmosphere of terror and xenophobia along many Mediterranean shores (Davis 2003; see also Friedman 1983).

Why did the European powers accept this system, and what eventually moved the British to radically change their relatively lenient attitude toward the Barbary pirates in the early nineteenth century? One might rightly argue that the British had no incentive to eliminate Barbary piracy: these pirates had scarcely harmed English nationals since the 1750s, and more often than not they actually benefited British commercial and naval interests by preying on Britain's competitors and providing port services to British men-of-war. This was still the case in 1816, when Britain decided to suppress the pirates in a decisive and relatively costly maritime attack, demanding an unconditional end to piracy and slavery.

And as the influential Tory-inclined *Quarterly Review* wondered, "If England is to be constituted *pirate-taker-general,* she had better commence with the Malays and Ladrones of China, who plunder her ships and murder her subjects; the Barbary pirates do neither. . . . What has England to do with it, that she must stand foremost as the avenging power, and sacrifice her seamen to evince her humanity toward Sardinians, Sicilians and Neapolitans?"[13] The British, then, moved to suppress the Barbary pirates at a time when the latter were not causing them any material harm.

On the other hand, two centuries earlier, the Spanish monarchy—then the most powerful European state in the international system—had done little to suppress the pirates even though thousands of Spanish nationals were taken into captivity and slavery in Barbary each year and hundreds of others were killed in corsair attacks and raids. Mortality among the Spanish captives and slaves was high because of epidemics, cruel treatment, and hard labor. The corsairs not only attacked Spanish vessels at sea, but they also raided Spanish territory and kidnapped civilians from settlements located miles inland. Not surprisingly, Spaniards were terrorized by the corsairs and the prospect of slavery in Barbary. Miguel de Cervantes—the famous Spanish author who was himself a captive in Algiers between 1575 and 1580—described Algerian captivity in his *Los tratos de Argel.*

> Sad and bitter enslavement!
> Where the sorrow is as long
> as the good is short and abbreviated!
> Oh purgatory in life,
> Hell placed in this world,
> evil that has no equal,
> strait that has no exit! (Quoted in Garcés 2002, 137)

Spain did attack the corsair bases with intensive armed force several times between 1500 and 1570. But during this time, the pirates posed a threat mainly to Spanish imperial garrisons in North Africa and the western Mediterranean, not to the general Spanish civilian population. Paradoxically, though, when the corsairs focused on the Iberian Peninsula itself in the late sixteenth century, the Spanish Crown diminished its armed efforts against the corsairs considerably, even when corsair attacks reached records in the number of Spanish captives and slaves taken and civilians killed.

Other European societies suffered a great deal as well. England, the Dutch Republic, and France were routinely attacked too by the corsairs, and thousands of these states' nationals were enslaved in Barbary. Yet international anticorsair cooperation among these states was very limited and rare, and even when such cooperation did materialize it was so guarded and fraught with mutual suspicions among the Europeans that it was rendered completely ineffective. In fact, the most powerful European states constantly worked to divert the threat of the pirates toward each other. And although throughout the centuries many European nations sent their navies to bombard Algiers and the other Barbary ports (Tunis and Tripoli), these were fitful effort, and none of them intended to completely and unconditionally eliminate this system of piracy and slavery. Furthermore, it was not until the British attack in 1816 that any European nation demanded that the corsairs absolutely cease their white slave trade and piratical raids, regardless of their victims' nationality.

Why were the pirates tolerated by the Western states to such an extent that the leader of the Tripolitan corsairs—the bashaw—could boast even in 1801 in front of the American consul that "all nations pay me" and that he knew his "friends" (i.e., tributaries) by the value of their "presents" (U.S. Congress 1832, 350)? Revealing his self-confidence, the bashaw added that "in Tripoli, consul, we are all hungry, and, if we are not provided for, we soon get sick and peevish. . . . Take care that the medicine [in other words, tribute] does not come too late, and, if it comes in time, that it will be strong enough" (ibid., 345). Statements like this by the "prince of ruffians" or the "ringleader of a banditti of Corsairs" (Parkinson 1934, 435) could not have been made without the "anxious competition of the European belligerents for [the Barbary pirates'] goodwill" (Lewis 1982, 46).

But as this book shows, the prevailing attitude toward such nonstate transnational harmful actors has dramatically changed since the time of the Barbary pirates. Great Powers created a structure of authority and hierarchy in world politics that excluded nonstate harmful actors who did not yield to this authority. One might intuitively suppose that the degree of material damage or harm that various PATHs caused a Great Power would be the main factor determining the response of the latter. However, I show that what determines PATH exclusion and the specific form of counter-PATH policy has actually been the threat the agents posed to the order the Great Power is interested in or committed to. In some cases, PATHs that have caused more material harm to a Great Power have been treated with more toleration than PATHs (or even states) that have caused less or no material harm. The important factors were how the Great Powers defined their constitutive entitlements and obligations toward their own domestic society and toward the society of states and how the PATHs interacted with the Great Powers in the context of these definitions. PATHs that overtly violated these rights and duties were treated more harshly than those that simply infringed on them. The former were perceived as predators of authority, the latter as parasites.

The Barbary pirates moved from the status of parasites of authority in the sixteenth and seventeenth centuries—precisely the time when their depredations reached their zenith—to a status of predators of authority in the early nineteenth century—when they no longer posed a material threat to the most powerful states in the system. This happened when their practice openly defied the international moral authority of Britain, the hegemonic power in the aftermath of the Napoleonic Wars. While the intentions of the pirates had been essentially the same since the sixteenth century—namely, self-interested plunder—the British saw them now as predators precisely because they openly *refused* to abide by an explicit British ultimatum to abolish sea robbery and white slave trade. Through the ruler of Algiers—evidently afraid for his life if he disobeyed the pirates—the corsair community flouted British authority, not only challenging the British in the specific context of white slavery but undermining the moral stance of Britain as a Great Power in the Congress of Vienna. This led the British to construe the corsair base of Algiers as a "bird of prey" and to severely punish the pirate stronghold.

In this case from 1816, the rest of the Great Powers were relatively indifferent to the British operation against the pirates. This was because the corsairs challenged a new norm in the international system (antislavery) that only Britain eagerly sought to advance. But whereas in the sixteenth century the other European powers actively interfered with the Spanish efforts to curb Barbary piracy, the early-nineteenth-century Great Powers did not disturb the suppression of piracy by Britain. There were many material and self-interested reasons for this avoidance of interference, but as we shall see in chapter 4 the mutual empowerment among the Great Powers and their recognition in each other's authority were highly important in this regard. And as opposed to these two cases, after the terrorist attacks on the United States in 2001, all the Great Powers considered the transnational harmful practice of al Qaeda to represent a predatory menace to their authority. The terrorist network, and more significantly the terrorist idea, challenged the most fundamental norms and values that are important to all these powers and are essential for the preservation of their authority. Thus, all the other Great Powers offered help·to the United States in its War on Terror in Afghanistan (ranging from China allowing an American aircraft carrier to harbor in Hong Kong to Russia helping with search-and-rescue missions to active British and French combat participation). Other countries as well sent armed forces to Afghanistan, offered help in logistics and intelligence, and showed solidarity with the United States.

The most obvious and immediate explanation for the intense American and international response and cooperation against al Qaeda and its host, Afghanistan, is that global terrorism and "asymmetrical" warfare threaten to wreak further mass destruction on the American homeland— and perhaps on other states as well. This reasoning is compatible with John Stuart Mill's (1955) argument that punishment should be rationally administered according to the degree of harm done by the offender. However, if the material and harmful aspects of terror were the sole or major reason for the intense reaction to it, then why has the United States avoided escalating its War on Drugs to the levels of the War on Terror?

Although drug trafficking has put a much heavier material toll on America than terrorism, the "war" on drugs has basically remained a law enforcement operation ever since its declaration by President Nixon in the early 1970s. Despite the fact that between 1979 and 2000 more than three hundred thousand Americans have died from illicit drug-induced causes and many thousands of others have been murdered due to drug-related violence and that hundreds of billions of dollars have been lost to the American economy due to various illicit drug damages, the United States has not invaded or bombed Colombia as it did Afghanistan. Colombia is the largest source of cocaine trafficked into the United States, and in it are based some of the most sophisticated, entrenched, persistent, and violent drug-trafficking organizations and networks of the world. Indeed, these actors probably do not want to kill drug consumers—on the contrary, they want to broaden the circle of drug users. However, I still consider drug traffickers as PATHs in the sense that they almost never relinquish their practice unless physically coerced to do so by the state, and at times they are ready to resist this coercion through violence. Furthermore, drug traffickers are well aware of the fact that their *illicit* product kills thousands each year and that the American state strictly prohibits their practice, but they persistently continue their practice notwithstanding[14] (as opposed to tobacco producers, who in America alone sell a product that kills three hundred thousand a year *under state permission and regulation*). Hence, despite certain U.S. measures to militarize the War on Drugs,[15] the war remains essentially an enterprise of law enforcement.

Of course, one might argue that invasion or bombardment of the source states from which the drug networks operate would not have ended the drug flow because of the "balloon effect": the tendency of the drug producers and traffickers to move to other regions and countries when pressure is applied on their original locations. But there are two problems with this argument. First, the United States does demand that the governments of the source states establish the rule of law through military means in the regions where the traffickers operate; to this end, the U.S. government finances the militarization of the War on Drugs in Colombia and Mexico. Second, the balloon effect should apply to all transnational wars; therefore, the U.S. bombardment of Afghanistan in the War on Terror will not root out global terror either. Terrorists, their networks, and their ideas will spread out to other states, and future terrorists might come from states in which America has no military presence at all. The 9/11 bombers, after all, spent a great deal of time in Germany and the United States itself. The main reason for the different approaches to terror and illicit drug trafficking, I suggest, is a difference in the social construction of the two phenomena.

Terrorists are now perceived by the United States, and also by an overwhelming number of other states, as predators of authority: they are believed to aim to *destroy* structures of rule on both the domestic and the international levels. Mass destruction terror undermines the current state monopoly of large-scale transborder violence and calls into question the modern state's role as a protective Leviathan to its citizens. It also threatens the international status and prestige of the hegemonic power of the international system in that this hegemony is first and foremost based on the possession of certain material capabilities that define *legitimate* power in world politics and the *acceptable* ways and means to resist it. Terror networks such as al Qaeda, with their elusive and global nature, openly defy this structure of authority. They emerge and are able to operate precisely because states have adopted intrinsic limitations on their use of violence, limitations that were crucial for the construction of the modern and open world system in which we live. Al Qaeda exploits this openness and turns it into an acute vulnerability. It is perceived by the United States as wishing to destroy the existing order for another, not to bargain *within* an order as previous terror groups did.

Al Qaeda is also not believed to aim to abuse the order as previous "traditional" terrorists did or to stop short after one attack. Drug traffickers, on the other hand, are seen as parasites of authority; they are considered as intent on *abusing* authority but requiring it to continue their business. This is because they do not directly clash with the system of states and its constitutive principles and institutions, and they do not pose an alternative to it. In this they are different from terror groups such as al Qaeda, whose practice and rhetoric directly confront the constitutive institutions of international society, institutions that enable Great Power authority. This difference constructs a perception of the drug traffickers as actors and networks that basically supply an illicit and immoral form of happiness to their consumers—people who die from drug use are usually private *individuals* who (at least in the first stages) choose at some level to use drugs. In other words, drug-related deaths are in a sense a form of self-destruction. While the victims of terror die as *citizens* of the state, drug peddling is supposedly crime without victims, crime that results in harm mainly to the participating individuals themselves. Whether or not we consider drug-related deaths to be more tolerable, however, destroying oneself through a drug overdose is prohibited and criminalized, and hence the facilitation or enabling of this death by selling illegal drugs *is* harmful. Drug traffickers, nonetheless, are perceived by the "target" state as having a parasitic nature in that they do not threaten to overturn the social and political order by presenting an idea and praxis alternative to the sovereign states system and its hierarchy. Furthermore, and most important, they do not openly question and defy the social basis on which the Great Powers are constituted in international society as a source of authority.

Within the overall plan of the book, chapter 1 presents a theory of Great Power authority. Chapter 2 explains the concept of predators and parasites of authority. In chapter 3, I explore the case of the Barbary corsairs' depredations on Spain in the sixteenth and early seventeenth centuries. Chapter 4 turns to the British effort against the Barbary corsairs in 1816 and accounts for the bombardment of Algiers in light of the British campaign for the abolition of the slave trade (this chapter is based on an article I published in *International Studies Quarterly* in 2003). Chapter 5 deals with the U.S. War on Terror that ensued from the September 11, 2001, attacks on the United States. And in the conclusion, I compare the cases and present some questions on discipline and punishment in Great Power policy, reflecting in particular on the notion of the *authority dilemma*.

My approach is qualitative and comparative. My main research methods are process tracing, historical investigation, and discourse analysis. Thus, the book takes "pictures" of various historical configurations of thought patterns, material conditions, and institutions of violence and authority. Case selection was guided by two principles: examination across time and across issue areas. The first two cases examine the same phenomenon across time and thereby analyze changes in the concept of Great Power authority. Although they deal with the same issue area and geographic region—Barbary pirates in the sixteenth and seventeenth centuries and then in the nineteenth century—these two cases are nonetheless distinct in methodological terms. First, they are separated by more than two centuries of international history. Within this time span, changing norms and institutions of Great Power authority constructed new definitions of the same harmful transnational practice (sea predation and the enslavement of white Europeans in North Africa). Second, the Barbary cases focus on the distinct responses of two different dominant powers: Spain and Britain. Third, and most important, the pirate cases differ considerably in terms of the explanatory factor: the degree of authority predicament the pirates represented to the most powerful state in the system. In addition, the internal variation in each case can teach us a great deal about how threats to authority are constructed.

In the earlier centuries, as I mentioned previously, the more the pirates threatened Spanish civilian society, the less the Spanish Crown tried to suppress them. The reason behind this conundrum is that, in an era when Great Power authority was rudimentary and based on very different values than in our time, the corsair attacks on Spanish civilian population would have been perceived as no more than a nuisance. Crossing borders and harming civilians of low social orders was not seen as a threat of any significance to sovereignty nor as a deviation from the principles of actorhood and the laws of war. Consequently, there was no threat to Spain's international authority. It was only when the corsairs, serving as the vanguard of Ottoman expansion in the western Mediterranean, menaced the imperial interests of the House of Habsburg that they warranted offensive suppression. In this international system, the most powerful states (Spain and the Ottoman Empire) did not consider each other capable of authority and nonstate violence was taken for granted. The pirate issue was therefore interpreted through the lens of the intense enmity between these two powerful states. After the 1570s and 1580s, the threat of the Ottomans considerably subsided and the pirates' practice was disassociated from the Spanish-Ottoman conflict. As an independent phenomenon, corsairing was not understood in Spain to be a significant deviation from the existing institutions of violence. Spain, therefore, refrained from intense offensive efforts against the corsairs, even though the pirates stepped up their depredations on the Spanish civilian population.

The 1816 case of the British attack on Algiers is diametrically opposed to the sixteenth- and seventeenth-century case: the British attacked the corsairs despite the fact that the latter did not cause them any material harm. This was because new norms instituted by the British obliged them to perceive the pirates as deviants who challenged and undermined British authority in international politics. As a Great Power, Britain was expected—and indeed was called upon—by smaller states who suffered from the pirates to end the scandal of the Barbary corsairs. In other words, Britain and other European states perceived that ending the Barbary slave trade was a British duty. When the pirates explicitly refused to abide by Britain's demand, they pushed it into an authority dilemma. Whereas Spain did not feel an obligation to protect its own—much less other nations'—civilians against the pirates, the British knew that their role identity as a Great Power was at risk if they did not show a commitment to install international order and provide security for foreign nationals. The British could not allow themselves to authoritatively demand other states to stop their slave trade in black Africans and at the same time permit the continuation of Barbary piracy. These two cases thus complete each other: they highlight the relationship between the perceived threat of PATHs and the prevailing conception of Great Power authority. In addition, each case manages to isolate the role of material harm (the competing explanatory factor of this study) within the overall authority predicament posed by the PATHs.

In a similar manner, the third case study (the War on Terror) shows variance in the independent variable through the cases of anti–United States terrorism in the 1980s and mass destruction terrorism of the twenty-first century. I study the response of the United States to the terror attacks of Hizb'allah in Lebanon and the state-sponsored terrorism of Libya's Qaddafi and then compare these events with the American response to 9/11. Although anti-American terrorism in the 1980s was much less materially destructive than the attacks of 9/11, a comparison of Hizb'allah's threat with Libya's reveals how an explicit and open challenge to U.S. authority by Qaddafi in 1986 elicited a much greater U.S. military response than the more materially destructive—but less overt in terms of challenge to authority—attacks of Hizb'allah in 1983. The immense material damage suffered in 9/11, in its turn, was integral to the challenge to America's superpower authority. But this does not mean

that *any* form of material damage is by definition a challenge to authority; as discussed previously, although the harm caused by the drug trade
is considerably higher than terrorism's, the United States has avoided
intensive military response. In addition, a critical examination of the military response of the United States to 9/11 ("Operation Enduring Freedom" in Afghanistan) reveals that in many ways this response was more
than a simple utilitarian harm-prevention reaction to the material threat
of terror. Chapter 5 shows how this military response was in fact also a
disciplinary act in the Foucauldian sense.[16]

Moreover, although the harm inflicted by the Barbary pirates on six-
teenth- and seventeenth-century Spain was not the same as the harm
caused by the al Qaeda terrorists on 9/11, it was still objectively
significant enough to allow us to distinguish between material harm
per se and material harm that is interpreted as a challenge to Great Power
authority. Closely related to this issue is the fact that both terrorism and
piracy terrified the civilian societies of these powers. Of course, we cannot accurately measure the level of fear of five centuries ago, but there are
many qualitative indications that Spanish society was indeed terrorized
(in the emotional sense) by these attacks. This again helps to emphasize
that the level of threat to authority is crucial to determining Great Power
response to PATHs. In Spain, the fact that large segments of the civilian
population were terrorized by the pirates did not translate into an
authority threat to Spain's position in the international system because
sovereignty—one of the constitutive institutions that enables Great
Power authority—did not prescribe defense of civilians as the primary
duty of the state. As opposed to this, 9/11 clearly threatened the authority of the United States in the international system: modern sovereignty
and state power *are* about ensuring the security of individuals from both
domestic and foreign threats. By harming civilians through such overt
terrorist methods, and by taking pride in these methods, al Qaeda was
defined by the United States as a predatory actor willing to resist and
challenge America's superpower status in a manner that is in complete
opposition to the institutions of international society. In this regard, I discuss authority's second facet: beyond the power of positively and legitimately ordering actors what to do, authority defines acceptable ways of
resisting power (i.e., what not to do) and of punishing those who deviate
from these rules of resistance.

Thus, through the comparison of the three cases I hope to gain a
broader and historical perspective on the phenomenon of PATHs with
relation to changing meanings of power and authority.

◄ ONE ►

Great Power Authority
in World Politics

What accounts for the variance in Great Power policy toward persistent agents of transnational harm? This book argues that the specific nature of this policy depends on whether the PATHs are construed as parasites or predators of Great Power authority. In developing this claim, I first explain what authority is and how the Great Powers come to possess it in world politics, and then, in chapter 2, I turn to discuss the specific modes through which the Great Powers categorize PATHs as predators or parasites of authority.

In the first section of this chapter, I define Great Power authority and present empirical evidence and operational indicators for its existence in international politics. I also explain why this book focuses on the coercive and forceful elements of Great Power authority. The second section provides a conceptual framework that accommodates Great Power authority in an anarchical system built on the principle of sovereign equality. The third section accounts for Great Power authority through discussion of the effects of three fundamental institutions of violence: sovereignty, actorhood, and the laws of war. Finally, the fourth section highlights the centrality of moral consistency in the preservation of Great Power authority.

I. Authority and the Great Powers

What is Great Power authority and how does it come to exist in world politics? In this book, I conceive authority to be *legitimized power that invests its bearer with special rights and duties.* While many scholars would not dispute the central role of authority in domestic politics, fewer would agree that authority as defined here exists in world politics. Unlike authority within states, which is based on a formal legal structure of rights and duties, the presence of authority among juridical, equal sovereign states in the international system would be disputed by most IR scholars. Furthermore, the conventional wisdom of IR theory posits that the Great Powers do not possess a formal status in international politics and international law in any official sense. Although they wield *influence* over smaller states and nonstate groups, this influence is directly related to their superior material capabilities (economic and military) and does not represent authority in the sense of a legitimate *right* to command. The conventional argument is that, although the various branches of domestic government are official organs of the municipal law, the Great Powers are not official organs of international law. And so, while domestic politics are based on legalized and binding hierarchies, international relations take place in an anarchical environment of sovereign equality.

Thus, although neorealism has at least two theories of order—hegemonic stability and balance of power—it excludes authority in IR. In fact, Kenneth Waltz's seminal *Theory of International Politics* contrasts anarchy and hierarchy and defines the first as the absence of central authority among sovereign states (whereas in hierarchies a central authority does exist; see Waltz 1979, 95; Donnelly 2000, 89, 94). In contrast to this view, I argue that in order to understand Great Power policy against PATHs we have to include more ordering principles between the two ends of anarchy (as lack of authority) and formal hierarchy (as central legalized authority). I build on Gerry Simpson's (2004) concept of legalized hegemony and suggest that an intermediate possibility could be a *cartel* or directorate of authoritative actors (as opposed to a monopoly of authority). I will argue that the Great Powers in international politics function as the authoritative gatekeepers in a cartel of sovereign states. Thus, we can talk about *fragmented* or *diffused* authority as an intermediate condition between Waltz's anarchy and hierarchy. The main role of the Great Powers in this structure of authority is the regulation and institutionalization of transborder violence; at the same time, however, Great Powers are constituted through these regulations and institutions of transborder violence. PATHs that the Great Powers perceive as aiming to destroy or replace these institutional structures that define power from the outset are categorized by them as predators. PATHs that are seen as merely abusing these institutions are deemed parasites.

However, before I go on to provide a conceptual framework to account for Great Power authority (i.e., what makes it possible and, consequently, how exactly PATHs challenge it), I wish to outline some empirical and operational indicators for Great Power authority's actual presence in international politics. Hedley Bull's famous discussion of the Great Powers' special rights and duties sets the stage in this regard.

> [G]reat powers are powers recognized by others to have, and conceived by their own leaders and peoples to have, certain special rights and duties. Great powers, for example, assert the right, and are accorded the right, to play a part in determining issues that affect the peace and security of the international system as a whole. They accept the duty, and are thought by others to have the duty, of modifying their policies in the light of managerial responsibilities they bear. (Bull 1977, 202)[1]

Similarly, Gerry Simpson (2004) situates the special rights and duties of the Great Powers in what he calls a system of legalized hegemony. He defines legalized hegemony as "the existence within an international society of a powerful elite of states whose superior status is recognized by minor powers as a political fact giving rise to the existence of certain constitutional privileges, rights and duties and whose relations with each other are defined by adherence to a rough principle of sovereign equality" (68). In this sense, a good operational indicator for the presence of Great Power authority could be the existence of Great Power directorates and the fact that other states accept these hierarchical bodies as legitimate (I. Hurd 2002, 2004). While states might be dissatisfied with the decisions of Great Power directorates in systems of legalized hegemony (such as the UN Security Council or the Directing Committee of the Congress of Vienna) or even evade compliance with the decisions of these bodies, the very existence of these directorates reflects Great Power authority. Note that even resentful states do not call for the disassembly of the Security Council, for example (although calls for reform of the council increase; see Hurd 2002). Similarly, in the Congress of Vienna, dissatisfied states did not deny the right of the Directing Committee to redraw the borders of Europe. On the contrary, they made great efforts to appear before the Great Powers and present their cases in the conceptual language authored by the Great Powers (namely, the principles of "dynastical legitimacy" and "just equilibrium"; see Osiander 1994). In fact, states strive to attain a permanent seat in such bodies and to acquire for themselves the recognized status of Great Power (e.g., Germany and Japan in the Security Council, France and Spain in the Directing Committee). Such conduct on the part of the smaller powers and states reifies the authoritative directorship of the Great Powers.

A second indication of Great Power authority emerges through an examination of common perceptions, practices, and discourses of Great Power duties and responsibilities in international politics. As noted previously, authority consists of special rights *and* duties. Bull considers the Great Powers' primary duty to be to maintain international order and the global balance of power. They should achieve this by avoiding and controlling crises among themselves[2] and by restraining their regional allies and associates. The importance of this duty and its relation to the legitimization of the Great Powers' position (in other words, their authority) is highlighted by Nina Tannenwald's (2005) discussion of the origins of the nuclear taboo. She contends that "[t]he superpowers, both of which were pursuing nuclear arsenals, nevertheless felt obliged, *for purposes of moral legitimacy,* to engage in disarmament talks—however cynically" (19; emphasis added) and that "the historical record shows that the actors themselves have viewed the [nuclear] nonuse norm as more than simply a rule of prudence. They have thought about it and talked about it as a taboo with an explicit normative aspect, *a sense of obligation,* attached to it" (36; emphasis added).

But beyond the special obligation of mutual restraint, Great Power authority also consists of direct and positive obligations and responsibilities toward smaller states (i.e., not just restraining regional states but granting them some of *their* legitimate demands). Thus, if states apply to the Great Powers and argue that it is their duty or responsibility to intervene in a certain issue, crisis, or conflict, then this signifies that they perceive the Great Powers as bearers of authority (e.g., the numerous appeals of states to the Security Council). In these cases, the Great Powers are called to act not simply due to self-interest or bilateral obligation vis-à-vis a regional ally, but because the action is understood as a special duty ensuing from their role identity as Great Powers. In other words, the very possession of superior power capabilities creates certain obligations for the Great Powers. These obligations are a result of the legitimization of the power of the Great Powers: in return for recognition of the Great Powers' superior rights, the weaker actors in the system expect the powerful to accept special duties. In this chapter, I show how duties and rights are correlative and how authority is an attribute that can only be possessed if granted by others. And in chapter 4, I show how Britain, "the mistress of the seas," was called upon by the smaller powers of Europe to end the scandal of the Barbary pirates. In this case, the British were deemed to have a special obligation and responsibility to "civilized" humanity due to their overwhelming naval capabilities and the special rights they were granted in the Congress of Vienna. Similarly, during the Cold War the United States, beyond its various interests and contractual alliance commitments to the smaller states of the North Atlantic Treaty Organization (NATO), also felt a moral duty to protect these states—which in turn continuously demanded this duty (Lundestad 2003). Cuba as well strained the Soviet Union's duty to protect a "fellow revolutionary" country, and indeed the Soviet Union conceived it had a duty to secure Cuba (Steinberg 1991; Fursenko and Naftali 1998).

In this sense, authority does not necessarily have to be based on formal-legal concepts; it can be constituted by customs and traditions and implicit understandings, as Max Weber noted. A sense of a special moral obligation can therefore reflect authority in its traditional nonlegal manifestation. Accordingly, beyond the recognition of the Great Powers' special rights, the conception that they also have special duties signifies that they have an authoritative position in international politics. Therefore, I strongly agree with Bull's assertion that "[s]tates which, like Napoleonic France or Nazi Germany, are military powers of the front rank, but are not regarded by their own leaders or others as having these rights *and responsibilities,* are not properly speaking great powers" (1977, 202; emphasis added). This means that being a Great Power is a special social class as much as it is a material categorization.

A third indication of Great Power authority emerges through the language that states use to resist the decisions and policies of the Great Powers: in these cases they couch their opposition in terms of the fundamental institutions of international society. "Sociologists and anthropologists report that resistance works best when presented in terms borrowed from the language of the authority," argues Hurd. He then shows that Libya's strategy against the sanctions imposed on it by the Security Council in 1992 and 1993 "could be used as a handbook for the internalization of this advice" (2002, 47). Thus, most small states and even nonstate violent groups (e.g., "traditional" terrorist organizations such as the Palestinian Liberation Organization [PLO] or the Irish Republican Army [IRA]) endeavor to show that their conduct is based on and congruent with the norms, laws, and rules of international society. These fundamental institutions, as this chapter shows, are ideational structures that the Great Power themselves author and authorize as gatekeepers.

The presence of Great Power authority can also be deduced from what states and other international actors *don't do*. Beyond the ability to legitimately instruct others what to do, authority also consists of establishing acceptable definitions of what actors should avoid and the legitimate limits of resistance to power. This point is one of the most crucial elements in my argument throughout this book because PATHs are essentially actors that resist power by transgressing the normative and legal limitations on international behavior.

In a system of authority, not only do the most powerful limit their use of force to the rules of the game, but the weaker actors do as well. Thus, for example, the latter do not look for ways (such as bombing skyscrapers with passenger airliners transformed into cruise missiles) to exploit the nonmilitary weaknesses of the Great Powers. However, a realist might argue that small states are deterred simply because of the overwhelming military capabilities of the Great Powers and that this is the reason they do not devise such ploys as megaterror à la bin Laden, even if they resent the authority of the Great Powers. (States are territorially bound and thus cannot "escape" the wrath of the Great Powers, while terrorists like bin Laden can move to other territories and dodge retaliation.) The weak are either deterred or coerced into maintaining the social order of hierarchy, or they find it to be in their self-interest (see Krasner 1985).

But it is important to note here that from a constructivist point of view the interests of actors—along with the benefits they strive to attain and the costs they want to minimize—are defined by the shared norms and concepts of what is rational from the outset. Rationality is socially constructed (Weber 1978, 63–211; Hollis and Lukes 1982; Habermas 1984; Katzenstein 1996; Ruggie 1998; Reus-Smit 1999; Bukovansky 2002), and in the international system the Great Powers have considerable input in the social construction of rationality. Thus, for example, tolerating the high costs of religious wars—or, for that matter, waging religious wars at all—was rational for seventeenth-century states. Yet from the perspective of modern states this seems completely irrational, precisely because the constitutive norms of the international system have changed. In the 1648 Peace of Westphalia, the powerful states of Europe decided to leave out religious reasons from the legitimate motivations for war. In doing so they delegitimized religious wars, an act that reverberated with secular ideas and philosophies within states that led to the eventual distinction between the so-called rational sphere of secular politics (both domestic and international) and the irrational sphere of religion.[3] Taking into account that the Great Powers are central agents in the formulation of such constitutive ideational structures, we can see the deep effects of Great Power authority in the context of the construction of rationality.

Most small states and nonstate groups do not even contemplate ploys such as 9/11—not just because they are deterred and think it is irrational but mainly because they do not *want* to inflict such massive damage on the Great Powers with such horrific methods (terrorism) and for such illegitimate reasons (religious war). Even if actors do not constantly contemplate these issues, this knowledge constitutes the realms of possibility that establish their interests and identities (Giddens 1985, 11–12; Weldes 1999, 12–14). In this sense, Great Power authority has profound influence on the "minds" of international actors—by not only defining rationality but constructing standards for normal and deviant or shameful conduct. In this way, the Great Powers effectively institutionalize social hierarchy; they create a symmetry of ideas that allows for an asymmetry of power and right (more on this issue later).

A further manifestation of Great Power authority in international politics is the phenomenon of "spheres of influence," which demonstrates that the Great Powers themselves view each other as capable of authority (a necessary condition for authority; see Simpson 2004, 110). Over the last two centuries, Great Powers have acknowledged to varying degrees of explicitness the existence of geopolitical regions from which one Great Power excluded other Great Powers (Keal 1983; Miller 1995; Wendt and Friedheim 1996; Lake 2003), where the excluded powers accepted the hegemonic position of that power in its sphere of influence. The mutual exclusiveness of spheres of influence is even more striking if we take into account the intensive contests among the Great Powers in what we may call "spheres of competition." Realists tend to see spheres of influence as determined solely by interest, geographical proximity, and the presence of the relevant power's armed forces. However, this perspective does not explain why such spheres are sometimes acknowledged (even tacitly) when the very claim to such a sphere could be rejected (e.g., the 1975 Helsinki Accords, which effectively legitimized the territorial division of Europe and the existing political status quo,[4] and the British nonrejection of the Monroe Doctrine in the 1895 Venezuelan Crisis[5]). Neither can material considerations and interests solely explain why certain regions or states that represent an important interest to a Great Power, are geographically proximate to that power's borders, and contain a large military presence of that power are more prone to a rival power's intervention than other similar regions or states (think of the American military aid to the Mujaheedin rebels in Afghanistan during the Soviet invasion of that country in the 1980s versus American noninterference in the Soviet suppression of Czechoslovakia in 1968). It is beyond my ability here to delve into the intricacies of spheres of influence, but in my view we have to take into account an element of mutual Great Power recognition and empowerment—or authority—when we discuss them. Thus, it could be useful to dub them "spheres of recognition" rather than simply spheres of influence (see also Suri 2003).[6]

Further evidence of Great Power authority is the legitimization of material inequality in the international system. This phenomenon is highly manifested in the norm of territorial integrity (Zacher 2001), which became an established tenet of international society in the post–World War II system. The territorial integrity norm, which the Great Powers had a central role in instituting and guaranteeing, entails that states have effectively frozen their territorial property rights. The current Great Powers thus possess very large and habitable territories, and no state has the legitimate right to *forcefully* dispute these possessions. These territories are often rich in natural resources, energy deposits, and water and food. In addition, large territories provide strategic depth and preferential access to airspace and oceans, and they can ameliorate problems and pressures associated with environmental pollution, population growth, and so forth. Although some believe that the importance of territory considerably diminished in the age of the trading or "virtual state" (Rosecrance 1986, 1999), I think that this aspect cannot simply be ignored. Thus, the territorial integrity norm perpetuates inequality of territorial rights. Perhaps even more significantly for the preservation of Great Power authority, however, the territorial integrity norm also provides the Great Powers with a *legitimate* reason to prevent aspiring states from acquiring certain coveted territories, the possession of which could propel changes in regional and even global balances of power among states (e.g., the 1991 Gulf War). And considering that the Great Powers (and especially the United States) enjoy preferential access to the material resources of states such as Saudi Arabia, Kuwait, and post-Saddam Iraq,[7] the norm of territorial integrity actually helps to perpetuate not only territorial rights inequality per se but inequality in access to the territories of others.[8]

Here it is important to ask why powerful actors strive to maintain legitimate authority. In other words, what is authority "for"? From an instrumental point of view, as we have seen earlier, authority can bestow special material benefits. Authority also reduces the material costs of social control (no need to exert extensive coercion in every conflict) and increases the physical security of the holders of authority (no need to constantly monitor others for their violent ploys). Based on Max Weber, we can also stipulate that international authority increases the popularity and legitimacy of the domestic regime (see Weber 1978, 911–12). But I believe that there is something deeper and more constitutive in authority than this. In this regard, I can think of five major motivations for authority.

First, authority enables its bearers to construct social relations, structures, and agendas in a manner that allows the authoritative agent to feel comfortable in the community (e.g., by reflecting and reifying the moral values and ideologies of that actor; see Hall 1997).

Second, authority enhances one's self-esteem, which is an important human motivation (Wendt 1999, 236; Khalil 2000; Johnston 2001, 500). Except for rare cases of narcissism—in which, by definition, self-esteem is limitless and cannot be threatened by external forces because of the extreme autofocus of the narcissist—most social actors derive a large part of their self-esteem from the societal rights they possess. When superior material power is converted into superior or preferential entitlements, the possessor of power is enabled to *rightfully* claim prominence. This in turn increases the self-esteem of that actor because it feels that justice is on its side (Wenzel 2000). The special responsibilities of authority also increase actors' self-esteem. Thus, we will see in the next chapters how nineteenth-century Britain took pride in rendering "a lasting service to mankind" by destroying the pirates of Algiers and how the United States today solemnly congratulates itself for pursuing a cause that "has always been larger than our Nation's defense" (Bush 2002a, 1).

A third motivation for authority, and related to the previous point, is that the legitimization of superior power through authority confers prestige. The pursuit of prestige is one of the most fundamental human drives (Markey 1999; O'Neill 1999). Although realists understand prestige as mere reputation for materialist power (Gilpin 1981, 30–33), I believe that it entails respect and admiration in a positive sense. An actor cannot inspire respect solely through fear: respect must be based on some sense of legitimacy and recognition. If these elements are missing, the feared holder of power is usually despised as well—and certainly not considered prestigious.

A fourth motivation is connected to identity: because authority reflects social recognition of the privileged political status of the bearer of authority, it confirms and validates the self-identification of the bearer of authority by revealing that significant others share this view. An identity that is validated by others (i.e., there is high congruency between others' and one's knowledge of the self) is more emotionally robust than non-validated identity (Baumeister and Smart 1996). Such validated identity (Franck 1990, 91ff.) also satisfies a need for a meaning or purpose in life that human beings seek both individually and through corporate associations. In this regard, authority confirms and legitimizes a sense of "manifested destiny," which is beyond a simple or specific sense of responsibility or obligation to international society.

And last, authority provides actors—both its bearers and its subjects—with routines and certainties that reduce emotional stress and existential anxieties. Authority brings a dimension of inevitability to political life. In this manner, authority makes the world a more orderly place and helps actors to prioritize and make sense of threats. Thus, authority reduces actors' ontological insecurity (Mitzen 2004; Steele 2005).

Now, one might object that actors' self-value is based on their material power per se, and some realists would add that "might is right" regardless of what others think of you.[9] But when rights are respected only because of instrumental considerations or the threat of naked force, the desired self-esteem, prestige, and identity of the powerful actor remain tentative and incomplete. Their recognition due to legitimacy, on the other hand, represents the highest level of internalization (Wendt 1999). And this legitimacy must be constituted on some reciprocal relationship, in which right is correlated with obligation. Thus, even material power as a source of self-esteem and prestige is to some extent dependent on social understandings and conventions, and although it invests one with entitlements, it also restricts one through obligations. Accordingly, self- and other esteem, prestige, validating identity, and acquiring ontological security could be strong motives for even very powerful states to seek authority.

II. Abandoning the Anarchy-Hierarchy Dichotomy

A. Anarchy, Sovereignty, and Authority in World Politics

As mentioned previously, mainstream IR literature tends to deny the possibility of authority among equally sovereign states. Furthermore, it does not consider harmful nonstate actors to be an issue of authority but a problem of control. A further and related neorealist objection to the possibility of authority in world politics is that because the international system lacks a central authority to enforce international law, anarchy is the organizing principle of the system. Thus, realists come full circle: states are sovereign equals with no authority above them; this constitutes anarchy as the organizing principle of the system. But at the same time, anarchy presupposes sovereign equality and the lack of central authority (Bukovansky 2002, 23). In an effort to untie this logical problem, Stephen Krasner (1999) claims that the fact that certain states (usually strong ones) impose their will on other states—despite the alleged equality of states and the alleged resultant principle of nonintervention—means that sovereignty is actually a system of organized hypocrisy. This is a powerful argument, but I will try to show that sovereignty is not organized hypocrisy and that in fact the only way out of the sovereignty-anarchy problem is to relax the mutual exclusiveness of sovereign equality and the lack of authority in world politics. I come back to this in the following pages.

Similar to the neorealist focus on international anarchy and the consequent lack of authority as the distinguishing features of international politics, many constructivists maintain that international politics take place in an anarchic environment (at least in the meantime, if we take Wendt's inevitability-of-a-world-state argument into account). Although constructivists do not see inescapable implications of anarchy as neorealists do (such as self-help, the security dilemma, and balance of power), they still connect anarchy and sovereignty (see, e.g., Lipschutz 2000, 140). Alexander Wendt and Daniel Friedheim (1996) consider the presence of hierarchy under anarchy in special situations that they dub "informal empires," and Nicholas Onuf and Frank Klink (1989) see international politics as a heteronomy based on a principle of "rule." However, the concept of Great Power authority in international politics is underdeveloped in constructivist literature,[10] which still accepts the assumption of anarchy in international politics.[11] Wendt and Friedheim do not elaborate on the possibility of authority and hierarchy outside informal empires, and Onuf and Klink do not explain who it is exactly that "rules" in the heteronomous system of rule. Finally, while Bruce Cronin (2001) talks about hegemonic authority as a social property, he distinguishes between the hegemonic power and the other great powers. Cronin argues that only hegemonic states possess authority in international politics, while the other great powers lack this attribute. Hegemony and Great Powerness are role identities, which according to Cronin compete with each other. Hegemony is related to authority and multilateralism; Great Powerness is associated with unilateralism and anarchy.

The principle of sovereign equality—the alleged foundation of international anarchy and therefore the cause for the lack of authority in world politics—as well is not problematized enough by constructivists and English School scholars. Thus, Reus-Smit, for instance, claims that "the principle of sovereign equality is an unquestioned given" today (1999, 102). Chris Brown notes that "[s]tates are legally equal, differing in capabilities (Great Powers, Medium Powers, Small Powers) but with the same standing in international society" (2002, 34). Stephen Kocs believes that the "content of the three long-established norms [of international law: sovereign equality, nonintervention, and good faith] is well-defined and provokes little disagreement among states" (1994, 539). Finally, Barry Buzan maintains that "[s]overeignty as the defining quality of states (pieces/players) cannot be disentangled from anarchy as the defining quality of system structure (and therefore the rules of the game)" (2004, 178). Although he considers "great power management" of the international system to be a "primary institution" in world politics, Buzan stops short of arguing that this oligopolistic order vests the Great Powers with authority.

I, on the other hand, do want to question the nature of so-called sovereign equality and its relationship to anarchy and authority (over both state and nonstate actors), and therefore I problematize sovereignty in a manner different from most constructivists. I follow such authors as David Lake and Gerry Simpson in arguing that sovereignty, and institutions of violence in general, *can* establish some degree of authority in international politics. As such, the Great Powers have the highest interest in preserving the institution of sovereignty because it creates a structure of authority and status according to principles of *legitimate* power (as opposed to illegitimate power). In the institution of sovereignty in international politics, the holders of superior coercive capabilities acquire not only more avenues for influencing smaller states in the strict material sense but a privileged social status. Although Great Powers might compete with each other over the leadership of the system or forcefully intervene in small states, they usually share an interest in preserving the rules and norms by which other transborder actors accept their leadership and define them as Great Powers from the outset—"power over opinion" à la E. H. Carr.

B. Great Power Authority and Sovereign Equality

We have seen previously that the Great Powers do possess special rights and duties in international politics. But how can the authority of the

Great Powers exist at the same time as the principle of sovereign equality? Here we have to untie the mutual exclusiveness of sovereignty and authority. The first step is to explain what the term *sovereign equality* means. Simpson's analysis is extremely useful here. As Simpson explains, there are actually three forms of sovereign equality in international law: (1) formal, (2) legislative, and (3) existential. On the first, he writes,

> [F]ormal equality encompasses the principle that in *judicial settings* states have equity in the vindication and "exercise of rights." No state can be barred . . . from bringing a claim to international law that its rights have been violated, and in bringing such a claim the state will be treated equally before law.
>
> In this way, the distinction between formal equality and equality of rights becomes an important one. All states do not have the same rights (absolute equality or equality of rights) though all states have the legal capacity to enjoy the rights they already possess in *judicial* settings (formal equality). . . . The point is that rules that do apply to the same states should apply equally. (2004, 43–44)

Legislative equality is based on two principles: first, "that states are bound only by those legal norms to which they have given their consent"; and, second, that states have equally weighted votes and equal representation in the decision-making process of international bodies "and an equal role in the formation and application of customary law and treaty law" (Simpson 2004, 48). However, Simpson shows that the Great Powers possess constitutional privileges within international organizations and that international law recognizes certain law-making privileges of the Great Powers, as in the case of the doctrine of specially affected states (ibid., 52). Finally, existential equality includes a state's sphere of domestic jurisdiction, its right to territorial integrity, its right to political independence, and its right to participation in international institutions. Simpson views existential sovereignty as a negative right, or a threshold immunity, that does not preclude preferential positive rights of certain states. Simpson concludes that "the classic principle of sovereign equality can accommodate, and indeed justify, a number of material hierarchies" (ibid., 61). This is why he believes that legalized hegemony can exist side by side with sovereign equality.

The international law perspective is thus very important for understanding the possibility of authority in an international system of sovereign equals. However, authority could be conferred not just by legal structures but also through informal or semiformal mechanisms, customs, and codes. Note that the legalized model of authority is not the only kind of authority in social and political relations. And indeed, "primitive" societies without a formal juridical system are by no means without authority (Snyder 2002). According to Weber (1968), authority can come in three basic types: legal, traditional, and charismatic. Authority constructs a hierarchy of rule within the issue area. Hence, we can see that in modern international politics there is some clustering of the various forms of authority discussed previously. The Great Powers have some legal authority as embodied in their privileged membership in international organs and forums such as the Concert of Europe and the UN Security Council as well as in their special role in the formalization of international law. Some Great Powers are also said to possess "soft power" (which could be equated with Weber's charisma), which is the attractiveness of their domestic political, societal, and economic systems. And they enjoy traditional authority, which is probably what Bull conceives of as their managerial or operational rights and duties. In this sense, Hans Mommsen's perception of authority as something that is "more than advice and less than a command, an advice which one may not safely ignore" (quoted in Arendt 1958, 100) sounds very apt with regard to the Great Powers' special status in international relations.

III. Institutions of Violence and Authority

In general, Great Power authority comprises two main clusters of institutions and norms. The first, or primary, cluster includes the institutions of violence in world politics. These institutions govern the employment of transborder violent force. The secondary cluster is made up of norms and institutions that prescribe the generation, regulation, management, and control of transborder flows. The second cluster of norms has been dealt with extensively by literature on hegemonic stability and by neoliberalism, which focus on the role that powerful actors play in the construction and maintenance of regimes and institutions of transborder flows and on the special and authoritative status they enjoy within them. However, I believe that the implications of the institutions of violence for Great Power authority have not thus far been fully understood. The main thrust of my theoretical argument, therefore, will deal with this aspect.

This book focuses on institutions of violence because Great Powers are commonly defined in IR literature, as well as in political practice, as first and foremost holders of superior coercive and destructive capabilities and resources that can be converted into coercive and destructive power.[12] Most IR scholars would probably agree that a necessary condition for being a Great Power is the possession of a certain level of *transborder* coercive and destructive capability (on top of other resources such as economic power, a large population, and natural resources). Of course, debates abound about the utility of violent force in the contemporary world (see, e.g., Mueller 1989, 2004; Rosecrance 1999). It is not my intention in this book to enter this debate. Rather, I argue that as long as states retain armed forces and have not renounced their right to use them across national borders—even if various normative and material inhibitions prohibit the activation of these forces—an intrinsic link exists between the concept of Great Power and organized violence. In this sense, realists and constructivists both seem to agree that, as long as transborder organized violence is a *possibility* (due to either the permissiveness of anarchy or the legitimate right to use violence), power politics in the most literal sense will have important ramifications in world politics (Mearsheimer 2001; Wendt 2003).

It is important to note too (as many authors before me have done) that the regulation and management of organized violence—the "forces of destruction" in Daniel Deudney's (2000) terms—is one of the basic problems of social life. The nature of technologies of violence, who controls them, and how and why they are employed have an impact on all other spheres of life. Social relations—within states and across their borders—cannot exist independently of the various aspects of organized violence. Because the use of violence endangers all social relations and constructs, they are dependent on certain institutionalization of violence and definitions of legitimate and illegitimate violence.

Thus, to many the regulation of organized violence represents the primary problem of politics and social life (Deudney 2000, 88). But control and regulation of the forces of destruction also facilitate politicolegal structures (Giddens 1985, 16). Accordingly, the distinction between legitimate and illegitimate violence, the regulation of the forces of destruction, and the reproduction of these distinctions and regulations constitute and enable political authority (Volkov 2002). From this point of view, violent power and legitimate authority "are not antithetical, but complementary," as Inis Claude contends (1966, 368). Hence, if we wish to understand how authority is enabled in international politics, we first have to have a notion of which mechanisms and processes legitimize violent force. Institutions of violence, I argue, carry the potential to legitimize the power of the Great Powers and to vest them with authority. Institutions of violence convert raw material power into social conventions that specify the limits of the allowable in the sphere of international force, and, hence, they establish rights and duties. In other words, "[t]o say that a person has authority is to say not that he actually has power but that the political formula *assigns* him power, and that those who *adhere* to the formula expect him to have power and regard his exercise of it as just and proper. The regime may now be described as the structures of authority and authority practices" (Lasswell and Kaplan 1950, 133; emphasis added).

In my view, institutions of transborder violence in world politics consist of three main interrelated and mutually constitutive elements: sovereignty, actorhood in the sphere of transborder force, and the laws of war. These elements correspond to the following questions: (1) *what* are actors entitled to do to each other and *why?* (sovereignty); (2) *who* is allowed to exercise transborder violence and through *which* type of wielder of force? (actorhood); and (3) *when* and *how* are actors allowed to do it? (the laws of war and armed conflict). Thus, I conceive of institutions of violence in their constitutive meaning as ideational structures that define realms of possibility in the sphere of transborder force, and not in their organizational or bureaucratic manifestations (such as alliances or international organizations). I view institutions in general as not merely regimes that actors accept or reject depending on their self-interest or on instrumental calculations but as deep constitutive structures that effect the very construction of the identity and interests of the actors (Hurd 1999; Reus-Smit 1999; Philpot 2001; Buzan 2004). Institutions "are of a primary order. . . . Institutions are the permissive context of many social transactions" (Holsti 2004, 18). Or, as Douglass North put it, "institutions are the humanly devised constraints that structure political, economic and social interaction. They consist of both informal constraints (sanctions, taboos, customs, traditions, and codes of conduct), and formal rules (constitutions, laws, property rights)" (1991, 97).

A. Sovereignty

i. What Is Sovereignty?

In the literature of IR theory and political science, sovereignty is broadly understood to have two meanings: the effective control over a territory (empirical sovereignty) and authority (the legitimate right to wield such control). Of course, the two meanings are powerfully linked (for instance, effective control cannot be kept in the long run without legitimate authority and vice versa). Nonetheless, exclusive and final territorial political authority is the trademark of sovereignty that distinguishes it from other forms of political systems and organizations (Hinsley 1986).

Janice Thomson (1995) asserts that sovereignty is an institution of metapolitical authority: it gives the state the monopolistic right to decide what is political and hence subject to coercion within its territory (see also Barkin and Cronin 1994, 107). But such authority could not be maintained for long within the state if other states (and also other transborder actors) did not intrinsically acknowledge the state's right to exercise this capacity. Here the connection between sovereignty as authority and sovereignty as effective control becomes important. Thus, as Wendt argues, the second key element of sovereignty—which makes it an international institution—is self-restraint among states. This self-restraint is an admission of each state's right to metapolitical authority within its borders, and hence it is an important factor in facilitating the materialization of this right into effective control. Sovereignty is therefore an internationally acknowledged institution of mutually empowered state rights and duties, both domestic and international. This mutual empowerment necessitates self-restraint, but self-restraint also requires reciprocal recognition or empowerment (Spruyt 1994). In this sense, I find the two to be mutually constitutive. This mutually constitutive element of self-restraint and mutual recognition serves as the *primary norm of sovereignty* (Löwenheim and Paltiel 2004).[13] Thomson's working definition for sovereignty seems to capture this view: sovereignty is "the recognition by internal and external actors that the state has the exclusive authority to intervene coercively in activities within its territory" (1995, 219).

Accordingly, for sovereignty as domestic metapolitical authority to exist and persist over time, states have to be embedded in an international culture of rights. However, this culture of rights does not necessarily preclude the right to be free of violence in times of conflict, as Wendt argues. Yet sovereignty informs states and other actors of the *legitimate limits* of transborder violence. These limits are important in two interconnected ways.

First, they represent the normative scope for the employment of transborder violence in terms of *territorial boundaries* (since state authority is linked to territoriality). In this way, they define whether states are entitled by the norms of sovereignty to conquer other states and completely annihilate their independent existence, to effect a change in other states' territorial boundaries without annulling their sovereignty, or to leave other states' territorial integrity intact but infringe on their borders in order to coerce them to do something or not to do something.

Second, sovereignty also sets constitutive limits as to what counts as *legitimate reasons, motivations,* and *interests* that warrant or allow the employment of transborder force. Mlada Bukovansky's discussion of sovereignty is very important in this regard. Bukovansky conceives of sovereignty as a variable in terms of its legitimate locus (with whom sovereignty resides, e.g., absolutist sovereignty versus popular sovereignty). To her, various legitimating principles of sovereignty within states represent changing hegemonic cultures in the international system. Such different hegemonic cultures of sovereignty construct various legitimate motivations and interests that states pursue through transborder force. In my view, the identity of the subjects of security (the people for whom the state should supply security) is also defined by the changing conceptions of sovereignty's locus. It goes without saying that states strive to defend their sovereignty. But the important question is, Who is legitimately entitled to demand that the state supply them with security? In this regard, it is important to highlight that although liberals—such as Moravcsik (1997)—might conceive that issues such as the identity of the subjects of security are determined by domestic politics, I believe that they are also largely influenced by systemic norms and ideas of sovereignty. Relying on Bukovansky, I argue that if sovereignty represents a hegemonic culture or order in the *international* system—"an order in which one mode of legitimacy is dominant" (2002, 50)—then ideas about why and for whom states should employ transborder force are not simply "domestic" issues: they represent hegemonic notions of sovereignty in the *international system.*

In this manner, ancien régime concepts of legitimate sovereignty resulted in an almost complete identification between the monarch and the state. Prior to the French Revolution, as Bukovansky demonstrates, "the relationship between state and nation was more distinct than fused" (2002, 73). Rather than being a specific characterization of France or any other European state, such conceptions of sovereignty were systemic in nature, permeating and transcending state borders. As such, these ideas had a great effect on the identity of the people whose security and protection were deemed to be a state duty and legitimate interest. Furthermore, systemic conceptions of absolutist sovereignty considered society to be composed of classes and "orders" and not of individuals. This too informed the identity of the subjects of security within that systemic configuration of sovereignty. Bukovansky concludes, "Reason of state viewed in terms of a monarch's interests could well be constituted differently than reason of state viewed as 'national' interest" (ibid., 74).

Hegemonic cultures of sovereignty thus define whether the state can wield transborder force to advance or protect private interests of state rulers or whether such violence is only warranted by broader political purposes. In fact, this is one of the differences between early modern sovereignty and modern popular sovereignty. In the first case, very few people were considered to be the subjects of state security and moral purpose, while under modern sovereignty all the citizens of the state are equally considered as subjects of security (Reus-Smit 1999). Another example of the effect of hegemonic cultures of sovereignty on the legitimate reasons and motivations for transborder force is the issue of whether a "civilizing" mission permits certain states to use force against other actors in world politics[14] (e.g., for the fulfillment of moral or humanitarian ends). Further, the hegemonic culture of sovereignty will define if other nontangible incentives and motives legitimize transborder violence (religious reasons; the pursuit of "virtue," glory, and prowess; the seeking of vengeance; ideological reasons) or if only ostensibly material and rationalist reasons (economic interests, commercial policies, geopolitical and security considerations) are deemed to be within the normative boundaries of the reasons for transborder violence. Thus, for example, absolutist sovereignty enabled personal wars of prestige and glory between monarchs and dynasts and led states to focus on protection or aggrandizement of royal interests. With popular sovereignty, however, war came to be seen as an instrument of public statecraft (Latham 2002, 253) and reasons such as dynastic glory and aggrandizement ceased to legitimize the use of transborder force. By the same token, in the 1990s a growing number of states considered the protection of human rights in *other* states as a legitimate reason for the use of transborder violence on their part.

The exact nature of the rights that sovereignty bestows on states—and on the individuals that make them up as corporate actors—was never fixed. We will see in the empirical chapters how the territorial and motivational limitations prescribed by the norms of sovereignty changed throughout history. Thus my conception of sovereignty is a minimalist one: sovereignty is indeed an institution of both domestic and international metapolitical authority. It is based on the primary norm of recognition and self-restraint, but self-restraint and recognition as such do not preclude the use of violence across state borders, nor do they guarantee the existence of states, regimes, and their people in *all* circumstances and historical periods (see, e.g., Korman 1996 on the "Right of Conquest"). In this sense, Jens Bartelson is correct when he notes that sovereignty is actually a line in water drawn and redrawn again and again inside knowledge and the history of political ideas (1995, 52–53).

ii. Sovereignty and the Great Powers

I defined authority earlier as legitimized power that is manifested and reproduced by the special rights and duties of its bearer. This legitimized power constructs a hierarchy of rule among the actors. In this section, I wish to elaborate on what legitimized power actually means by exploring the distinction between legitimate and *illegitimate* power in the context of sovereignty. This distinction is important to my discussion of PATHs because authority also entails the right to exact costs for deviance from social norms. But without a distinction between legitimate and illegitimate practices in the sphere of organized violence, norms cannot be deviated from and hence authority has no meaning.

When actors perceive each other as enemies (in the Wendtian sense), although the Hobbesian culture of enmity itself can become legitimate and authoritative from the perspective of the actors in it, no *specific* actors within it can possess authority over other actors. There are two interrelated reasons for this. First, smaller actors will simply be absorbed by the more powerful ones whenever opportunity arises and for any possible reason, and at the same time the powerful actors will not recognize each other as capable of authority. The powerful in this world do not share a common understanding of the legitimacy and limits of power in their respective spheres of influence. And while strong actors might let weaker actors keep their independence, this is not because they think it is right but because they benefit from it or cannot change it at that moment. When the powerful represent each other as enemies, they cannot become authoritative actors, because even if they avoid abolishing the weaker actors, the threat that the powerful actors themselves will eliminate each other voids the concept of Great Power privileged rights and duties. In a system of Great Power authority, on the other hand, argues Simpson, rough equality (in rights) among the Great Powers is the norm: "hegemony appears to require the fiction of equality (albeit extended only to the hegemons themselves) in order to sustain it" (2004, 110).

A second reason that Great Power authority is impossible within an internalized Hobbesian culture is that rights that constitute authority have to be anchored in certain long-standing obligations, but the logic of enmity that characterizes the Hobbesian culture precludes such obligations. Authority is given by consent, and consent to authority requires some long-term commitments on the part of the strong actors with regard to the rights of the weak. The smaller powers might abide by the commands of the stronger ones even if the latter profess no commitment to norms that guarantee some (minimal) rights of the weak. But this would be more like involuntary and fearful obedience to force than intrinsic compliance with privileged rights of holders of authority. Society accords privileged rights to certain actors when the latter are also bound by certain obligations, as minimal or negative as they might be. Rights as an intersubjective set of legitimate entitlements that an actor possesses have no meaning unless accompanied by obligations on the part of the bearer of rights; these aspects are correlative (Gewirth 1988). Rights that are not correlated with duties represent tyranny and not a system of authority. Thus, Weber argues that during history even divinities were perceived as engaging in semicontractual relations with man and therefore as having some obligations toward him (1966, xxxi). And in the institution of sovereignty, even the most powerful actors are bound by certain normative limits in the employment of transborder force—the primary norm of sovereignty. In the Hobbesian culture of anarchy, on the other hand, states are not obliged by any norms of sovereignty, and therefore authority among states cannot exist. In addition, as no distinction between legitimate and illegitimate scope and ends for projecting transborder force exists, there will be no authoritative role of exacting costs for deviance.

Thus, in sovereignty brute violent force is converted into authority and social conventions, but this requires that states adhere to the regulations and restrictions that sovereignty places on the use of transborder force. Krasner (1999) believes that states—especially the powerful ones—often violate these norms and still pay lip service to them, a condition he dubs "organized hypocrisy." Great Powers intervene in other states and infringe on their sovereignty when their interests necessitate it or when opportunity presents itself, argues Krasner. But I agree with Brown that this does not turn sovereignty into a hollow or hypocritical concept.

[T]o claim to be sovereign is to assert a claim to valid authority in accordance with rules without which international society could not exist; hence, even when actually intervening, the rulers of states are obliged to explain how their behaviour can be understood in terms of the rules. . . . they offer such explanations, not,

as Krasner suggests, as a matter of hypocrisy, but because failure
to do so would, as it were, end the "game", and, at the same time,
end their capacity to claim the status of sovereign since this status
only exists by virtue of the existence of international society.
(Brown 2002, 36)

Therefore, the excuses that states provide when infringing on the
norms of sovereignty do not necessarily point to hypocrisy but indicate
that actors wish to justify their actions within the limits of the allowable
(Hurd 1999, 391). And as Carl Friedrich notes, authority consists of the
capacity to justify oneself in meaningful terms—meaningful to the community (1958, 36).

Accordingly, despite the fact that in the world of sovereignty Great
Powers might infringe on the domestic metapolitical authority of smaller
states, they look for justifications that will legitimize their conduct. This
might sound close to Krasner's definition of hypocrisy—a condition in
which the logic of consequences predominates the logic of appropriateness while keeping rhetorical allegiance to the logic of appropriateness.[15]
However, this is only a situation close to hypocrisy, because hypocritical
actors do *all* that they can to achieve their ends while swearing allegiance
to a professed normative principle, whereas in sovereignty strong actors
still stop short at certain acts that the professed normative principles prohibit (e.g., avoiding, since 1945, the formal annexation or physical annihilation of another state). This is a quantitative difference that amounts
to a qualitative difference. In other words, the institution of sovereignty
allows the small powers a (minimal) degree of security by exercising a
restraining influence on stronger powers. In this sense, I endorse a constitutive and institutional approach to sovereignty that sees the logic of
consequences as *enabled* by the logic of appropriateness.

This qualitative difference between organized hypocrisy and sovereignty as a constitutive institution of international relations gives the
Great Powers privileged rights and duties in the society of states. The
institution of sovereignty with its primary norm of recognition and self-
restraint establishes the rules of the international game. Rules "tell us
how to carry on" (Burch 1998, 11). But rules also constitute forms of
social rule that order social relations, assign resources, and characterize
interactions. They also assign institutional positions and roles for the
agents. Rules legitimize certain forms and employment of material power
and delegitimize others and are therefore the connection or link between
rulers and ruled. Rulers and ruled are bound in a nexus of rules (Onuf

and Klink 1989). And this is why the principle of sovereign equality—or international legal sovereignty, in Krasner's terms—still exists: sovereignty constitutes international rule. It legitimizes the power of the Great Powers and at the same time guarantees to a certain extent the security of the smaller states by reducing the arbitrariness in the use of transborder force. Sovereignty and the concept of sovereign equality thus enable the very feasibility of authority in international politics. Authority can exist only among subjects in a moral community of rights and duties. After all, masters have no authority over the slaves they deem their property[16] in as much as one cannot have authority over an inanimate object. Great Powers that treat other states and international actors as slaves or objects without any rights can have no authority. Only the recognition of others as moral persons can enable authority, because, as I argue throughout this chapter, authority is given by consent.

Precisely because violent power as such is not delegitimized in the international system, the possessors of superior material capabilities gain a privileged status within that system as long as they abide by the fundamental rules of the game. They obtain a right to lead the system because their power is now justified in the sense of being subjected and conditioned by at least a minimal set of obligations. Power is now more than mere material capabilities—it is a social convention. Thus, the very fact that states—Great Powers included—employ transborder violence against each other does not mean that authority is absent from this realm. Not all forms of such violence are antithetical to authority. This stands in contrast to Hannah Arendt's contention that "where force is used, authority itself has failed" (1958, 82)[17] and seems to vindicate Sebastian de Grazia's claim that "[i]n the obtaining of authority, the use of force will make authority impossible to achieve, *if force is detested by the public. If force is esteemed, then it can lead to authority*" (1959, 329; emphasis added). As long as the employment of transborder force remains within the institutions of violence, authority has not failed.

Recognition of other states' rights increases certainty for these states, which in turn facilitates more regulation and ordering of the system, mainly through the establishment of further norms of security. These norms confirm and prove the value of the Other as a moral subject. While Great Powers rise and decline, some of the norms they institutionalized survive and become part of social reality. Although norms that the Great Powers author can be said to reflect their interests, they also present incentives for smaller powers to participate in the system by defining realms of possibility and rules in international politics. Despite the fact that there are no clear-cut formal relations of pyramidal hierarchy between the Great Powers and smaller states (as in a bureaucracy or a military chain of command), rules authored or adhered to by the Great Powers nonetheless generate a structure of authority that lies somewhere between directive rules (formal political domination) and instructive rules (ideational domination), exactly the form of authority that Mommsen envisaged: an advice that cannot be safely ignored. The authority of the Great Powers is thus based on their compliance with the normative limits of sovereignty and is augmented by their being the *authors* of the international system's norms of security.

By authoring and authorizing rules and norms of security *and abiding by them,* the Great Powers create the distinction between on the one hand "normal" states and on the other "rogue" or "outlaw" states and other transborder actors. The normalization process that Great Powers engage in constructs an institutional framework within which international politics take place. This authorization and institutionalization of international politics, and especially of organized violence, provides actors in the system with ready-made answers for questions that otherwise might be invoked. Precisely because there is no central legal authority in world politics to enforce international law, the Great Powers become authoritative gatekeepers that distinguish between legitimate and illegitimate violence.[18] Hall and Biersteker argue that "authority entails both a social relationship between author and subject, and a definable domain of action. The consent to authority is socially constructed through a variety of different rhetorical and political practices—ranging from behavioral consent to routines, norms and public declarations of recognition" (2002, 6). Behavioral consent to routines, or the rules of the game, then is similar to Bull's operational rights of the Great Powers.

In this sense, hierarchy and authority exist in international politics in a way reminiscent of domestic politics: instead of a monopoly over legitimate violence, we have in international politics a cartel of wielders of legitimized power. PATHs are outsiders to this cartel, as I discuss in the next chapter. The cartelization (instead of monopolization) of legitimate power by states, and the resulting function of the Great Powers in the cartel as gatekeepers, serves as the connecting link between the primary and the secondary norms of sovereignty, which I discuss in the next section. Namely, not only does the cartel of sovereign states and Great Powers establish legitimized power and relations of rule—or *Herschaft,* as Onuf and Klink argue (1989, 162–63)—among the members of the cartel, but the cartelization of legitimized power also excludes unruly nonstate actors. By this exclusion I mean to the principle of legitimate actorhood in the sphere of extraterritorial violence. Legitimate actorhood developed hand in hand with sovereignty, and in the following section I explore this second constituent of Great Power authority.

B. Actorhood in the Sphere of Transborder Violence

Since the late nineteenth century, only sovereign states have been acknowledged by international law to possess the legal and customary right to employ transborder violence. In fact, "[w]ar came to be characterized as a 'right inherent in sovereignty itself.' Moreover, the war-making right was thought of as the paramount attribute of sovereignty" (Dinstein 2001, 71). Today, only a sovereign state has the privilege to issue a transborder-armed challenge to another state. Thus, international war also became a practice of exclusion and a device to set a group (of states) apart from other wielders of force. Historically, however, sovereignty and actorhood in the sphere of transborder violence were not identical. Between the sixteenth and mid-nineteenth centuries, nonstate extraterritorial wielders of violence—such as mercenaries, brigands, filibusters, pirates, and privateers—often practiced transborder violence either independently or in the official service of sovereign states (Thomson 1994). In addition, nonsovereign polities claimed the legitimate right to order and authorize transborder violence. However, as Thomson and Spruyt have shown, states gradually delegitimized nonstate and nonsovereign violence and its wielders and avoided using it as a resource—initially because it was seen as counterproductive and later because it was considered immoral as well. States constructed a cartel of sovereigns that prohibited other actors from ordering and employing intensive transborder violence. In effect, sovereign states today constitute an elite club in world politics that excludes nonsovereign and nonstate authorizers and wielders of transborder force. In chapter 5 I argue that the 9/11 attacks alerted the members of this club to the efforts of outsiders to change the rules for admission. Part of the trauma of 9/11 was precisely related to the realization that this elite club of states had been invaded by predatory nonstate actors thought to have disappeared two hundred years ago.

In modern history (the nineteenth century and onward, especially the Cold War system), PATHs were an almost nonexistent problem of authority because sovereign states, and especially the Great Powers, effectively monopolized intensive *transborder* violence and because nonstate actors had not perpetrated or presumed a right to order acts of significant transborder violence that grossly transgressed the laws of war (as opposed to many cases of intensive *intra*border violence in failed and weak states). Thus, in modern history, nonstate transborder actors issued no severe challenge to what I argue became the monopolistic right of states and especially the Great Powers. This may have created the notion that sovereignty and the right to order and use intensive transborder force are one and the same. Nonetheless, the 9/11 attacks clearly showed that nonstate actors are capable of intensive transborder violence that grossly violates the laws of war. And not only did the perpetrators of these terror attacks reveal themselves materially capable of inflicting such damage, but they claimed to possess a *right* to do so. "Ordinary" criminals do not claim a right to murder, vandalize, steal, smuggle, and so forth. Thus they are really a problem of control. But once a nonstate actor claims the right to intensive transborder violence, I believe that we have to consider the implications for Great Power authority. In effect, the post-9/11 world is haunted by the specter of norm decay in the sphere of actorhood.[19]

Thomson views the process of the delegitimization of nonstate transborder violence as an outcome of the domestic monopolization of violence by the state from the late seventeenth century and onward and also as a consequence of the intensifying connections between states (mainly in the commercial sphere). States gradually understood that unruly nonstate transborder wielders of intensive violence might cause unpredictable outcomes for them and complicate interstate relations in an undesirable manner. Currently, if states restrain themselves and regulate their mutual use of violence, the implication is that they focus on preparing themselves precisely to ward off the self-restrained and regulated violent capabilities and policies of other like-minded states. This means that states leave "structural holes" (Burt 1992) in their territories (e.g., civilian population centers) or in their overseas interests (e.g., international commercial shipping) as unprotected targets. Historically, although states gradually avoided exploiting such structural holes, nonstate wielders of transborder violence (maritime pirates, terrorists) tended to abuse them. In other words, while states became more rule oriented as actors in their mutual enactment of violence, nonstate actors remained unruly.

Thomson and Spruyt note that eventually states provided mutual empowerment for each other, and thus they excluded other authorizing actors and wielders of transborder organized violence from the international system. This was mainly because sovereign states recognized that it was preferable to conduct regular relationships with like units, who represented the most reliable and predictable international actors. Increasing levels of international interactions since the eighteenth century, especially in the commercial sphere, necessitated some intrinsic reliability in the relations between states, including in the use of organized violence. As states consolidated and elaborated the primary norm of sovereignty (mutual recognition and self-restraint) along with domestic property and civil rights, isomorphism evolved among sovereign states. This process highlighted the differences between them and nonsovereign polities, as well as between states and nonstate transborder wielders of violence, who were usually unruly and less vulnerable to sanctions because of their greater mobility (pirates are a prime example). This growing isomorphism and mutual empowerment among states gradually led to the delegitimization of nonstate transborder violence and to the selection of states among the other organizational types as the cartelizers of the social and legal right to wield and order not only domestic coercion but also transborder violence. Thus, a more regulated and centralized system appeared in the early eighteenth century, and the sovereign state gradually appropriated the right to legitimately wield transborder coercion by the mid-nineteenth century (Thomson 1994, 1995; Holsti 1996, 28–32).

Nonstate transborder violence did not completely disappear from that point onward. Terrorists, organized criminals, and even pirates continued to operate transnationally, usually from weak states or nonsovereign polities that did not possess an effective domestic control over organized violence. Other states also kept using nonstate actors to advance their interests well into the twentieth century, among them the Great Powers themselves (especially during the Cold War). But there are two important differences between these phenomena and the realities of the sixteenth through eighteenth centuries discussed previously. First, most intensive nonstate violence in the modern age, especially in the twentieth century, occurred within the context of domestic strife or decolonization and not in interstate war. Thus, it did not violate the containing function of sovereignty. Nonstate violence in the West was minimal (in terms of costs in human lives and property), but it had terrible consequences in the Third World (as in such cases as Rwanda, Liberia, and Angola). However, although the damages of nonstate violence within certain failed states in Africa or Asia often dwarf the loss of life in interstate war in bellicose regions such as the Middle East or Central Asia, the former is almost always contained within state borders or specific regional settings. This is quite distinct from the nonstate violence of the early modern period, which recognized no borders and was much more intensive than twentieth-century transborder nonstate violence. The second distinguishing element of modern nonstate violence is illustrated through the Cold War, during which the superpowers tried either to hide their support of substate violent groups (guerillas, insurgents, etc.)—often denying allegations that such support existed—or to ideologically justify their involvement with them. In either case, their reaction is telling: they knew they were infringing on international norms. In the sixteenth and seventeenth centuries, on the other hand, state rulers did not feel any strong obligation to explain their interaction with nonstate wielders of violence or to justify these relations. Furthermore, as opposed to the powers of the early modern period, who openly and officially used the services of nonstate extraterritorial violent actors within their mutual competition, the superpowers of the Cold War avoided this. Thus, we have today a norm of excluding nonstate actors from extraterritorial violence.[20]

C. The Laws of War

The third element of the institutions of transborder violence—the laws of war (formal and informal)—is made up of two parts: first, norms that govern the turning to war or the immediate acknowledged justifications for war (*jus ad bellum*); and, second, norms that prescribe acknowledged behavior and conduct within war (*jus in bellum*) by identifying the legitimate targets in war and the acceptable weapons of war.

Thus, under the UN system, states are prohibited from engaging in wars of aggression for any reason (as defined by the UN General Assembly in 1974), and they have set the principles of self-defense and collective security as the sole legitimate justifications for wielding international war (Articles 2(4) and 51 of the UN Charter). Even preemptive war must be legitimized in the vocabulary of self-defense. Although states do not always agree on what *aggression* or *self-defense* mean, this does not imply that they do not consider these rules as constraints. And so, "[g]overnments, however they understand or misunderstand the *jus ad bellum,* are not prepared—in this day and age—to uphold the proposition that there are no legal restraints on the employment of interstate force. . . . When governments charge each other with infringements of Article 2(4), as happens all too frequently, such accusations are always contested. The plea that Article 2(4) is dead has never been put forward by any government" (Dinstein 2001, 89).

But self-defense and the avoidance of aggression were not always the sole legitimate justifications for initiating war. During the sixteenth to nineteenth centuries, states often justified their wars or conquests in terms of aggrandizement. This, of course, was possible because the restraining content of the institution of sovereignty in terms of the legitimate reasons for war was different from today's. The pursuit of glory or the augmentation of absolutist rule, for example, were deemed as legitimate reasons to use transborder force. Thus the legend *non sufficit orbis* (the world is not enough) informed Spanish expansionist policies and the aggressive use of transborder force in the sixteenth century. Seventeenth- and eighteenth-century perceptions of raison d'état enabled aggressive wars and the Right of Conquest. In the nineteenth and twentieth centuries, sovereignty's capacity to prescribe reasons for transborder violence also affected the emergence of humanitarian intervention as justification for war.

In other words, *jus ad bellum* as a causal or immediate justification for resorting to transborder force (such as "NATO forcefully intervened in Kosovo because a humanitarian crisis ensued there in 1999") is informed and enabled by perceptions and concepts of constitutive reasons and rights to employ such force (such as "States are entitled to protect human rights across national borders because the gross violation of certain inalienable human rights is outside the limits of sovereignty's metapolitical authority"). These constitutive rights and reasons lie within the purview of sovereignty, and the causal or immediate justifications for transborder violence are embodied in the *jus ad bellum* part of the laws of war. Similarly, the right to self-defense is also informed by the specific reasons and entitlements for resorting to violence constituted by sovereignty: once self has been attacked, it has a right to defend itself (the laws of war). But the crucial question is *who* exactly is the self that bears this right or who is the subject of security: is it the state as a corporate actor, the regime, influential interest groups within society, certain dominant classes and sectors, and so forth (sovereignty)? Thus, *jus ad bellum* provides states with an answer as to *when* they are allowed to wield transborder violence—for example, when another state actually attacks them (self-defense), when they fear another state will attack them (preemption), or when another state exceeds its limits of domestic sovereignty with regard to its civilians—but sovereignty informs them of the underlying reason *why* they should do this—for example, to protect monarchical interests, to propagate a revolutionary ideology, or to acquire more power resources.

Jus in bellum, with its various prohibitions on the use of certain weapons (designated means of destruction) and delineation of legitimate targets in war, manifests the second regulative function of the laws of war. Thus, for example, the modern laws of war define the status of prisoners of war and their rights (Morrow 2001) and establish the prohibition of targeting noncombatants in interstate war (the 1899 and 1907 Hague Protocols, as well as the 1947 and 1977 Geneva Protocols). There is no general definition of noncombatants, but legal categories include civilians, prisoners of war, and wounded soldiers (Johnson 2000). During the 1960s and 1970s, several international conventions also prohibited violence against civilian aircraft and sea vessels. *Jus in bellum* also prohibits violence against state leaders and diplomats. Accordingly, since the late seventeenth century, international assassinations of heads of states were considered illegitimate in world politics (Ward 2000), although this norm may be declining since the 1980s with the alleged U.S. attempts to target Libya's Qaddafi (1986) and Iraq's Saddam Hussein (2003).

Jus in bellum is also informed by concepts of reasons and rights to transborder violence within sovereignty. In the sixteenth and the first half of the seventeenth centuries, when sovereignty prescribed almost any reason for war, there was little respect for the life and property of private individuals and barely any intrinsic limitations on the nature of the means of destruction. We shall see in chapter 3 how Spain seriously thought of flooding the rebellious Dutch provinces, for example. Furthermore, when waging transborder violence was not the monopolist right of sovereign states (in other words, when the principle of actorhood did not denounce the private wielding of force), civilians were not considered off-limit targets of cross-border violence. Thus, privateering as a form of privately waged war allowed the indiscriminate attack of civilians of other states for private purposes (e.g., retrieving one's property through private reprisals). This led to a system that included only minimal regulations on the use of violence once it was enacted. However, as the limitations and restrictions on the reasons for war and on actorhood in transborder violence became more elaborate, *jus in bellum* grew to be more codified and clear. This codification, in turn, solidified the defining mechanism that informs states that a certain violent action warrants the use of force on their part and entitles them to infringe on another state's sovereignty. Thus, we will see that in the sixteenth and seventeenth centuries, in the absence of codified and restrictive *jus in bellum,* the dominant maritime powers of the time did not define the Barbary pirates' intensive attacks on civilians as warranting a harsh response, nor could the powers overcome their own conflicts in order to suppress the pirates cooperatively. This perpetuated Barbary piracy as a system of sea predation and captivity for more than three hundred years. On the other hand, the attacks of 9/11 took place in an international system where the deliberate targeting of civilians is strictly prohibited, a factor that enabled the intensive response of the United States against the Taliban and al Qaeda in Afghanistan and also the cooperation of the other Great Powers in the War on Terror.

IV. Great Power Authority, Institutions of Violence, and Moral Consistency

We have seen that in international society the Great Powers intrinsically reduce the harm they do to each other and to smaller actors. This self-restraint, as G. John Ikenberry notes, indeed reduces the "return to power" (2001, 32). But institutions of violence do not simply reduce the utility of power for the powerful actors, as neoliberals seem to believe; they also can invest key actors in the institution with authority that increases their own security. When an authoritative agent employs power, although he is restricted and restrained by the institutions that enable his authority and thus has to retain some of the rights of those actors on which power is exerted, he also guarantees a measure of security for *himself*. Of course, no one wishes to be a subject of coercion, even if it is practiced by an agent of legitimate power. The real effects of direct violence cannot be denied. From the perspective of the individual victims of a bomb, for example, it does not matter whether the bomb was exploded as part of a "limited" or "total" war or whether the bombing party was a state or a terror group: the destruction and death are the same for individuals in any case. However, from the perspective of the states system, the institutions of violence construct power in symmetrical terms—not in the material sense of the distribution of power capabilities but in the sense of the distribution of ideas: what one can do with the power possessed and who is entitled from the outset to possess and employ transborder violent power. Paradoxical as it may sound, this symmetry of ideas constitutes and reproduces an asymmetry of rights—or authority.

This highlights the fact that authority is defined by both the powerful and the weak actors at the same time. In the same manner that contractual theories of (domestic) sovereignty see sovereignty as the outcome of the willingness or decision of the individuals to transfer their natural rights to practice coercion and violence to the state (and in return enjoy security), so too do the institutions of violence represent a social contract in the international realm. Robert Jackson (2000) argues that a global covenant exists in international politics and that states are joined in it through three major practices: sovereign equality, noninterference, and territorial integrity; however, I claim that the essence of the global contract is authority or legitimized power. In international politics, small states and nonstate actors maintain some autonomy (or, in other words, "security") in return for their acknowledgment of Great Power authority. But although the Great Powers acquire authority because of their self-restraint toward each other and toward the smaller states, unless the latter also practice self-restraint toward the powerful, Great Power authority cannot exist.[21]

"In general," writes Ikenberry, "a leading state will want to bind weaker and secondary states to a set of rules and institutions of postwar order—*locking in these states to predictable patterns of behavior*—but remain unbound itself, free of institutional constraints and obligations. *But to get the willing participation and compliance of other states,* the leading state must offer to limit its own autonomy and ability to exercise power arbitrarily" (2001, 51; emphasis added). While Ikenberry talks about order in the sense of peaceful interactions and international stability, I argue that metaorder rests on social agreement about how to define the limits of destructive power from the outset. In a stable metaorder, the use of force is legitimate within certain circumstances and justifications—in other words, it is institutionalized. When weak and strong agree on the boundaries of self-restraint, actorhood, and the laws that govern the actual use of force, metaorder is achieved.

Stable metaorder is achieved when actors avoid "asymmetrical" warfare as a matter of course (the "secret machinations" of Hobbes's state of nature). Thucydides notes in his famous Melian Dialogue that "the strong do what they can, and the weak submit" (1943, 267). On a certain level, this indeed reflects the reality of power politics. However, as I understand it, the weak submit only as long as they accept the *idea* that the power of the strong is right. I do not mean that the weak believe that the enactment of force against them is desired and good but that they accept the idea that the power of the strong is enacted within the boundaries of legitimacy in international politics (Franck 1990). Resistance to the powerful is thus framed within the institutions of violence too. These institutions eventually maintain the authority of the Great Powers in international politics.

In this sense, moral authority is pivotal for hegemony, as Daniel Garst (1989) claims. In other words, power is "powerful" as long as it is not absolute and based on (minimal) obligations that produce consent. In addition, moral authority means that the powerful cannot be at variance with the norms they themselves authored or accepted from previous Great Powers. Recourse to "barbarism," as Ivan Arreguín-Toft dubs the "systematic violation of the laws of war in pursuit of a military or political objective" (2001, 101), can significantly risk the authoritative position of a Great Power, especially if this barbarism includes a considerable deviation from the other institutions of violence as well. Of course, Great Powers can employ their superior material capabilities against weaker actors and compel them to accept their will. But that would suffice only as long as the weak do not search from the outset for a secret machination—or some form of asymmetric method of warfare—to resist the superior violent capabilities of the strong. The possibility and intensity of such asymmetric warfare depend to a great extent on technological realities (e.g., civilian airliners converted into cruise missiles). But various destructive means or techniques have been employed asymmetrically even in less technologically advanced times (e.g., assassination of heads of state, state-sponsored piracy, inciting rebellion). Chapter 3 explores a case of asymmetrical warfare in the factual sense (Barbary piracy in the early modern period) that caused considerable material harm but was not perceived as asymmetrical warfare in the institutional sense, precisely because there were almost no rules at the time to define legitimate versus illegitimate violence.

In a system of authority, the weak and strong, despite their material power imbalance, have to possess collective knowledge of what constitutes legitimate and illegitimate means and methods of violence from the outset. Or, in Simpson's words, "Raw power must be given some normative meaning" (2004, 72). Thus, security depends upon the small not defying the privileged rights of the Great Powers, but at the same time it stems from these very rights. In this context, Reus-Smit considers what he calls "constitutional structures" of international society to condition the "identity and behavior of strong and *weak* states alike" (1999, 33; emphasis added). Constitutional structures, and the norms of procedural justice they contain, make some practices mandatory, but they also make other practices unthinkable. Reus-Smit shows how it is possible to infer from Thucydides that Athens's use of "naked power" eventually led to her demise. Athenian domination after the massacre of the Melians was based solely on force, "losing sight of the fact that stable rule depends on moral authority" (ibid., 61). In this sense, instead of "might is right," we may conceive of authority as might *that makes and abides by* right (Garst

1989). Therefore, authority—as legitimized power and the set of rights and duties ensuing from it—is reproduced by practice, of both the strong and the weak. Each has to convince the other of its sincerity and to accord consent to maintain the rules of the game. Consistency, consent, and hierarchy are the key words of Great Power authority (Wheeler and Dune 1996, 96).

◄ TWO ►

PATHs as Predators and Parasites
of Great Power Authority

In principle, Great Powers could tolerate PATHs and abstain from countering their harmful practice. Nonetheless, when opposing the practices of PATHs, Great Powers can respond to the transnational challenge through various measures and policies. I suggest that there is a spectrum of Great Power counterharm policy or interruptive measures with regard to PATHs' practices. Ideal points on this spectrum would be as follows:[1]

1. Attempting to induce the PATHs to stop their practice through unarmed means and incentives or sanctions or pressuring another state that has leverage over the harmful actors to restrain them.
2. Attempting to contain or ward off the harmful transnational agents through policing, law enforcement, and defensive efforts within one's territory or on one's borders (e.g., border patrols, coast guard operations, capturing and jailing of the PATHs' leaders and operatives, or reconnaissance missions).
3. Ordering limited military offensive strikes against the PATHs.
4. Launching a full-blown military offensive strike against the PATHs, including occupation of territorial bases that serve the PATHs and annihilation of the PATHs' leadership and organizational structure through the use of military destructive platforms.

In a sense, these policies represent degrees of tolerance, or intolerance, toward PATHs. The task of this book is to provide a theoretical framework that will help us to understand this variance, an understanding that is important not only from a policy-oriented perspective (i.e., to better understand the behavior of the leading actors in the international system) but from a theoretical perspective as well. It will in fact shed light on theoretical aspects of world politics that have not been adequately developed in IR literature. This chapter, then, seeks to provide a theory of challenges to authority in world politics and to link it to the various counterharm policies discussed previously.

A realist would argue that the only condition that would make it necessary for a Great Power to interrupt a transnational harm is when the harm is inflicted on either the Great Power itself or its key allies. The aim of the counterharm policy, according to this logic, would be to ward off, dissuade, or incapacitate those doing harm. The specific nature of Great Power response would depend on the objective degree of harm the PATHs were causing to the Great Power or its allies: the more severe the material damage incurred by the Great Power, the more likely the Great Power to use offensive and destructive means to incapacitate the transnational harmful agents. But, also from a realist perspective, Great Powers rationally match the most effective means and methods to the end of interrupting or countering harm. Accordingly, a Great Power might use less destructive capabilities against a PATH even if the degree of harm caused by the latter is high if less costly expedients could bring the same results. For example, one could argue that containing a PATH through law enforcement strategies, or even buying it off, could under certain circumstances be cheaper and more effective in terms of stopping its harm than could a full-blown military operation against it. In other cases, a certain response might be chosen because other responses would be irrelevant for the case (e.g., if the PATH has no distinct territorial bases that could be attacked by conventional military forces). Realists would also tend to compare the material harm caused by the transnational actor and security threats that originate from other sources (mainly, other Great Powers) and argue that the policy of the Great Power would also depend on the balance of threats the Great Power faces at a specific time. Namely, at times when other Great Powers represent a significant threat, the said power will reduce its interruptive efforts against the PATH because the degree of harm that a hostile Great Power is capable of inflicting on the state is much higher than the PATH's. A hostile power has the potential to destroy or conquer another power; but a PATH—

while it could inflict severe harm—cannot annul the existence of a Great Power. Thus, from the material point of view, a powerful enemy state is a first-tier threat and a harmful transnational actor is seen at the most as a second-tier or second-rate threat. And indeed, Great Powers often behave according to these expectations: they tend to respond more aggressively against PATHs that cause greater material harm to them, rationally match their ends with the most effective means to achieve them, and prioritize threats according to their degree of (potential) harm. If this kind of logic is absent from the behavior of a Great Power, then many commentators and scholars will interpret it as a result of misperceptions, incomplete information, or mistaken calculations—but not representing some general theoretical rule.

However, other cases exist in which such realist expectations and predictions are not vindicated—but *not* as the result of disruptions of the kind enumerated previously. In one example of this, a Great Power employed a limited—but costly—military offensive strike against a territorial base of transnational harm doers who caused damages to other states and people but not to the Great Power or its key allies; indeed, in this case the damages generated by the PATHs actually benefited some material interests of that Great Power (see chapter 4 on Britain and the Barbary pirates in 1816). In another case, a dominant military power avoided almost all measures against PATHs that were causing considerable material damage to its civilian population precisely at a time when that power and its archenemy disengaged from each other (see chapter 3 on Spain, the Ottoman Empire, Britain, Holland, and the Barbary pirates in the sixteenth and early seventeenth centuries). And a final illustration is a Great Power that was greatly harmed by a PATH and responded with a full-blown military strike but whose rationale—the matching of means to ends—is questionable given that it is doubtful that this military strategy will prevent further harm by that PATH or similar groups (see chapter 5 on the U.S. War on Terror). How are such aberrations from realist expectations accounted for? Do they have some general theoretical implications?

I. On the Constitution of Predators and Parasites of Authority

I argue that the explanation for interaction between Great Powers and PATHs lies in how Great Powers understand transnational harmful actions and constitute them as challenges (or not) to their authority in world politics. Accordingly, the hypothesis of this research is that the policy employed toward PATHs is a result of the *authority predicament* that PATHs represent to Great Powers. And more formally, *the stronger the authority predicament posed by a PATH to a Great Power, the more this Great Power will tend to intervene against the PATH and the more offensive and destructive will be its anti-PATH policy*. In addition, the Great Powers as a group will cooperate against PATHs (passively, by putting their own competition aside and allowing one or several of them to act against the PATHs; or actively, by contributing resources and forces to a joint operation) when the PATHs are constituted as a high threat to the normative structure that enables Great Power authority in world politics.

Great Power perception of the authority predicament posed by PATHs is based on the following clusters of variables. First are the type, intensity, and identity of the subjects of the PATH's propagated or facilitated harm. These variables stand for the "what kind," "how much," and "address" of harm—whether, for example, the harm was a result of the use of designated means of destruction, what the objective material magnitude of the harm was, and who suffered it (e.g., civilian populations or armed forces, upper or lower orders of society). Another important variable determining the authority predicament is the "why" of harm: the professed reasons, ideologies, motivations, and interests that the PATHs provide—or that are deduced (e.g., through secret intelligence)—for their propagation or facilitation of harm. Finally, how the PATHs consider themselves vis-à-vis states in general and the Great Powers specifically in terms of rights is also very important to the authority predicament; they could publicly claim to have rights equal to the Great Powers and states or superior rights over states, or they could remain ambiguous or silent in this regard.

Together these elements determine the deviation of PATHs from the institutions of violence and thus construct a perception of the degree of their defiance of authority. The further PATHs deviate from the institutions of violence in these respects—and the further they advance opposing or alternative norms, concepts, and ideas to those embedded in and sanctioned by these institutions—the more predatorial they will seem to the Great Powers. Since Great Power authority is first and foremost based on the regulation and institutionalization of organized violence, predators are those actors whose acts, ideas, and discourse risk deregulating and deinstitutionalizing organized violence in the system. They arouse strong objection on the part of the Great Powers—the regulators and rule suppliers of the system. Conversely, the less extreme the deviance of the PATHs is from these institutions (in act, speech, and idea), the more likely they will be perceived by the Great Powers as *parasites* that abuse authority. Great Powers tend to be more tolerant toward parasites than predators, because the latter's extreme deviation from the institutions of violence exposes the social conventions behind the concept of power, and thus predators undermine the elements of inevitability, ontological security, self-esteem, and prestige that authority as legitimized power gives to the Great Powers. In effect, predators in their most extreme manifestation are those PATHs that overturn not only the system leaders' stable expectations about world politics but also their very understanding of international reality in the ontological sense. In other words, not only does a predator cause others to doubt the Great Powers, but it causes the Great Powers to doubt *themselves*.

It is important to note in this context that, although the Great Powers (and also we as analysts) can often have a good idea as to the specific motivations of a PATH, it is more difficult to know with full certainty the overall intentions of PATHs toward the global structure of authority itself. Some PATHs may have only limited regional or domestic ambitions. In addition, and as opposed to states, PATHs may not always be aware of the intricacies, traditions, and history of authority in international politics,[2] and therefore it is doubtful whether they intrinsically and systematically endeavor to undermine Great Power authority. Furthermore, because these groups are often clandestine, whimsical, disorganized, and small, the Great Powers cannot study their strategic intentions in as rigorous a manner as they can other states'.[3] Thus, unless a PATH explicitly states that it specifically challenges Great Power authority, it is not always easy—even if the PATHs harm the Great Powers themselves—for the Great Powers to determine their intrinsic intentions toward authority. Nonetheless, those reasons, interests, and motivations of the PATHs that the Great Powers *do* know of, together with the intensity and address of the transborder harm they propagate or facilitate, create a perception of these actors as predators or parasites in relation to the authority of the Great Powers.

Thus, for example, a PATH may openly state that it propagates violent harm for political reasons that, from the Great Powers' perspective, are legitimate within the parameters of violence in the institution of sovereignty. In this case, the Great Powers can assume that the PATH does not intend to challenge the institution of sovereignty—and along with it Great Power authority—itself. On the other hand, when a PATH's reasons for violent force are not sanctioned by sovereignty, it is a predator.

Even if the PATH did not clearly admit or "know" that its intention was to defy the institution of sovereignty, it is still defined by the Great Powers as a predator—because the extreme defiance of its practice and ideology might severely harm this institution. And if the deviation is persistent, well-planned, and intense—or, further, accompanied by direct and explicit provocations (in deed and/or word) against Great Powers—it could be reasonably supposed that such PATHs consciously intend to undermine or even destroy Great Power authority.

Granted, a PATH defined as a predator by one Great Power may not be by the next. Because Great Powers have divergent conceptions of the institutions of violence, they have differing perceptions of PATHs. Norms and rules of the game are of varying importance among powers. Certain norms of transborder force, for example, could be pursued and instituted by certain powers and avoided by others. Thus, for example, during the 1815 Congress of Vienna, when the British eagerly pursued the antislavery norm, the other Great Powers remained indifferent or only marginally interested in the issue.[4] As a consequence, the Barbary pirates' slave trade did not represent any authority threat for Austria or Prussia, for example, while Britain perceived that the continuation of this human traffic undermined its international authority. Another example of the varying conceptions of institutions of violence among the Great Powers is the nineteenth-century European Concert, which disintegrated because of diminishing consensus between liberal and conservative powers about the legitimacy of the principles of ancien régime sovereignty. And in 1999, the United States and its European allies pursued the norm of humanitarian intervention as a just cause for war in Kosovo, while China and Russia strongly objected to this type of intervention. The crisis before the 2003 Iraqi war also demonstrated a lack of agreement among the Great Powers on legitimate force in international politics.

Still, the Great Powers almost by definition share some basic conceptions of the institutions of violence. Thus, the prohibition of the use of designated means of destruction against civilians is accepted today by all the Great Powers.[5] Religious reasons do not count as a legitimate motivation for the use of force. The territorial integrity norm is well established. Nonstate groups are not entitled to use international force against state agents, civilians, and nonmilitary targets. Neither are they seen as having the right to command Great Powers and present them with ultimatums. And, finally, a strong norm existed, at least until the 2003 Iraqi war, against the assassination of heads of states (Ward 2000). A PATH that deviates strongly from the fundamental norms and concepts that the

Great Powers and other members of international society share becomes a predator of authority in the eyes not just of the specific power that was harmed but of the rest as well.

Those PATHs that are understood by the Great Powers as highly predatory might even induce cooperation between rival or opponent Great Powers (as opposed to "enemies"). When the Great Powers as a group consider that an institutional threat is on the rise, conservatism is invoked even among powers that had previously conflicting interests. This kind of conservatism is what Samuel Huntington calls "situational conservatism": it arises due to a fundamental threat to a specific social order in whose preservation all actors have an intrinsic stake. "The essence of [situational] conservatism is the passionate affirmation of the value of existing institutions" (Huntington 1957, 455). Accordingly, a strong predatory PATH threat to the principle of Great Power authority would push previous conflicts among the Great Powers into the background, providing a significant incentive for cooperation by invoking situational conservatism—or, better still, systemic conservatism. If an actor's identity and authority are anchored in a certain institutional structure, then threats to the system become a threat to that actor even if it is not satisfied with the current allocation of power within the system. "Westphalian states would not have the rights they do but for the society of states. Once this dependency on the group is appreciated we can expect mutually recognizing actors to exhibit solidarity toward the group qua group. In short, two actors cannot recognize each other as different without recognizing that, at some level, they are also the same" (Wendt 2003, 512).[6] This recognition serves as the basis of systemic conservatism, whether passive (not standing in the way of a Great Power peer in its actions against PATHs) or active (positively cooperating).

Thus, for the Great Powers, the way PATHs *interact* with them and the states system (rhetorically and in practice) in light of the international norms of the institutions of violence is the key indicator to understanding—and even constructing—their intentions and, therefore, to categorizing them as either predators or parasites. What PATHs actually do, who they do it against, and how they refer to their actions enable Great Powers to understand them in relation to authority through the normative and moral lenses of the institutions of violence. Therefore, the interaction of the PATHs with the Great Powers, which takes place through the institutions of violence, constructs their perceived nature externally as much as internally. PATHs may or may not have a strategy or intrinsic concerns with regard to authority itself. But from the perspective of the Great Powers, the nature of PATHs is determined by how the practice and discourse of the nonstate actors is filtered through the institutions of violence.

The perceived intentions of the PATHs thus play a crucial role in their categorization by the Great Powers as predators or parasites. In this manner, predators in their ideal or most extreme form are actors that are perceived not only as refusing to identify with the institutions of violence as discussed previously but as overtly advancing alternative or opposing basic concepts of authority. Therefore, they are construed as undermining the legitimacy of the existing institutions of violence—and hence the structure of authority that is founded on them. They not only are perceived as "deep revisionist" in the sense advocated by Randall Schweller (1994)—that is, actors that mainly seek material aggrandizement—but are constructed as deep revisionists in the institutional sense: they doubt, or even directly question, the idea that sovereign states and especially the Great Powers have preferential access to social power through their control of the definition of legitimized power.

Because the institutions of violence and the resulting Great Power authority are historically contingent, an encompassing and transhistorical list of what specifically makes a PATH a predator is difficult to provide. Of course, the use of organized violence is important here and could serve as a medium of defiance or even constitute the defiance itself. But the enactment of organized violence in itself does not necessarily mean that the PATH would be classified as a predator. As I demonstrate in the case of the Barbary pirates in the sixteenth and early seventeenth centuries, in an international system where Great Power authority as we know it today barely existed (because there was little regulation and institutionalization of organized violence), even the intensive violence of the pirates against the dominant maritime European states of the time did not prompt them to classify the corsairs as predators. They were seen at the most as "pests." This was mainly due to the weakness of the authority predicament. The same practice today would be construed as predatory for many reasons: the intense and wide-scale infliction of violent harm on civilians by nonstate actors; the lack of respect for fundamental human rights; the presumption of a right to enslave people; and the day-to-day armed incursions into the sovereign territory of states. Further, today a PATH would be considered a predator if it employed transborder force for religious reasons or rejected the principle of sovereignty by calling for the establishment of alternative modes of sociopolitical organization (e.g., dismantling state borders and creating a theocratic empire instead of a system of secular sovereign states). Again, a PATH does not have to "know" what sovereignty is in order to advocate an idea or agenda that conflicts strongly with it; but if its rhetoric reveals a conscious opposition to the concept of sovereignty, it represents a more extreme type of predator. Sovereign states are now comfortably established in a cartel of mutually empowering and hegemonic actors[7] who claim metapolitical authority in domestic as well as world politics. In the same manner as any ruling or privileged class, states—and especially the Great Powers who have the highest status within this cartel—find it difficult to tolerate alternative modes of order. The competition with and imitation of alternative modes of organization in other regions or states threaten the loss of institutional hegemony. Further, such diversity raises the specter of deconstruction of the self-restraints that govern interstate relations today. Alternatives to sovereignty might also undercut the concept of power itself by establishing units or polities that are sensitive to other costs and benefits than those embodied in current definitions and constructions of power (e.g., a theocratic empire is less sensitive to the material costs and benefits that the Great Powers can exact and supply). Nonsovereign polities could possess rationalities very different from those of sovereign states, and an asymmetry of rationality among actors means that power is redefined and problematized. No possessor of power wants to problematize the concept of power and thus risk losing what has always been seen as obvious, inevitable, and unproblematic. Utilitarian and material interests are very important in this context, but also significant is the fear of losing one's distinct identity, stable expectations of the world, and elevated social status—precisely the identity, expectations, and status conferred by authority as legitimized power.

If the ideology of the PATH (or the way this ideology is interpreted by the Great Powers) calls for imposing and spreading this alternative mode of sociopolitical organization, it further challenges the institution of sovereignty. A PATH that deviates not only from the principles of sovereignty but also from the laws of war through the intensity and direction in the use of force would become a predator today. The infliction of intensive and indiscriminate violence on noncombatants is especially important in this context and is construed as even more ferocious and predatory when meted out through methods of violence that are proscribed by strong international norms (e.g., weapons of mass destruction). Such violence, beyond its terrible material consequences, arouses strong moral objections and is considered an outrage or even a shattering of taboos (Price 1997; Tannenwald 1999, 2005).

Finally, a PATH is construed today as a predator when—in addition to the previously mentioned deviations from the institutions of violence—it actually claims a superior position over states in terms of prerogatives. Such a PATH would be openly skeptical of the primacy of states in world politics, claim to have an equal or preferential right to order and execute transborder violence, and presume to know better than states the best interests of human societies. For example, when a nonstate group purports to be the sole and true voice of God (who obviously knows right and wrong better than any human being or secular authority) and argues that the Great Powers or their key allies act against God's expressed will, then it effectively claims an uncompromising and superior right over states. Its demands of these states are then seen as the unacceptable ultimatums and unilateral dictates of an illegitimate actor. Thus, such a PATH is perceived as not recognizing *any* element in the authority of the Great Powers and the states system. When a PATH's rhetoric highlights and harps on these aspects and also directly challenges the Great Powers (e.g., by declaring their power to be merely a "myth"), it is perceived by the latter as a predator of authority that will try when possible to establish its own idea of how world politics should be constituted and managed.

Parasites, also outsiders to authority, are actors that are perceived by the Great Powers as *abusing* the institutions of violence and Great Power authority and feeding on them. They are not seen as a destructive phenomenon in this regard but rather as a corrosive force. In a sense, parasites are similar to free riders. But there are important differences between parasites and free riders. In the realm of international security, free riding represents a problem of burden sharing, whereby the small powers exploit the Great Powers who provide them with security without the small bearing the proportional cost required by their share in the public good of security.[8] The "balance of efforts," in Eiko R. Thielemann's (2001) terms, is not proportional to the actors' share of security. In this way, free riders can cause harm to the providers of their security. Parasites, however, either *deliberately* cause harm to the Great Powers or their key allies, or the essence of their interaction with the Great Powers *entails the propagation* of harm. In other words, while the enabling or toleration of free riding provides *some* positive utility to a Great Power (e.g., self-esteem or prestige), there is nothing in the interaction between a Great Power and a parasite *but* harm or cost to the Great Power.[9] Furthermore, parasites, in contrast to free riders, must be forcefully prevented or materially rewarded to stop their feeding on the system of

Great Power authority. Free riders can be brought to bear the costs of their security if the Great Power threatens to stop its disproportionate participation in maintaining their security or to abandon them. Of course, disengagement from either a free rider or a parasite might have a cost in itself. But in the former case, the Great Power's costs derive mainly from loss of benefits or positive values (e.g., losing a friendly or ideologically affiliated state or losing a market for the Great Power's products) or from domestic disapproval. Moreover, "the fear of abandonment limits confidence in collective security and decreases the attractiveness of free riding [for small powers]. Instead, fear of abandonment enhances allies' voluntary contribution to the alliance by motivating allies to seek self-reliance" (Lee and Heo 2001, 826). Disengagement from the parasite, on the other hand, requires the employment of coercive force against it; because of the persistent nature of the parasite, it will not let go on its own. The Great Power could alternatively supply the parasite with incentives to purchase exemption from its harm, but this will only reinforce the parasite and comfortably institutionalize its position vis-à-vis the Great Power. Thus, both parasites and free riders are tolerated to a certain extent by the Great Powers, but free riders are generally tolerated due to positive interests and benign policies on the part of the Great Power (Gilpin 1981), while the parasites are tolerated due to negative interests. Put differently, free riders are, to a certain degree, willfully tolerated by the Great Powers; parasites are reluctantly or grudgingly tolerated.

The reason for this toleration is that the harm that parasites cause does not explicitly defy the authority of the Great Power. Even if they use organized violence to advance their goals, other aspects in their practice and rhetoric reveal them as extra-institutionally *manipulating* an order, not aiming to end or destroy it. Parasites are thought by the Great Powers to abuse the system of authority by exploiting this cooperative institution to achieve an unfair advantage or utility. What they do is understood as breeching the social order established by the Great Powers, and their practice and rhetoric are not interpreted by the Great Powers as advocating either its destruction or an alternative system. Often, parasites are lawbreakers without any manifest political ideology or agenda ("criminals"). They are conceived to be working to maximize their utility *through* the system of authority, because instead of challenging the system directly their practice and rhetoric circumvent it by means and techniques such as corruption,[10] blackmail, and crime.[11] Therefore, they represent merely a control challenge—not an authority challenge. Corruption, blackmail, and crime are commonly understood as conservative forces because they preserve a favorable status quo for the parasite—a status quo, however, that it can illegally or extra-institutionally exploit. Because of their less confrontational practice and rhetoric, parasites are not construed by Great Powers as wanting to take over the system or replace it. Parasites keep a low rhetorical profile and do not deliberately try to bring themselves to the attention of Great Powers. For Great Powers, this in turn means that the interests of the parasites are partially defined in terms of the system and that instead of seeking to replace it they look to exploit it (e.g., to make illegal financial profits or to achieve national liberation or statehood through "traditional" methods of terrorism). However, even "conservative" methods such as corruption, blackmail, and crime might eventually cause a political system to collapse because of their corrosive effects. But as long as PATHs keep a relatively low profile by not publicly and explicitly advocating competing or alternative principles or ideas, they will be regarded as parasites that pose a less dramatic, immediate, or acute threat (Löwenheim 2002). Thus, it is not merely the physical or material *security predicament* that leads to the construction of a certain policy toward PATHs; rather, it is the *authority predicament*.

The process through which the Great Powers distinguish between predators and parasites is important for at least four reasons. First, from the perspective of the defining power, once a PATH is named a predator the state actually gains greater communal legitimacy to deal with it more harshly—even through intense military measures. If a considerable number of states—other Great Powers and also smaller states—concur with the categorization of a certain PATH as a predator, the harmed power will face less material opposition (or even gain others' cooperation) in dealing with the predator. In other words, collective action will be more feasible. (This aspect correlates with the social control and utilitarian functions of authority that I discussed in chapter 1.) Second, from a theoretical point of view, if other states identify with a Great Power's categorization of the PATH as a predator, it indicates the authority of that power. Assuming that the general international acceptance of the definition was at least partially achieved due to identification with the defining Great Power (as opposed to simply material pressures/rewards or self-interest), then this clearly stands as an operational sign for Great Power authority. The definition of a PATH as a predator *and* the social acceptance of that definition articulate that aspect of Great Power authority that concerns the normalization of world politics through the distinction between legitimate and illegitimate actors. Third, through the process of categorization and definition the defining state gives a meaning to social life. And once such a categorization is generally accepted, the power feels more comfortable in its social environment due to the fact that other states identify with (at least some aspects in) its understanding of the world. In my view, this is one of the most fundamental features of why actors pursue authority at all. Fourth, the labeling of a PATH as a predator is important because it carries the risk of a self-fulfilling prophecy. As mentioned previously, the Great Powers cannot be certain of the overall intentions of PATHs toward authority, and sometimes these groups do not have systemic intentions. However, if the group is externally constituted and labeled a predator by a Great Power and other states accept this definition, then the PATH indeed might develop more intrinsic, comprehensive, conscious, and systemic aims than it initially had. While some PATHs could be deterred by the systemic conservatism response of international society, for others the response will validate and sharpen previous notions they had about the world. These latter PATHs will thus become more estranged and alienated from the system as a whole, living up to the expectations of the labeling state or states. In such a case, they indeed might become true "enemies of all humankind." In my opinion, Great Powers should be very much aware of this possibility.

Lesser authority predicaments, on the other hand, lead to categorizing the actor as a parasite and employing mainly policing measures against it. Full-blown use of destructive capabilities on the part of a Great Power in the case of parasites would be hard to justify to international and domestic society, and, as I argued previously, just and normative conduct is no less important to authority than mere material capabilities. Justifying intensive violence against parasites is difficult because they are not seen to directly challenge the shared conceptions of the institutions of violence and Great Power authority. Even if a Great Power considered the intensive use of force as the most efficient way to stop the parasites' harm, the fact that these PATHs do not represent a severe authority threat from the point of view of the institutions of violence makes such a response illegitimate or problematic from the normative perspective. Indeed, a Great Power can redefine a parasitic actor as a predator for instrumental reasons, but this stretches the limits of its authority—and might cost that power its legitimacy. States and other international actors would see the Great Power's conduct as inconsistent and arbitrary, and, as discussed in chapter 1, these characteristics are highly detrimental to authority. On the other hand, once the institutions of violence themselves transform, a

Great Power could legitimately relabel a previously defined parasitic PATH as a predator without actually changing its practice and rhetoric. Within the new configuration of these institutions, if there is a consensus among the Great Powers about a new norm or principle (or at least if there is little contention), certain persistent harmful practices could be reconceived as directly opposed to Great Power authority, especially if the PATHs explicitly refuse to cease doing harm.

Returning to parasites, the intentions and interests of these actors, as opposed to those of predators, are interpreted by the Great Powers as dualistic: on the one hand, they seem to strive toward some rights established by authority; on the other hand, they persistently attempt to attain these rights by means forbidden by or circumvention of authority. Again, a state cannot know in absolute certainty what PATHs really want. Drug traffickers, for example, are usually thought to pursue illegal financial gains. Although this is their probable goal, some drug networks (e.g., due to ideological grievances) may actually aim to weaken social cohesion, undermine social morality, and cause public health problems in their "target" states. But what is important here is that no drug trafficking group publicly endorses such an agenda, declaring that its aim is to harm or corrupt. In fact, drug traffickers are overwhelmingly silent, not openly advocating any competing principles of authority. For the Great Powers, such silence is telling. In this respect, parasites are constituted as inherently paradoxical actors. On the one hand, their pursuit of property rights in the form of money implies that they want to be integrated into society. In fact, criminals employ *lawyers* to protect themselves from the laws that they break, and they use various other law-constituted means to ensure their personal safety and maintain their property rights. Criminals, when caught, couch their actions with words of compliance. By doing this, they do not deny the authoritative status of the state. They also effectively subject themselves to the state's moral judgment. "Traditional" terrorists such as the PLO or the IRA also opted for similar tactics, endorsing the discourse of the hegemonic international system and the institutions of violence to explain their deviance from these institutions. On the other hand, this alleged recognition of the law or institutions is largely instrumental or strategic. Criminological research shows that criminals generally don't feel guilty about breaking the law; even when complying with it they cannot be said to be law-abiding actors in the deep sense of the concept. The high rates of returning to crime, the failure of so many ex-convicts to "learn their lesson," and the fact that some organized crime bosses continue to direct their business even from prison indicate that many criminals are persistent and treat crime as a "career" or an ongoing enterprise (Gibbons 1968; Volkov 2002). Therefore the criminal apparently has no intrinsic interest in obeying the law, and therefore the essence of criminal practice is persistent illegality and a willingness to resort to illegal and illegitimate means for self-protection (such as unauthorized violence or corruption) if the structure of costs or benefits allows or encourages it. "Thus the criminal appears as a juridically paradoxical being. He has broken the [social] pact, he is therefore an enemy of society as a whole, but he participates in the punishment that is practiced upon him" (Foucault 1977, 90).

The perceived paradoxical nature of parasites suggests that at their most offensive they could be deterred by low-cost coercion (because they are assumed to be sensitive to the rights they seek through the system of authority and these rights can be denied by the state and the Great Powers) and at their least offensive they could be socialized or corrected. Accordingly, lethal or destructive violence is seen as an unnecessary[12] or unjustified response. Parasites are indeed outsiders to authority in the sense that they persistently violate or infringe on some of its fundamental norms and institutions. But their lack of explicit rejection of other fundamental norms and institutions of authority and their pursuit of some of the rights and benefits that authority enables construct them as actors that could be contained by international society—or even brought back into it. Law enforcement and penal correction then are more suitable strategies for society's defense from them, because in a sense these actors are less free of authority—and society—than predators. They are tangential to society—they chafe against its institutions or cross along its frontiers—whereas predators are seen as barbarian invaders of sovereign society. Parasites sneak into society through its many structural holes, but they are not believed to aim to destroy society. Predators also enter through structural holes but are thought to try to disintegrate society. Parasites try to take some of society's benefits with them (such as property rights) into the "outlaw" sphere. Predators are deemed to be interested in neither the rights nor the duties of society, and therefore they are considered to come in from the outside as destroyers. Thus, an economy of punishment is based on the principle of the challenge to sociopolitical authority.

I therefore argue that the degree of punishment that Great Powers mete out to PATHs is not dependent simply on the amount of harm per se the latter causes or facilitates with regard to the Great Powers or their key allies, but also on *how* the harm was caused and the perceived

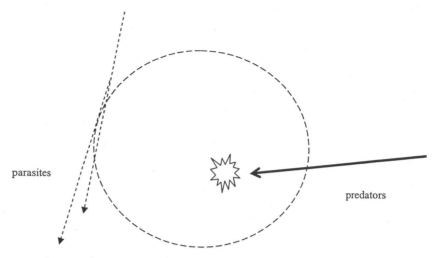

Fig. 1. The perception of parasites and predators as outsiders to authority

reasons—the *why*—for it. The means and manners of inflicting harm are significant in the formation of Great Power counterharm policy because variations in these represent different degrees of challenge to the international social order and its paramount attributes—the hierarchy of power that vests the Great Powers with special authority. Since this order is based on legitimized and cartelized violent force, the further a PATH is excluded from the institutions of violence and yet continues to use (or facilitate the use of) intensive unauthorized and illegal transborder violent force against a Great Power or other states (despite the Great Power's explicit will), the more defiant the PATH is considered to be. Harm caused by means or techniques other than designated destruction (e.g., by illegal drugs) would be considered a secondary challenge because it does not conflict with the underlying basis of the structure of authority in international politics. By harming the Great Powers in a manner that not only inflicts material damages on them but questions or undermines their top position and status in the international hierarchy, the PATH becomes a predator of authority. Punishing an actor that challenges Great Power authority—seeing the violator humbled—brings the damaged power a measure of satisfaction. It also represents a public shaming and a venue for moral indignation to be acted out. Punishment of challengers of Great Power authority thus goes beyond the preventive/incapacitating/deterring consideration: it also provides a theatrical setting in which authority roles are acted out. It projects spectacular images of authority, deviance, and cost for deviance.[13]

On the other hand, the less defiant a PATH is perceived to be—the less it propagates or facilitates harm that uses provocative, intensive, and recalcitrant *extra-institutional* organized violence—the less excessive is the Great Power's response. Great Powers also have a milder response toward PATHs when the harm is propagated through nonviolent means and practices, even when the objective degree of this harm is higher and more costly than that inflicted through organized violence. Again, this is because the social order and authority within it—domestic and international—are constructed on the basis of institutionalized violence. Paradoxically, then, parasites can cause a much greater degree of material harm than predators but garner less intensive Great Power countermeasures. The perception of the number of deaths involved in an issue area or a practice, argues Steve Smith,

> has much to do with how we see deaths by political violence as compared with deaths by "economics," or deaths by "naturally occurring diseases." . . . I believe that our discipline [IR] makes very important assumptions about what constitutes violence and what kinds of deaths are relevant to explaining the world of international relations; *I also believe that these assumptions rely on a prior set of assumptions about the social world, and that these in turn reflect social, political, and ultimately economic power.* (Smith 2004, 507; emphasis added)

Parasites are dealt with in a way that supposedly prevents repetition of their harm or contains it at a certain level but that will not physically eliminate them as actors. Thus, if the moral stakes of the parasite's practice are low from a Great Power's perspective, the Great Power might even consider buying the parasite off in order to induce cessation of the harm. Predators, on the other hand, are severely punished—to the extent of physical elimination—through a ritual designed to restore authority. The punishment is designed not only to prevent further harm but to show that harmful actors can be severely punished against their will, and thus it reestablishes the relations of authority. "The art of punishing, then, must rest on a whole technology of representation" (Foucault 1977, 104).

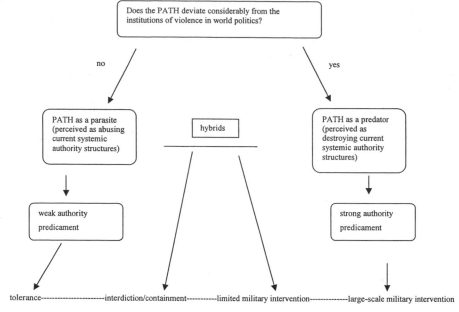

Fig. 2. The Construction of the authority predicament and the consequent policy toward the PATHs

II. On Punishment

Punishment then should be understood not only in the security (material) or judicial senses but also as part of a ceremony in which authority is manifested or made known—both to the holder of authority itself and to others—and reproduced.

> Punishment is not a behavior, but an institution. . . . To punish someone is not just to harm them because of something they have done. It is to stake a claim to a certain kind of institutional authority, even when the institution is only the family. To punish someone is to assert a right and accept an obligation to punish anyone similarly circumstanced and behaved. . . . to punish is to act as an officer or agent participating in a system for enforcing an authoritatively promulgated norm. (Bindert 2002, 321)

Whereas parasites are perceived mainly as attacking or abusing *individuals* within the order of authority, predators are seen as attacking authority itself. Parasites might interfere with the administration of authority, but predators are construed as challenging authority's administration *and* ideational foundations.[14] Punishment is therefore not only meant to redress the injury and prevent similar events in the future; it is also designed to restore the sovereign's authority. As Michel Foucault notes regarding public execution, "[It] has a juridico-political function. It is a ceremony by which a momentarily injured sovereignty is reconstituted. It restores that sovereignty by manifesting it at its most spectacular" (1977, 48). The punishment and abolition of renegade actors in international politics entail inflicting physical destruction to varying degrees or occupying predatorial territory, thus imposing authority on the predator in the "most spectacular" manner.

Now, is spectacularity in punishment inherent to the idea of authority, or is it specific to Great Power authority in international politics? In discussing this issue, it could be useful to keep in mind Carl Schmidt's argument that "sovereign is he who decides on the exception" (quoted in Michaelsen and Shershow 2004, 295). The purpose of exclusionary punishment is to differentiate between the holder of authority and the challenger: to highlight, on the one hand, the elements of order, normality, justice, control, and inevitability that make up authority and, on the other, the reclusion, futility, and even wickedness of the challenger. Severe and intense punishment highlights the exceptionally negative nature of the subject of punishment; the punishing actor's authority is thus demonstrated and reified. Severe punishment also reassures the punishing agent of its ability to exact cost for deviance and defiance. And because political authority is based first and foremost on the legitimizing of violent force (by the state in domestic politics and by states in international politics), political authorities tend to inflict harsh physical punishments on those actors who challenge the foundations of this authority. In other words, for exclusion to be meaningful, it has to be made in the language of authority that is relevant to the issue area. In religious affairs, for example, authority's exclusionary function could be asserted through excommunication of "heretics." In politics, ultimate exclusion is made through physical coercion. However, Foucault's discussion of criminal punishment shows that since the nineteenth century states have become more refined, so to speak, in punishing criminals. The emphasis of punishment has shifted from publicly inflicting physical damage and pain on the *body* of the criminal to disciplining and "correcting" his *soul* in a secluded prison.

Yet note that outrageous defiance of political authority still entails extreme and sometimes very violent punishment, not only in world politics but within states too. In cases where the authority's exercise of authority itself is threatened, states still harshly punish the bodies of criminals who provoke strong moral outrage. And although this punishment is no longer carried out in public, the focus of the news media brings them to wide public attention. In certain cases, the state actively facilitates such media coverage. Consider, for example, the highly publicized trial and punishment of Ethel and Julius Rosenberg, executed on the electric chair in June 1953 after being convicted of treason and conspiracy to pass nuclear secrets to the USSR. Note that other Cold War spies and traitors were not executed: the Rosenbergs were the only spies ever put to death in peacetime America. Their harsh punishment stems from the fact that they allegedly violated one of the then most sacred and valued aspects of U.S. international authority—the monopoly over nuclear knowledge—and handed this knowledge to the enemy of the United States. When declining the Rosenbergs' last-minute plea for clemency, President Eisenhower argued that he "could not justify commutation which would open up the possibility that these 'arch criminals' could be paroled in as few as fifteen years" (Radosh and Milton 1997, 378). Another example is Timothy McVeigh, the Oklahoma City 1995 bomber, who was killed by lethal injection in June 2001. His execution was witnessed by an unprecedented number of news media representatives, as well as broadcast on close-circuit TV to hundreds of relatives of his victims. The Bureau of Prisons went so far as to build a special media center to accommodate the multitude of journalists covering the event. McVeigh was the first federal prisoner to be executed in thirty-eight years. And although executions in the United States today are no longer a public spectacle (the last public hanging took place in Owensboro, Kentucky, in 1936 with a crowd of twenty thousand attending), this does not mean that they are less violent or more humane. None of the methods for "putting people to death" guarantees a death that is quick, painless, and clean. Horrific and very graphic scenes of bodily suffering accompany each of the execution methods. Ethel Rosenberg, for example, had to be electrocuted twice before she was killed. "Botched executions knock down the ritual frame and expose the gruesome reality of actually putting a human being to death" (Conquergood 2002, 361–62).

Even in countries in which the death penalty does not exist (most states in the world), some criminals are treated more harshly than other perpetrators of the same category of crime. Yigal Amir, for example, the murderer of Israeli prime minister Yitzhak Rabin, was sentenced to life in solitary confinement with no human contact except the occasional visits of his close relatives. In addition, Amir was forbidden to marry, this despite a law permitting all prisoners to wed and have children and despite the fact that other "regular" murderers serving lifetime sentences in Israeli prisons are allowed to marry and consummate their marriages. The Israeli High Court in fact has stated that the right to have sexual relations is a basic human right and is related, among other things, to the human desire to procreate. But because Amir was defined by the court as an extremely dangerous, ideologically motivated, insistent, and uninhibited terrorist (in other words, a predator of authority) he was not entitled to realize this right due to alleged security considerations.[15] Amir's crime outrageously defied the authority of the Israeli state because his act was widely interpreted as intending to literally kill the state (as one of Rabin's close advisers said). As a result, the state has done its utmost within the boundaries of the law to inflict mental *and* physical pain upon him and has also prevented him from passing on his genes. It is interesting to note that in all these three cases (the Rosenbergs, McVeigh, and Amir) the punished individuals were perceived as monstrous traitors, not the least because, in addition to the morally outrageous aspects of their crimes, they refused to express repentance, thus exacerbating their defiance of state authority.[16]

Having said this, it is nonetheless clear that in general the intensity (in terms of inflicting physical pain and harm) and purpose (in terms of causing physical suffering per se or correcting the soul of the offender) of criminal punishment within "developed" states have moved in the manner Foucault discusses. This shift was closely related to the ascendance of rationalism during the Enlightenment, the evolution of human and civil rights, the emergence of popular sovereignty, and the strengthening of the rule of law within states. The almost universal abolition of the death penalty is probably the most important development in this context (Schabas 2002). Yet note that punishment became more refined and rationalized in international politics as well—or the Great Powers at least try to create such an image. Thus, the United States highlights its use of "precision guided weapons" in an effort to demonstrate its attempts to "surgically" minimize "collateral damage" and "unnecessary suffering" in war. Acts of revenge and excess are forbidden in international law, and as opposed to previous historical periods, states now never admit that they take revenge[17] on their enemies. Also, the treatment of prisoners of war has become much more humane over the last centuries; they are no longer considered criminals deserving cruel punishment. However, noteworthy in this context is the post-9/11 U.S. distinction between soldiers fighting for a recognized sovereign state and nonstate fighters. The United States dubbed the al Qaeda and Taliban fighters who were captured by American forces in Afghanistan "unlawful combatants" and consequently did not treat them as prisoners of war. The Guantanamo Bay detainees were not given the protections the status of prisoner of war entails and faced court marshals. In essence, they were stripped of the law's—international and American—protection.

The modes of punishment discussed in these examples—domestic and international—seem to validate Schmidt's argument about the power to exclude: by deciding which challengers deserve exceptional and unusually severe punishment, the authorities make their authority known and reproduce it. The exceptions highlight the rule and thus reify it. And, as discussed in chapter 1, rules establish social rule.

Foucault notes that the spectacular public torture of the offender in early modern society was meant to display and confirm the sovereign's authoritative power. Public torture represented the activation of absolute monarchical power on the body of the criminal; witnessing the infliction of acute pain and torture on the offender imprinted in the mind of the crowd the absolute authority of the monarch, an authority derived from divine right. The monarch himself derived validation of his authority through such punishment. Prison, human and civil rights, and the various other coercive disciplining techniques and technologies brought about by the Enlightenment and modernity have made public torture redundant and have constructed it as an inhumane cruelty. The "disciplines," claims Foucault, enabled the state to exercise a much deeper and subtle form of authority over the individual. But when these mechanisms do not work— or do not emphasize enough the desire to exclude (as in the cases of the Rosenbergs, McVeigh, and Amir)—publicized bodily punishment is still used (although in a more "refined" manner). In international politics, on the other hand, there is no direct equivalent to the Foucauldian prison. While states maintain prisoner of war camps in times of war, these are not penal institutions. They are only meant for military incapacitation during battle or for political bargaining in the aftermath of war. War crime tribunals are the exception and not the rule in international war, and they are established only after a decisive and often very costly military victory. Indeed, the Great Powers can seclude a "rogue state" by imposing economic and diplomatic sanctions on it. Even terrorists can be excluded in this way, as the financial elements of the War on Terror are designed to do (e.g., the measures against money laundering and the increased international supervision of various money flows that could be used for terror funding). But such sanctions, even when highly efficient, do not speak directly in the language of coercive and physical power that is inherent to Great Power authority. Thus they only partially satisfy the need and desire to exclude such states or nonstate predatory groups, and partial measures are not enough for validation of an authority that is challenged by a predator.

In international politics authority is not constituted on the legal-formal-hierarchical model, where all legitimate coercive power in society is monopolized by a single actor (the state). It is constituted on the exclusion of nonstate actors by a *cartel* of states and on the legitimization of certain violent capabilities and policies *among* the members of this cartel, thereby establishing hierarchy among them. Hence, in international politics the last resort in the exercise of authority is the activation of military power. By nature, the employment of military power is an especially visible event. But when Great Powers want to highlight the fact that in a certain case their use of force is not normal or conventional (i.e., in the institutional sense) but is rather intended to exclude an actor, they have to revert to a spectacular show of force. The spectacularity in the use of force is thus evidence of the Great Power's extreme excluding and delegitimizing function as well as of its humbling of the challenger—and, hence, of its being the ultimate instrument of international authority.

Because PATHs are nonstate actors by definition—and in the contemporary international system there is barely a land territory left out of the formal jurisdiction of a recognized state (the Antarctic, Taiwan, the West Bank, and the Gaza Strip are probably the sole exceptions)—in order to punish predatory PATHs, Great Powers must infringe on another state's territorial integrity. Here the connection between authority's outsider states (or "outlaw/rogue states"; see Simpson 2004) and PATHs becomes important: Great Powers will not intervene unilaterally in the territory of a state that they consider to be a law-abiding actor or an insider to authority, even if a predatory PATH used the territory of that state as a base. Indeed, such states would be encouraged or pressured to act against the PATH—and even "offered" Great Power help—but they will not be coerced to do this by an explicit military threat or offensive force (as in the case of Germany and its treatment of the 9/11 cell in Hamburg).[18] In fact, insiders to authority will often act on their own against PATHs that operate from within them. The material cost of becoming an outlaw state—the "source" state that refuses to punish the PATHs—is a significant incentive to act against a "resident" PATH. But beyond such considerations, insiders to authority states have intrinsic motives to punish PATHs that used their territory.

On the other hand, states that knowingly and intentionally host PATHs, or decline or ignore Great Powers' demands to confront them, would be considered outsiders to authority, or outlaw states, and would be susceptible to attack by military force in the Great Powers' efforts to abolish the predatory PATH. These states, on top of openly flouting Great Power authority, are seen by the Great Powers as refusing to contribute their share to the general good by accepting international standards and norms of uniformity in the sphere of transnational harm.[19] Simpson argues that "[i]n an encounter between a Great Power and an outlaw state, the sovereignty norms associated with a traditional conception of international law are suspended. The legal scope for the use of force by Great Powers is widened while the territorial integrity and political independence of the outlaw state shrinks. The result is a highly permissive environment in which the use of force can be more readily employed" (2004, 336). In my view, however, the institution of sovereignty and the resultant Great Power authority not only permits an attack on an outlaw state knowingly and intentionally harboring predatory PATHs, but it also *necessitates* the (attempted) elimination of predatory PATHs by the Great Powers. Herein lies an important difference between the treatment of outsider states and predatory PATHs. According to Simpson, from the nineteenth century onward the Great Powers avoided eliminating the independent existence of their defeated enemies and did not declare them criminal states as such. An exception here is the Versailles settlement of 1919, where Germany as a nation was burdened with the guilt of the Great War. At the Congress of Vienna in 1815, in contrast, France was not dismantled or declared responsible as a state for the Napoleonic Wars. And "[a]t the end of the Second World War, the Versailles model was rejected in favor of a regime of individual responsibility. The Nuremberg Trials, then, were important as a method of punishing the major Nazi war criminals but they served another function by deflecting attention away from the criminal conduct of the *state* of Germany" (Simpson 2004, 273; emphasis added). Similarly, Serbia was not declared a criminal state as such in 1999, nor was Afghanistan in 2002 or Iraq in 2003. In these cases, a distinction was made between leaders and regimes that were outsiders to authority and the *right* of their state to continue to exist as a member of international society after their removal.

I claim, in effect, that we have to distinguish between micro- and macroperspectives here. From the microperspective, states can be outsiders to authority once their leaders or ruling regimes endorse policies that violate the institutions of violence or when they collude with predatory PATHs. From the microperspective, these states *behave* as outsiders to authority. This might help to explain Krasner's organized hypocrisy thesis: he claims that state rulers, and not states as persons, are those who make decisions in international politics. No hierarchical structure exists to prevent state rulers from violating the logic of appropriateness of Westphalian sovereignty or international legal sovereignty (Krasner 1999, 8). However, seen from the macroperspective, state rulers as individuals might indeed behave as outsiders to authority, but once other states have removed these leaders (as has indeed happened in several cases), they are compelled to treat the defeated state as an insider to authority with all the rights and duties that this status confers.

My explanation for the modern practice of not punishing the state as such but rather its leadership and regime is that the modern institution of sovereignty treats the state as a corporate or public person in itself, as Wendt argues (2004). This personality vests the state with what Simpson (2004) dubs "existential equality." At first (in the early nineteenth century), the existential equality in sovereignty was the privilege of the Great Powers themselves (in order to preserve the "just equilibrium"). Later on, the "standard of civilization" promised existential equality to other "civilized" nations, and after 1945 existential equality became an international standard with the norm of territorial integrity. Thus, the distinction between the state and its individual leaders who might be considered deviants, outsiders, or criminals was enabled. Abolishing states as corporate persons is perceived as politically unwarranted in the post-1945 institution of sovereignty precisely because states came to be defined as integral and undividable persons from the ontological perspective.

On the other hand, and here I come back to PATHs, abolishing a predatory PATH is seen as rightful—and necessary—because *by definition* a predatory PATH is an antinomy and illegitimate entity. Not only an outlaw, a predatory PATH is also beyond the protection that the law provides to "regular" offenders (i.e., parasites). A predatory PATH in the modern states system *must* be eliminated,[20] because allowing it to survive would endanger the cartel of states and the concept of power and therefore the authority of the Great Powers. Such PATHs cry out loud that the king is naked. And as Inis Claude notes, "emperors may be nude, but they do not like to be so, to think themselves so, or to be so regarded" (1966, 368).

◄ THREE ►

Enemies of All Mankind?

The Barbary Corsairs in the
Sixteenth and Early Seventeenth Centuries

This chapter tells the story of the North African Barbary corsairs and their depredations on Europe during the sixteenth and early seventeenth centuries. Because Spain was the foremost victim of the corsair attacks and also was the dominant European power of the time, I will focus mainly on its response to this practice of persistent transnational harm. I will also examine in this chapter the 1620 attempt of European cooperation against the corsairs.

Why examine this case and period? In terms of the theory outlined in chapter 1, the period investigated here most likely represents the beginning of an "international" system, that is, a system composed of sovereign states that had broken away from the superior and formal authority of the "universal" Church and the Holy Roman Empire (Wight 1977, 130–34; Tilly 1990, 81, 181). Moreover, this era represents the Golden Age of Spain—a period in which Spain was the chief military power in Europe (Davies 1964; Elliott 1977, 41–61; 1986; Lynch 1992)[1]—and it also corresponds to the height of the Ottoman Empire's power. This is important because despite the fact that the Ottomans represented a civilization very different from the European one in many ways, in terms of transborder violence they had similar practices and norms. The heyday of Barbary corsairing thus coincided with the emergence of the early modern international system of sovereign states and the high point of Spanish power, allowing an examination of the concepts of legitimized power and the authority therein of the dominant powers. My analysis reveals that during this period of an emerging international system, concepts of authority—in the sense of legitimized power based on well-defined institutions of transborder violence—were at best very narrow, and therefore the dominant powers could not have "known" the Barbary corsairs as anything more than parasitic actors.

I. The Corsairs of Barbary as Persistent Agents of Transnational Harm

A. The Damages and Injuries They Caused

The Barbary corsairs operated mainly from the North African ports of Algiers, Tunis, and Tripoli. But even though these ports were regencies or provinces of the Ottoman Empire, they became de facto independent polities from the 1580s onward. Eventually, they maintained only nominal and ceremonial relations of allegiance with the Ottoman sultan. The further the Ottoman imperial control over the Barbary regencies waned, the more developed became the organized and persistent system of sea predation in the major Barbary harbors—to such an extent that plunder became one of the major income sources of these centers of transnational violence (Braudel 1973, 884).[2] Algiers, Tunis, Tripoli, and at times Salee became homes to corsair fleets that operated for more than three hundred years in the Mediterranean, preying on the commercial shipping of almost every seafaring nation and raiding the littoral settlements of the Mediterranean Christian states.

The coasts of Spain, France, and Italy suffered the most, but from the late sixteenth century and well into the seventeenth century the shores of countries such as England, Ireland, and even Iceland and Sweden were visited by the Barbary corsairs (Lewis 1982, 32). Their extensive reach and intensive sea predations caused Charles Molloy, a renowned seventeenth-century English jurist, to refer to them as *hostis humani generis* (the enemies of all mankind) (Molloy 1682, 31, 61). Yet, as we shall see in this and the next chapter, the European powers did not consider the corsairs to be such a threat. The Barbary corsairs were tolerated and at times even encouraged because of the rivalries among the Europeans (see, e.g., Lee-Wiess 2002). In the theoretical terms of this book, the Barbary corsairs were not construed as deviants from the institutions of violence of the early modern period; at the most they were viewed as parasites.

Accordingly, although European powers sent many expeditions against the bases of the corsairs, they were usually not aimed at stamping out piracy altogether but more often than not had ulterior and sinister designs against European rivals (Thomson 1987, 128). This chapter explores the origins of Barbary corsairing in the sixteenth and early seventeenth centuries and tries to illuminate why it persisted for so many years.

Sea predation was a traditional occupation of the inhabitants of the Barbary Coast. North Africa's rough environmental conditions, difficult climate, and half-barren terrain constrained the economies of its littoral settlements. One of the earliest methods developed by the inhabitants of Barbary already in antiquity to confront these dire conditions was sea predation (de Souza 1999; Pennell 1994, 272–82). In the late Middle Ages and during the Renaissance, when commercial shipping in the Mediterranean reemerged, Barbary corsairing intensified, and at the turn of the sixteenth century Barbary sea predation took a new form and scale. Previously, piracy had been a relatively sporadic and unorganized phenomenon. But the completion of the *Reqonquista* of the Iberian Peninsula by the Catholic monarchs Ferdinand and Isabella in 1492 brought about an abrupt change in the nature and extent of Barbary sea predation. Tens of thousands of people escaped or were expelled into a land that could barely support a sparse population of petty craftsmen and peasants. The Muslims exiled from Spain were not only desperate for sources of livelihood, but they had intense religious motives for revenge—against Spain in particular and the Christian world in general (Hess 1968, 7). One of the most expedient methods of achieving these two goals—subsistence and revenge—was sea predation on the Mediterranean shipping of Spain, France, Venice, and other Christian seafaring nations.

Preying on Christian shipping thus became the main occupation of the Barbary corsairs, but from the 1570s onward they increasingly focused on kidnapping Europeans into captivity and slavery in the Barbary Coast itself. Gradually, slave trade became their primary activity. The people enslaved by the Barbary corsairs were taken from ships captured by the corsairs and in raids on coastal settlements around the Mediterranean. The captives might spend the rest of their lives as agricultural or household slaves, quarrymen, or rowers in a galley (Colley 2002). In fact, the slave trade was so lucrative that the corsairs often went to sea solely to kidnap.

But more profitable than the slavery business were the ransom deals:

the Barbary corsairs demanded forfeit from the families, communities, and friends of wealthy prisoners in return for their release. Redemptionist orders such as the Mercedarians and Trinitarians kept representatives in the Barbary regencies, and from the mid-seventeenth century most European powers maintained consuls in Barbary with a mission to bargain for the liberation of rich prisoners or groups of less well-to-do persons (Clark 1958, 106–7). Jewish middlemen played a role too—as transnational financiers (Clissold 1977, chap. 8). Between the sixteenth and the early nineteenth centuries, hundreds of thousands of European Christians were kidnapped into slavery or ransomed in this manner. Bruce Taylor estimates that by the mid-sixteenth century probably as many as fifteen to twenty thousand Spaniards were captives in the Barbary Coast (Taylor 1997, 86). Robert Davis finds that between 1530 and 1580 the corsairs brought three hundred thousand European slaves to Algiers alone, the strongest and best-known Barbary regency. An average of twenty-five thousand Christian slaves were kept in Algiers every year between 1580 and 1680. Another ten thousand on average were most likely held annually in Tunis and Tripoli during these years (Davis 2003, 23; 2001, 106, 108).

During the sixteenth century, most corsair activity was directed against Spain and its Mediterranean possessions in Italy. But France and Venice suffered a great deal as well. According to Alberto Tenenti (1967), corsairing was one of the major reasons for the decline of Venice in this era. Between 1580 and 1620, the depredations of the corsairs reached a zenith, and during this period northern European states such as England and Holland also began to feel the harm.

The depredations of the corsairs resulted in high losses for Spain (Elliott 1989, 116). The ransoming of thousands of Spanish nationals from Barbary;[3] the resources allocated to defend the coasts against corsair attacks; and the loss of men, ships, and commerce were serious costs for Spanish society, especially since most of the burden was borne by local communities and not by the Crown. In addition, the raids of the corsairs created an atmosphere of terror and a mentality of siege in many regions in Spain. Barbary corsairing greatly increased feelings of xenophobia for the Spanish people at that time. Spaniards were terrorized by the prospect of captivity in Algiers (see Garcés 2002, 137).

In actual fact, many Spanish captives fared well in Barbary, especially if they were lucky enough to be sold to benign masters or were valued because of their professional skills. Often captives were allowed to maintain private business and commerce while in captivity, sharing their profits with their Barbary master.[4] Rich captives were usually also treated well because of the high ransom price they were expected to command. Nonetheless, slaves who were sold to the city of Algiers often suffered torture, and mortality among them was high. The experience of most Spanish slaves and captives in Algiers involved cruel treatment and daily confrontations with death. Furthermore, and perhaps more important, the perception of Barbary slavery and captivity at the time was as depicted previously by Cervantes. But beyond the suffering of the individual Spanish captives and slaves in Barbary,

> [t]he sustained corsair threat led to the abandonment of large sectors of the Spanish littoral, and by 1600 long stretches of coastline had been deserted. . . . the Granadan littoral was largely depopulated and the Murcian coast completely deserted except for Mazarrón and Cartagena. Local economies suffered commensurately, especially those dependant on fishing, and coastal trade and communications were badly disrupted. . . . Constant vigilance was necessary, with alerts often causing settlements to be temporarily evacuated. (Taylor 1997, 87)

From the early 1600s, the English suffered no less than the Spaniards. At the beginning of the seventeenth century, the corsairs gained access to the Atlantic and began raiding English ships. Petitions from merchants and families of those kidnapped to Algiers were frequently brought before Parliament and the Privy Council (Matar 1997, 111–18). After 1617, Barbary corsairs were spotted even in the estuary of the Thames in England. Between 1609 and 1622, 556 English and Scottish vessels were taken, along with about six thousand captives (Davis 2001, 92). Between 1622 and 1642, seven thousand English nationals were kidnapped and more than 300 ships plundered (Hebb 1994, 139–40). But these numbers—as in the Spanish case—refer only to the captives who were ransomed; many others left no record. As in the Spanish case, the corsairs not only kidnapped people from ships: they also raided British coasts and literally snatched people from their beds (Matar 2001, 13). In 1627 they invaded Irish shores, and as late as 1654 they stormed fishing villages in Cornwall. During the early seventeenth century, their vessels sailed every summer in the Bristol canal and the English Channel. Fear of Barbary corsairs reached such a level that special prayers for protection from them became a part of Anglican church services (Perkins and Douglas-Morris 1982, 22).

The Dutch entered Mediterranean commerce in the early years of the seventeenth century. They soon became the main carriers in the Mediterranean trade, and during the Twelve Years' Truce between Spain and the United Dutch Province (1609–21), the majority of Spanish exports to Italy were actually freighted by Dutch vessels. Dutch merchantmen were in fact responsible for a great deal of intra-Spanish trade (van Royen 1990, 69–102; Israel 1982, 45). As such, the Dutch were much exposed to the corsair threat as well. At first they tried to neutralize the corsairs through a treaty with the Ottoman sultan, the nominal sovereign of the Barbary Coast (de Groot 1985, 131–47). That did not help: hundreds of Dutchmen were soon being sold in the slave markets of Barbary, and Dutch vessels and goods were taken as prizes. Although the Dutch had diplomatic and friendly relations with the Ottoman Porte since 1612, when they approached the sultan to restrain the attacks of the Barbary corsairs on their Mediterranean shipping, his high admiral—the *kapudan pasha*—replied that the sultan's authority did not reach far enough for him to be able to give them hope in this matter (de Groot 1978, 65). This was, again, a result of the independent nature of the Barbary regencies and the unruliness of the corsairs themselves. Thus, between 1613 and 1622, the Algerian corsairs made prizes of 447 Dutch ships (Wolf 1977, 190). These losses prompted the Dutch merchants to exert strong pressure on their government to do something about the corsair threat. In response, the Dutch States General (the governing body of the Dutch Republic) tried to reach an agreement with the many Dutch renegades among the Barbary corsairs to respect the merchantmen of their home country, "but this was broken upon some pretext."[5]

B. The Corsairs as Persistent Agents of Transnational Harm

The renowned French historian Fernand Braudel aptly captured the transnational and frontierlike nature of the Mediterranean world in the early modern period: "[M]en passed to and fro, indifferent to states and creeds, pursuing instead their own private, unofficial, and sometimes rebellious vision of what they wanted from life" (1973, 889). Within this world, the Barbary corsairs were private and mobile violent entrepreneurs: soldiers and seamen from diverse ethnic and national backgrounds who specialized in sea banditry and had relations of mutual benefit with the Barbary regencies and the Ottoman Empire. Although the majority of the corsairs were Muslim in origin, Christian renegades—"Turks by profession" as they were known—were also drawn to or kidnapped by the Barbary corsair community. Greek, Italian, Spanish, Albanian, and especially Dutch and English (Corbett 1917, chap. 2; Senior 1976) renegades who "turned Turk" (opportunistically converted to Islam) were among the hundreds of Europeans who were warmly welcomed in Barbary in the late sixteenth and early seventeenth centuries. They brought with them maritime skills and new sailing technologies that soon allowed the corsairs to brave the Atlantic. I. A. A. Thompson has characterized the corsairs in the late sixteenth and early seventeenth centuries as a "multi-national fraternity" (1976, 198), and Nabil Matar also refers to their multi- and transnational nature: "English, Scottish, Welsh, and Irish pirates flourished under Muslim flags. While many of them converted to Islam and settled in North Africa, *others 'worked' there until they made enough money to buy a pardon and return home. For them, settling among the Muslims was financially lucrative and professionally rewarding*" (1999, 63; emphasis added). Friar Diego de Haedo, an early seventeenth-century Spanish chronicler, argues in his book *Topografia e historia de Argel* that among the *renegadoes* of Algiers one could even find Indians from Brazil and Russian nationals (Fuchs 2001, 139n3). Renegade Europeans continued to fill the ranks of the Barbary corsairs well into the late eighteenth and early nineteenths centuries (Abun-Nasr 1987, 197).

In Arabic the corsairs were dubbed *al-ghuzat,* "the same term that had been used to denote those who fought with the Prophet Muhammad. . . . The term is connected with early Islamic conquests when men fought for both faith and gain" (Matar 2001, 11). But for the Christian states of Europe, the corsairs were simply infidel pirates, criminal sea robbers (Lewis 1982, 45). In this context it is important to distinguish between piracy and privateering. The latter practice was very similar in essence to piracy, but it differed in one important aspect: privateering was sea robbery authorized by a state (or by other political entities). Privateers were actually sea robbers with license. In times of war, states issued privateering permissions, which allowed their subjects or other nationals operating under this permission to plunder enemy ships. The privateer usually paid some percentage of his booty to the issuing state and kept the rest for himself. Occasionally, peacetime pirates turned to wartime privateers and vice versa (Thomson 1994).

And indeed more often than not the Barbary corsairs exceeded the terms of their privateering licenses and thus became "simply pirates recognizing no law above their will" (Wolf 1977, 114). In numerous cases they attacked vessels of states that were at peace with the regencies or the Ottoman Empire and thus crossed the already blurred line between privateering and piracy.[6] According to Jamil Abun-Nasr, the holy war waged by Algerian corsairs in the sixteenth century against Spain and other Christian states degenerated in the seventeenth century into unruly piracy (1987, 159). John Wolf elaborates on this unruliness: "If the legality of the capture was questioned [in terms of the corsair's privateering licensee], the simple expedient of looting the vessel, enslaving the crew, and sending the ship to the bottom of the sea destroyed most of the evidence" (1977, 184). Often, when Barbary corsairs came upon a vessel from a state that was at peace with their commission-issuing regency, they would simply hoist the colors of a Barbary regency that was at war with the state in question. And because the Barbary regencies had to constantly be at war with some states in order to keep the supply of booty and captives coming in, this was not an unusual tactic (Bennett 1960, 76; Davis 2003, 41). Corsairs would also board ships of neutral or friendly states and have one of their renegades accuse a passenger of being an enemy national—a Spaniard, for example, as happened to one French cleric who protested "that I did not know a single word of that language [at which] they whipped me with blows of a rope to the head, swearing that they would teach it to me well. Then hearing me speak French and seeming to willingly believe that I had nothing in common with Spain, they insisted that I was a Jew" (quoted in Davis 2003, 48).

But this practice of crossing back and forth over the privateering-piracy line according to the self-interests of the violent entrepreneur was not unique to the Barbary corsairs at this time (Thomson 1994). The English Elizabethan Sea Dogs used similar tactics, as did the knights of St. John's order in Malta. These were designated by the Holy Roman Emperor Charles V to defend Christendom from the "Turk," but they nevertheless frequently shifted into self-authorized piracy—and at times robbed even Christian vessels (mainly Venetians; see Earle 1970; Fisher 1957, 153; Braudel 1973, 868). Thus, the Mediterranean in the sixteenth and seventeenth centuries was a chaotic place, in which Christian and Muslim privateers and pirates operated almost unchecked (Nadal 2004).

As mentioned previously, the corsairs kept close relations of mutual benefit with the Barbary regencies (Braudel 1973, 870, 884). But they were not an official organ or branch of the regencies' government. The organization of the corsair navy was based on *private* funding and resembled the concept of the joint stock company in Elizabethan England (Kelsey 1998). Namely, private investors and financiers bought shares and stocks in a corsairing enterprise or in a corsair corporation and received shares of the corsair booty and plunder according to their investment (Davis 2003, 30–33). Although the rulers of the regencies—the beys, pashas, and deys—often bought large shares of corsair stocks themselves, they did this not in their capacity as the government of the regency but as private persons (Wolf 1977, 140). And many other persons invested in corsairing as well—governmental officials, janissary elite soldiers, merchantmen and craftsmen, and private civilians. What was left after all the shareholders took their cut was divided between the owner of the corsair ship and the crew. The plunder was then sold in the markets of the regencies or was resold to representatives of European trading companies who, after the early seventeenth century, held consuls and agents in Algiers and the other Barbary ports (Braudel 1973, 880–87; Abun-Nasr 1987, 159, 165, 177, 194). And so corsairing was symbiotically intertwined with Barbary society, politics, and economics. The corsairs were private violent entrepreneurs who operated in close cooperation with hosting communities that like them lacked a clear legal and political (European) conceptualization at the time; they were denoted at various times as "states," "city-states," "kingdoms", "military republics," "warlike cities," "regencies," or "vassals of the Porte."

But the symbiotic relationship between the corsairs and the Barbary polities did not mean that the sea rovers were disciplined actors. To a considerable extent they seem to have more closely matched the definition of persistent self-interested actors—as this concept was outlined in the introduction to this book. The previous examples illustrate the recalcitrance of the corsairs and their independent nature. But their persistence is revealed through the fact that the rulers of Barbary "had to request, rather than to order, the [corsairs] to help fight the [Christian] enemy and police the Turkish Empire's lines of naval communication" (de Groot 1978, 34). The real power in Algiers and the other Barbary regencies rested with the divan (the council of the local militia, or janissaries) and with the *taifa* (the council of the corsair captains, or *reis*)— not with the Ottoman-appointed rulers: "no authority that was ever set up in [the Barbary regencies] could maintain itself unless it complied with the wishes of the janissaries and the corporations of sea captains." Accordingly, "even when the constituted authorities wished it, which was not always the case, they were often unable to make the rovers behave otherwise in peace than in war" (Clark 1944, 24; see also Arenal and Bunes 1992, 180).

Even in the 1540s, when Algiers was ruled by beys who were indeed loyal to the sultan in Istanbul, powerful *reis* imposed their own will and disregarded commands that were contrary to their interests or wishes. The *reis* were private sea captains who turned war into a business and a way of life, and they depended on plunder and booty for their income. Accordingly, although the Ottoman Empire and Spain were at truce in 1544, the corsair *reis* Dragut of Algiers refused to recognize this and soon led the Algerian corsair community to continue the depredations on Spain (Wolf 1977, 34–35). Similarly, despite the fact that during the sixteenth and seventeenth centuries the Barbary regencies were for the most part at peace with France—and that under Franco-Barbary treaty French vessels were exempted from looting and captive taking—unscrupulous *reis* often simply destroyed any documents they could find on board and took the ship as a prize (Lee-Wiess 2002, 46).

After the Spanish-Ottoman disengagement of the 1580s, the corsairs became more persistent and independent in their raids. They ceased to serve as auxiliary units of the Ottoman navy and became a hazard to maritime commerce, even to Turkish vessels in the eastern Mediterranean. In a desperate effort to control the corsairs, Sultan Murad III (who reigned 1574–95) ordered them to let his janissaries participate in their raids. But this decree actually encouraged the janissaries to turn into frontiersmen themselves and engage in a private enterprise that pulled the periphery further away from the center (Hess 1978, 109).

II. Spain and the Barbary Corsairs

As mentioned previously, during the sixteenth and seventeenth centuries the Spanish empire (the Iberian Peninsula and Spain's possessions in Italy) was one of the primary targets of the Barbary corsairs. But, paradoxically, the more intensive the depredations of the corsairs became against Spain itself (in other words, against the Iberian Peninsula), the less intensive were the Spanish Crown's responses to them. Spain acted vigorously against the Barbary corsairs during the first three-quarters of the sixteenth century, but at that period the corsairs were a threat mainly to Spanish imperial garrisons on the North African coast, to the western Mediterranean shipping of Spain, and to Spanish possessions in Italy. After the last quarter of the sixteenth century, however, as the corsairs intensified their operations against Spain's Iberian coasts themselves, the intensity and frequency of Spanish counterharm measures decreased dramatically.

How can this paradox be explained? How can we account for the fact that, during the first three-quarters of the sixteenth century, Spanish monarchs sent navies of hundreds of ships and tens of thousands of soldiers to eliminate the Barbary corsairs, but in the last quarter Spain's interest in eliminating the depredations of the corsairs declined considerably? In order to answer this question, I will first present a chronology of the Spanish policy toward the Barbary corsairs (the dependent variable) and then try to account for the variation in this policy using the theoretical framework outlined in the previous chapters.

A. The Spanish Response

By the beginning of the sixteenth century, Spain had already begun to employ naval and military forces against the Barbary ports of Algiers, Tunis, and Tripoli in an effort to suppress their growing corsairing enterprise. The Spanish king Ferdinand recognized that something had to be done against the corsairs, but he was unwilling to invest the money and manpower needed to conquer the territorial bases of the rovers. Ferdinand and his advisers thus opted for a policy that "can best be described as 'containment' rather than conquest; Ferdinand attempted to check the piracy by controlling the ports from which the pirates could operate" (Wolf 1977, 5).

And, indeed, Spain's response roughly matched a strategy of interdiction and containment. The Spaniards did not conquer Barbary ports, but they constructed *presidios*—fortified military posts—in their entrances to control them by artillery and thus prevent the corsairs from embarking. Thus, while Spain did not institute direct imperial rule over these cities and ports, Spanish fortresses with guns commanded the traffic in these harbors, effectively pushing the Christian-Muslim frontier onto North Africa (Wolf 1977, 7–8).

However, in 1516 the corsairs started pushing back the frontier. The arrival of the (in)famous corsair Arouj Barbarosa to Algiers was a crucial development in this regard. With five thousand corsairs and adventurers following him from the Levant, Barbarosa took control of the city and murdered the ruler, who had called on his help against the Spaniards. The Spaniards managed to kill Aroudj Barbarosa (in 1518), but his brother, Kheir el-din Barbarosa, took his place. Kheir el-din's first move as the ruler of Algiers was to ally himself with the Turkish sultan, who, in return for Kheir el-din's offer to name Algiers an Ottoman province, sent him a force of two thousand janissaries and four thousand enlisted men. Kheir el-din's main motive for forging this alliance was the knowledge that in the long run only the Ottoman Empire could secure his possession of Algiers against the Spaniards (Rodriguez-Salgado 1988, 258). But inviting the Ottomans to Algiers was also the decisive step toward expanding Turkish rule to the entire central Barbary Coast. For Spain, the tightening of the bonds between the Algerian corsair community and the Ottoman Empire signaled that the latter wished to strengthen its position in North Africa and the western Mediterranean. Thus, the corsairs' increasing connections with Spain's archenemy—the Ottoman Empire—turned them from a problem of commerce and coastal security into a strategic threat. This example, then, highlights the fact that nonstate actors can actually exacerbate inter–Great Power relations.

Soon after Kheir el-din established rule in Algiers and expelled the Spaniards from their *presidio* there, he renewed corsairing operations against Christian shipping in the Mediterranean and the littoral settlements of Italy and Spain. With the help of Istanbul, Barbarosa built a corsair navy that took to the sea on a regular basis and cooperated with the Ottoman navy. In fact, it was not long before the sultan made Kheir el-din his *Kapudan Pasha*—grand admiral of the Turkish navy. In this capacity, Kheir el-din even wintered the Ottoman navy in Toulon harbor in 1543–44, the year that the French allied with the Turks against Spain.

Barbarosa's corsairs continuously raided the Italian and Spanish Mediterranean littoral settlements, sacking many of them and taking thousands of Christians into slavery (Davies 1964, 93). In addition, in 1534 Barbarosa captured Tunis. This port was strategically valuable for Spain because of its proximity to Sicily—a Spanish granary that supplied much of the Iberian Peninsula. Wars with the Ottomans in central Europe distracted Charles V—the Holy Roman Emperor and Spain's Habsburg king—from the Tunisian threat; but upon the conclusion of these wars in 1535, Charles assembled an expedition against Tunis. A navy of more than six hundred ships, under the command of Andrea Doria—a Genoese condottiere admiral who for money made his war fleet available to various monarchs—made its way to North Africa. Christian privateers thus conducted the war against the corsairs, a situation that has arisen many times since then.

Doria's ships transported thirty thousand imperial soldiers (Spanish, Italian, and German), who were joined by a flotilla of the privateering St John's Knights from Malta. The timing was perfect: the Ottoman war had just ended, and Spain was at peace with its other major enemy, France. After a prolonged siege, the Habsburg forces defeated the corsairs, occupied Tunis, and sacked it. This was an act of pure robbery: the victims were not the corsairs but inhabitants of Tunis who previous to being conquered by Barbarosa had been sympathetic to Spain. Furthermore, this could not be explained as a spontaneous act of plunder on the part of undisciplined soldiers, because prior to the expedition Emperor Charles promised his soldiers that he would let them sack the city. Spain's conduct was thus not much different from its corsair enemies. As we shall see later in this chapter, piracy was not Spain's major concern with the corsairs: it was the corsair's threatening of Sicily and Spain's interests in southern Italy due to their Ottoman connections (Lane-Poole 1890, 86).

Emperor Charles's forces managed to free several thousand Christian slaves from Tunis, but Barbarosa himself escaped to Algiers (mainly due to the chaos during the pillage of the city). But the corsair *reis*, unwilling to let go of his pursuit, continued his conflict with Spain. In 1536 Barbarosa organized raids on the Balearic Islands and Valencia, and in 1537 he sent his forces to southern Italy. Again, a war with France (1536–38) distracted Charles's attention from the Mediterranean, and his campaign against the corsairs was renewed only after the truce of Niece in 1538. In October 1541, the emperor himself headed a Habsburg expedition to occupy and eliminate Algiers. Renowned Spanish generals—including Cortez, the conqueror of Mexico—also participated in the expedition. However, this armada of five hundred ships and thirty-six thousand men perished: bad weather conditions, defective planning, and poor command resulted in the loss of more than three hundred Habsburg officers and eight thousand soldiers, and many of the expedition's ships were lost to a storm. The slave *bagnos* (prisons) in Algiers were full of Habsburg soldiers (Gosse 1932, 27).

In 1556 Charles V abdicated and handed the Spanish Crown to his son, Philip II (the Imperial Crown was entrusted to Charles's brother, Ferdinand of Austria). Philip sent Spanish galleys to Tripoli to secure it for Spain and to remove the corsair threat to Sicily. But prolonged Spanish preparations for the expedition allowed the corsairs to call the Ottoman navy to their aid, and Philip's navy was defeated in 1560. Forty-two out of his eighty-two galleys fell into Muslim hands, along with eighteen thousand Spanish soldiers who were killed or taken captive (Lovett 1986, 134). The disaster prompted Philip to construct a standing navy for Sicily, Naples, and Catalonia. The result of this buildup was that by 1564 Spain possessed more than one hundred Mediterranean galleys (Thompson 1976, 16n10). Spain further strengthened its position in the Mediterranean after the 1565 Battle of Malta, which was successful in preventing the Ottoman navy from approaching the western sea.

But in 1566 the Spanish Netherlands revolted against Philip's rule. The king was convinced that the challenge to his rule in the Low Countries would be defeated only through military force, and he directed Spain's best armed forces and the thrust of the monarchy's military efforts to the Netherlands. This meant shifting most of the Mediterranean's financial and military resources to the Dutch revolt. Thus, Spanish counter-corsair response from the 1570s onward was mainly defensive, resorting back to containment: coastal patrols and construction of coastal watchtowers. This shift was especially notable after the Battle of Lepanto in 1571 (in which most of the Ottoman navy was destroyed by a coalition of Spanish, Venetian, and Papal forces) and the Ottoman-Spanish truce in 1580.

In addition, while in the first three-quarters of the sixteenth century the Crown bore most of the expenses in the war against the corsairs, after the 1570s the burden was shifted to the coastal communities themselves. It is important to note here that this was despite the fact that in the last quarter of the century the percentage of captives taken directly from the Spanish coast or from Iberian coastal shipping increased sharply (Friedman 1983, xxv, 4): in 1572 only 5 percent of Spanish captives in Barbary were taken from the Iberian coasts or their vicinity, but by 1589 this rose to 34.3 percent. This points to a considerable increase of corsair raids on the Spanish coast itself. In the long term, the Battle of Lepanto and the decline of the Ottoman threat to Spain in Italy and the western Mediterranean only aggravated the corsair threat to the inhabitants of Mediterranean Spain.

Paradoxically, then, when the corsairs ceased to be directly related to an imperial threat—that of Ottoman Turkey—and Spanish countermeasures against them diminished, their harm to civilians in Spain itself increased. Indeed, the failures of Charles V in Algiers (1541) and Philip II in Tripoli (1560) could account for Spain's pulling back from further direct assaults on the Barbary Coast. But Spain won a great victory in

Tunis in 1535, which meant that the Barbary Coast was not unassailable. And despite great military failures in Holland and England, for example, Spain was not discouraged from continuing to war with these states. In fact, these military defeats made Spain even more persistent in efforts to eradicate Protestant "heresy" there. As I will show later, it was *because* of these military failures that Philip II was determined to double his efforts in Holland and England; and his heir, Philip III, similarly renewed the Dutch war in 1621, knowing that it could not be won.

The corsair threat to Spain's coasts became even more pressing after the 1609 expulsion of the Moriscos from Spain. More than 250,000 Moriscos (Muslims forcefully converted to Christianity after the *Reconquista*) were expelled in 1609 to North Africa. The belief in Spain was that the Moriscos regularly cooperated with the Barbary corsairs, and their expulsion was partially carried out to improve the security of the coastal regions. Indeed, evidence confirms the connections between the Moriscos and the corsairs (Taylor 1997). The Spanish Crown perceived them as a fifth column, and their expulsion served to pacify the Spanish population through an easy victory (Lynch 1992, 57). Furthermore, since the Moriscos persistently refused to assimilate into Spanish Christian society, the presence of such an unruly and rebellious minority in Spain (they rebelled in 1570) was deemed to undermine the religious homogeneity of the state that led the Catholic Counter-Reformation campaign in Europe (Hess 1968; Payne 1973, 288). The Moriscos had maintained busy networks of people smuggling between Spain and North Africa since the middle of the sixteenth century. They also cooperated with the corsairs. This history of transnational cooperation between the Moriscos and the corsairs was the basis for the Spanish Crown's hope that the expulsion of the Moriscos would ease the problem of the Barbary sea rovers, who would no longer have access to their littoral assistance and intelligence.

The result of the expulsion of the Moriscos was the opposite of what its planners had hoped: the corsair attacks on Spain and its Mediterranean shipping actually increased after the expulsion of the Moriscos. Thus, many authors dub the early seventeenth century the golden age of Barbary sea predation (Julien 1970; Feijoo 2003). The expulsion of so many Spanish-speaking people who knew the Spanish coast intimately, together with their desire for revenge and the need to prove loyalty to their coreligionists in the Barbary Coast, made the Moriscos a much greater threat than they were in Spain. The fact that many Moriscos were phenotypically similar to Spain's "Old Christians" further aggravated the threat they posed once turned corsair, as they were often indistinguishable from "real" Spaniards once they landed on Spanish coasts (Taylor 1997).

The expulsion of the Moriscos brought about a significant change in the operational patterns of the corsairs. Between 1570 and 1609, an average of 31.9 percent of the Spanish captives in Barbary were taken from Spanish shores; between 1610 and 1620, this percentage jumped to 54.2. On average, in the first half of the seventeenth century 42 percent of Spanish people kidnapped were taken from their own shores (Friedman 1983, 13). But on top of the raids on the Mediterranean shores, the first decades of the seventeenth century also witnessed the encroachment of the corsairs into the Atlantic. At the height of the corsair operations in the Atlantic, between 1610 and 1639, a quarter of the Spanish captives in Barbary came from the Atlantic (as opposed to the mere 3 percent four decades before). Clearly, then, in the first half of the seventeenth century Barbary corsairing became an Atlantic threat too (ibid.). Thus, the corsair activity against Spain in the early seventeenth century did not diminish but rather intensified (ibid., 20–22).

These facts indicate that the corsairs were a significant threat to the personal security of many Spanish and Habsburg civilians. Although the Spanish Crown did provide certain measures for the protection of villages and towns against the corsairs, these were never sufficient. In fact, Barbary corsairing against Spain continued until the early nineteenth century: as late as 1816, the British navy under Lord Exmouth released Spanish nationals from captivity and slavery in Algiers (see next chapter). But back in the late sixteenth and early seventeenth centuries, protection against the Barbary corsairs ceased to be a high priority of the Spanish Crown.

In general, the efficiency of privately built and royal coastal defenses was low. Various counties and provinces commonly brought complaints to their respective Cortes (their parliaments and tax-voting bodies) about the insufficiency of coastal defenses. Continuous claims for better protection through fortification and strengthening of coastal regions and settlements were raised, especially in the Mediterranean kingdoms and provinces. Representatives of corsair-stricken regions urged the Crown to establish peace with other Christian kings and princes so that Spain could directly confront the Barbary corsairs. In addition, Mediterranean representatives constantly asked the Crown to pay the costs of arming their provinces' ships with guns to deter corsairs (Merriman 1962, 172). But the Crown usually remained indifferent (Amoraga 1999). Furthermore, in the early seventeenth century the Crown's galleys almost never patrolled the Mediterranean coasts of Spain. The coastal fortifications, on top of lacking ammunitions and guns, were undermanned and in an advanced state of decay. To complicate matters, finding men who were willing to enlist to coastal defense was difficult because of the risky and demanding nature of the work. Despite recurrent demands that the Cortes of the coastal provinces take some action, and despite the advice of engineers and experts, almost nothing was done. Evidence of requests and advice for a long-term policy on coastal defense abounds, but none exists of the Crown consenting to or implementing such a policy (Friedman 1983, 35–41).

Another indication of the relatively low priority the Crown ascribed to the corsair issue after the 1580s is the fact that the Crown did not establish a formal state mechanism for ransoming the thousands of Spaniards who were taken captive but rather left this to private religious orders. Ransom funds were raised through donations and contributions, not through a mandatory state tax. Although various organs of the Spanish government—among them the monarch himself—often donated large sums for the redemption of Spanish captives, no tax was levied. From the perspective of the Spanish state, ransoming was a traditional *charity* and not a legal obligation. Indeed, the government supervised the financial activities of the redemptionists, and the religious orders had to submit detailed reports on their expenses and uses of ransom money (albeit no evidence exists that legal penalties for failure to submit these reports on time were ever imposed) (Friedman 1983, 110). Moreover, the Crown turned a blind eye to the enrichment of the redemptionist orders, which actually benefited from corsairing due to their intermediary function. Organized redemption made Spaniards the most sought-after captives in the Mediterranean (due to the frequency of the redemption expeditions and the high prices the captives commanded). Therefore, many critics in early modern Spain saw organized redemptionism as a major incentive for the continuance of corsair captive-taking raids and an intolerable drain of money to Spain's enemies. In spite of criticism, however, ransoming activity continued unhindered (Taylor 1997, 86).

The Spanish Crown's relatively low-intensity post-1580s counterharm policy was reflected as well through its international stance: Spain made no effort to initiate international cooperation with other European states that were attacked by the corsairs. When such cooperation was suggested by England in the late 1610s, Spain was very reluctant. This can be compared to the Spanish willingness to cooperate with Venice and the pope in the Battle of Lepanto (1571). Admittedly, the fact that the other major victims of Barbary corsairing—England, France, and Holland—were all rivals or erstwhile enemies of Spain may have played a part in Spain's position. However, as constructivists believe, "[a]narchy is what states make of it" (Wendt 1992), and nothing necessarily predisposes states to be enemies. Historically, Spanish subjects constantly implored their king to make peace with other European states so that he could devote his resources to the defense of his realm against the corsairs. Moreover, when the option of international cooperation became serious due to the increasing harm suffered by other European states (namely, England and Holland) Spain was at peace with England (since 1604) and had a truce with Holland (1609–21). A joint operation against the corsairs—a block-ade[7] or an offensive attack—could have eliminated them or, at the very least, relieved the condition along the Spanish coast. This was most likely the reason behind Spain's final agreement to enter into negotiations with England (but not with Holland) in the late 1610s. Despite the shared interest to stamp out Barbary piracy, however, two facts must be remembered. First, the English—not the Spanish—initiated and pursued these negotiations. Second, the eventual anticorsair cooperation between England and Spain was ephemeral and guarded, and Holland looked for ways to exempt itself from the raids of the corsairs while at the same time encouraging them to continue to prey upon Spain.

Thus, in April 1617 the English approached the Dutch and the Spaniards with regard to a joint anticorsair expedition. The Dutch expressed an interest and willingness to participate in such an effort—without Spain—and asked Venice and France, two other victims of Barbary corsairing, to finance some of the costs.[8] But the Venetians were very suspicious, especially when they learned of the English contacts with Spain.

> With regard to the union against pirates, proposed by the States [Holland] to ourselves and the kings of France and England . . . after we hear by way of England of similar negotiations between the two crowns [England and France] and the States, and the Spaniards also, we suspect the last of deceit, and a desire to lull the suspicions of the other powers in this matter, to cover their preparations against the Gulf [of Venice]. We therefore warn you to be on your guard.[9]

In early 1618, the Dutch communicated to the English their strong objection to the participation of Spain. However, in the face of English insistence that Spain be part of the joint expedition, the Dutch finally withdrew their commitment to the operation. When the English insisted that the Dutch participate in the attack on Algiers, the Dutch responded that such an attack would mean an act of war against the sultan of Constantinople, with whom they were at peace—an obviously naive reply since the Barbary regencies were only under nominal Ottoman rule by this period (Corbett 1917, 82).

Parallel to the effort to solicit Dutch approval for the operation, English diplomacy concentrated on ensuring the support of Spain for this enterprise. In the summer of 1617, the English ambassador to Spain presented King Philip III a letter from King James I, proposing that the two monarchies cooperate against the Barbary corsairs. But the Spanish Council of War did not give a conclusive answer to the English offer. The *consejo de guerra* concurred with the English naval experts on the need to combine forces in order to subdue the corsairs, but by the spring of 1618 the Spaniards decided to act unilaterally—without the English and the Dutch. Cottington, Britain's agent in Madrid, noted that the Spanish "are very unwilling his Majesty [James I] should intermeddle in the clearing of the seas for them" (quoted in Hebb 1994, 67). Similarly, the Venetian ambassador in Spain observed that the Spaniards "are not pleased to hear of the English king joining his ships to those of Holland and they would much prefer that everyone should embark upon this undertaking for himself."[10]

Parallel to the decision to act alone, Spain also began an ambitious naval buildup program to restore and strengthen its declining fleet. Throughout the reign of Philip III (1598–1621), the Spanish navy had been reduced in tonnage, numbers, and operational readiness. But by 1623, the Spanish navy was entirely reconstituted. Only after the major thrust of this naval buildup did Spain became more open to the recurrent English appeals to cooperate against the corsairs. Thompson argues that the main reason for the Spanish naval buildup of 1617–23 was the need to check the increasing raids and attacks of the Barbary corsairs (1976, 198). Although this was the proclaimed reason for the naval buildup, one cannot ignore three elements in its timing. First, it came as the English and the Dutch were already entering the Mediterranean—or, in the latter case, forcing their way into it. Second, Spain was very much concerned with the activities of the Dutch and the English "beyond the line"—in the New World. And third, and most important, Spain was very preoccupied with the approaching expiration of the Twelve Years' Truce with the Dutch (1609–21).

The naval buildup coincided with the rise to power of Zúñiga and Olivares in Spain, who led a hard-line policy against the Dutch Republic. The replacement of the Lerma cabinet by Zúñiga and Olivares strengthened the move to restore the navy—these two influential ministers actually sought a renewal of the war with the Dutch in order to get an improved peace (Goodman 1997, 17). Strange as it might sound, a Mediterranean navy was an essential component in projecting Spanish power to the Low Countries of northwestern Europe when the war resumed; Spanish supply and communication lines to the Low Countries—known as the Spanish Road—started in the Mediterranean and from there went into Lombardy, Bohemia, and northwestern Europe (Parker 1972). In any planning to resume the Dutch war, a strong and big Mediterranean navy was necessary to safely transport soldiers, money, and provisions to Italy and from there to the Army of Flanders (Cooper 1971, 228). Without such a navy, Spanish transport and supply lines in the Mediterranean were exposed to corsair attacks. The need for a reconstructed navy and anticorsair measures rose mainly from the requirements of European warfare: the reconstructed navy's prime function therefore was *not* to reduce the corsair threat to Spain's coasts.

Although it did not embark on a joint operation with the English against the corsairs, Madrid finally allowed the English to operate in Spanish waters against the Barbary sea raiders and also to anchor in Spanish ports for provisions and to care for their ill and wounded. Nevertheless, this was allowed only after English assurances that they would not attack Spanish targets and exploit the situation for their benefit (Hebb 1994, 73–74). But the English proposal to actually join forces and conduct concerted naval operations against the corsairs was declined: Spain wanted to keep full control of its navy. Thus, in September 1620 an English fleet of six royal men-of-war and thirteen armed merchant ships, commanded by Sir William Mansell, was sent to the Mediterranean (Clowes 1898, 52). During the winter the fleet anchored at the Spanish ports of Majorca, Alicante, and Malaga and went out to seek the pirates only when weather permitted. However, already by July 1621, four of the larger royal ships were recalled to England. This, on top of the lack of sufficient supplies and victuals, rendered the expedition inefficient and its effect on the pirates negligible; the rest of the fleet was ordered back in September 1621 (Lane-Poole 1890, 272). In all of this, there were no joint operations between the Spanish and the English. In fact, the Anglo-Spanish cooperation was so guarded in this case that their navies' ability to properly deal with the corsairs was extremely reduced. Mansell, for example, was ordered to first negotiate with the Algerians; only if these negotiations failed was he to use force. But he was also told to be very cautious in the case of hostilities not to injure His Majesty's ships. Negotiations were meant not only to stop piracy but to secure an African base should war break out with Spain (Corbett 1917, 101).

The Spaniards were quite sensitive to the possibility of English defection and were closely monitoring Mansell's actions. Thus, on one occasion when Mansell was before Algiers, six Spanish men-of-war appeared.

> They excused their intrusion into the English sphere of operations by alleging that they were in chase of some pirates, who had recently taken a large ship off Cartagena; but Mansell was well aware this was not their real object. . . . there can be no doubt that they had been sent to see what Mansell was doing. Finding him quietly anchored in the road and in constant communication with the shore, their worst suspicions were aroused. The haunting fear that England meant to ally itself with the corsairs hurried them to the conviction that they had caught Mansell in the act of hatching the dreaded plot. (Corbett 1917, 103–4)

Mutual distrust after this incident was so high that the Spanish preferred that the English stay in harbor if they were not willing to risk their navy to really harm the corsairs. These constraints were the reason why Mansell's fleet was so idle: the ships, "besides their coming and going, spent not forty days at sea, but retired into harbour, where the pirates could find them; but not they the pirates" (Monson, quoted in Clowes 1898, 54).

B. Theoretical Analysis of the Spanish Counter-Corsair Policy between 1500 and 1620

In order to understand the variations in the Spanish response toward the Barbary corsairs during the sixteenth century and the early decades of the seventeenth century, I will now explore the three institutions of transborder violence—sovereignty, laws of war, and actorhood—during these times, examining how they informed the Spanish perception of the Barbary corsairs' threat.

i. Sovereignty

Sovereignty constructs the employment of transborder force in two important ways. First, it determines what states are allowed to do to each other in territorial terms. Second, it establishes why they are allowed to wield transborder force—what are the legitimate reasons states can pursue through the use of transborder force and who are considered the subjects of security (those to whom the state is committed to supply security).

Territoriality. Early modern norms of sovereignty tolerated the occupation of other states' territories. The conquest of the whole territory of another state was also acceptable (Weber 1995, 910; Teschke 2002, 13). Often, only technological, logistic, geographic, and other material extrinsic constraints prevented states from eliminating the territorial sovereignty of others. This created a strong security dilemma and a constant need to stand on guard against other powerful states. Legal claims to territory or international treaties were an extremely limited guarantee of territorial integrity (Sorel 1964, 16). In this sense, the dominant powers of the time barely considered each other as capable of authority.

For Spain, the menace of Ottoman and French territorial expansionism was constant during the sixteenth century. We have seen previously how the French, the corsairs, and the Ottomans allied themselves against Spain in the early 1540s. In 1558 an Ottoman navy of 150 galleys from Istanbul reached Minorca Island, and Ottoman troops landed and burned the city of Cuidadela, only 150 miles from the coast of Spain (Hess 1968, 11). When the Morisco revolt broke out in Granada in 1568, Sultan Selim II was resolved to send his galleys in support of the rebellion, with a design to reestablish Islam's rule in Spain. In the end, the sultan made do with instigating the Moriscos to continue their rebellion and sending them arms from Algiers. But he also approached the Dutch rebels to coordinate their attacks on Spain with the Moriscos.

Philip II was well aware of these threats, and he prepared his military for the possibility of an Ottoman invasion supported by the Moriscos. Philip was never sure that the Ottomans had given up their plans for an Islamic reconquest of Spain. On their part, the Ottomans had good reasons to suspect Spain: they perceived the Spanish advance in North Africa and the capture of strongholds in the central Mediterranean as Spanish imperialist expansion. And, indeed, after the Battle of Lepanto, the Duke of Alba, Spain's principal military commander, recommended that Philip "clean up" the Barbary Coast—not primarily as an antipirate operation but rather as a prerequisite for the conquest of Constantinople (Parker 1998, 7–8)!

In this sense, Geoffrey Parker is probably right to consider both the Ottoman Empire and the Spanish empire as "universal states" in terms of their bids for dominance and territorial expansion (Parker 1988, 18–19, 64–67; Abun-Nasr 1987, 144–50). But, ultimately, the military revolution of the sixteenth century, with the introduction of modern technologies of powder weapons and defensive warfare, posed increasing material constraints on the imperial expansion of both powers (Hess 1978, 71). In other words, the limits of Spanish and Ottoman expansion were not determined by intrinsic considerations of mutual respect for each other's sovereignty and territorial integrity but rather by the growing costs of defense and conquest, as well as the difficulties in long-distance sea transport and supply (Brummett 1999, 237). Although the enmity between Spain and the Ottoman Empire did not result in the conquest or annihilation of either of the belligerents, the deadlock the two powers reached in the 1580s was due to material and extrinsic factors. These two sixteenth-century giants clearly did not consider each other Great Powers in the sense discussed in this book—as authoritative actors possessing a mutually respected right to manage international politics.

In western Europe as well, state borders remained unstable, often transformed through armed force. In fact, "the first map of Europe to attempt to show state borders was not printed until 1602. . . . Everywhere political boundaries and political alignments were in flux, reshaped by the strategies of war and marriage. . . . The trend over the long term was for the larger states to consume the smaller states and digest them in a slow process of internal consolidation" (Gunn 2001, 102–3). Sometimes the strategies of war and marriage/inheritance combined: in 1580, for example, Spanish troops marched into Portugal claiming the Portuguese Crown for the Spanish king Philip II by descent through his mother. Portugal was thus absorbed by the Spanish Crown and ceased to be a sovereign actor in international relations for sixty years. Portuguese sovereignty was restored only in 1640 when the Portuguese took arms against Spain, assisted in this effort by Britain.

Even when material constraints prevented the conquest of another state, the belligerents often believed that the aim of the other was to conquer them. Fear of conquest was one of the main reasons behind the establishment of resident embassies in foreign courts in the early modern period—diplomacy's primary task was anticipating attacks, and diplomats acted on the principle of mutual distrust (Hale 1985, 25). The early modern period thus was one of high bellicosity. War was rife, and the dominant powers often tried to annul each other's independent existence (e.g., the Spanish-Ottoman enmity of the sixteenth century, Ottoman invasions of Habsburg Austria, Spain's armada to England in 1588, and the Spanish Eighty Years' War with the Dutch Republic). The powers also frequently used force to occupy and subjugate small states (as in the case of the sixteenth-century Italian Wars between Spain and France). The real possibility of extensive territorial changes and even complete conquest loomed always in the minds of state rulers (Parker 1998, 6).

Since this chapter focuses on Spain, this state's alleged quest for "universal monarchy" is of special concern here in the context of authority. Recall that, according to my theoretical argument, Great Power authority depends on the dominant powers respecting some minimal rights of their peers and nonpeers. Authority cannot simply be taken: it has to be given. The full conquest—or the desire for such conquest—of other states, especially other powerful ones, undermines authority. Spain's reasons for projecting transborder force were so broad (see next subsection)—and at times arbitrary—that other states could never be certain of Spain's motives and actions, resulting in constant suspicion of the strongest power in the system. The fact that by 1586 the legend *non sufficit orbis* (the world is not enough) had been incorporated into the royal arms of Spain as the monarchy's official logo surely did not help to ameliorate this tension (Gunn 2001, 106).

Thus, the actual efforts of Spain to achieve "universal monarchy," and the perception of others that this was what Spain indeed looked for, seriously hampered Spanish authority as a Great Power. Consequently, I argue, Spain and its opponents were locked in a system of realpolitik, very close to the Wendtian concept of Hobbesian anarchy, and the possibility of significant harm by other dominant powers was always imminent.

While matrimony was a primary strategy of Spain to achieve universal monarchy—or, in the aphorism of the time, *Bella gerant alii. Tu, felix Austria, nube* (Others make war. You, happy Habsburgs, marry)—Spain did not relinquish war and conquest as empire-building tactics. Thus, "Admiral Coligny in France warned his prince that Philip meant to be 'monarche of Christendome' and that France was to be the victim of Spain's dream for universal monarchy. Philip's II turncoat secretary, Antonio Pérez, further inflamed French suspicions by claiming that 'the heart of the Spanish Empire is France'" (Parker 1994, 120). In the last quarter of the sixteenth century, Spain made considerable efforts to invade England and to reconquer the Dutch Republic. These bellicose plans seemed to abate after the death of Philip II and the ascension of his son, Philip III. Thus, in 1604 Spain concluded a peace with England, and in 1609 it signed the Twelve Years' Truce with the Dutch. But this only reflected the exhaustion of Spain, not any deep internalization of a norm against conquest of other states (Trevor-Roper 1971, 263). But Spain itself was not free from the risk of dismemberment by hostile powers. In the 1580s Spain was threatened by a French invasion led by Henry of Navarre, assisted by the Turks and the Moriscos. In the early 1600s, upon becoming the king of France, Henry IV plotted with the Moriscos to raise eighty thousand men and conquer three Spanish cities, one of them a sea-port. Eventually, Henry decided that the moment (1604–5) was not favorable, and the plan was postponed. All of this took place when official peace existed between Spain and France (Lea 1907, 387). The separation of Portugal and Catalonia from Castile, through French conspiracy and support, also loomed constantly during the early seventeenth century (Rule 1999, 54). Earlier, in the 1570s, France had also threatened the Spanish rule in the Netherlands (Butterfield 1953).

Although Spain still contemplated expansionism in the early 1600s (or at least was reluctant to give up a vision of universal monarchy), it had to face not only the threat of French expansion but also the growth of Dutch imperial power. In fact, of all the new century's threats to Spain's international position, Dutch imperial growth was seen by Spain as the most dangerous. The Dutch, it seemed, preferred the expansion and increase of power to the status quo of their truce with Spain, and they were willing to risk another war with Spain to pursue these ends. The Dutch declined to cease infringement on Spanish possessions in the Far East and the Americas. Spain considered these regions of the globe to be its monopoly (by virtue of a papal bull from 1494) and defined any other nation venturing into these parts as pirate (Carter 1964, 36). But not only did the Dutch refuse to cease their current level of penetration into these regions; after the truce of 1609 they intensified their trespassing onto the Spanish overseas empire (Israel 1982, 28).

Hence, the general conviction in Spain was that the Dutch truce was a disaster. Furthermore, as Jonathan Israel has shown, Spain perceived Dutch imperial expansion as a real threat to the Spanish imperial system and consequently to the very survival of Spanish power. Clearly, the truce years were a period of dramatic expansion in Dutch navigation and trade, and Philip III's ministers were inclined to link the two phenomena as cause and effect. Furthermore, the Dutch were undermining Spain's position not only in the New World but also in Europe, especially Germany. By providing men and money elsewhere, they were assuming the lead in undermining Habsburg rule in central Europe (Israel 1977, 39).

As a result, although Spain indeed wanted universal authority, efforts to achieve this, or even simply to maintain the status quo, sometimes culminated in the complete denial of others' rights. And, as my discussion of Ottoman and Dutch expansionism has demonstrated, other powerful states did not remain aloof either. This led, as Parker rightly notes, to the intense security dilemma of the period (1998, 6). When dominant powers harbor designs to conquer each other, or when peers can and want to inflict significant harm on each other, the threat of PATHs like the Barbary corsairs lowers considerably; the PATHs are not deviating from the institutions of violence because these norms are so permissive in terms of the violent behavior they sanction that hardly any deviation from them can exist. The Barbary corsairs, therefore, were a predatory threat to Spain only when they were close allies or in direct service of the Ottomans (Arenal and Bunes 1992, 86). In 1541, for example, when Emperor Charles V tried to capture Algiers, "[i]t was clearly not against a mere piratical den or corsair base that the emperor so obstinately hazarded his fortunes and reputation. . . . His objective was essentially a political one of great importance"—namely, repelling Ottoman expansion in the western Mediterranean (Fisher 1957, 78). But once the Spanish empire and the Ottoman Empire disengaged in the 1570s and 1580s and the corsairs increasingly detached themselves from Istanbul, the corsairs simply became, from the Spanish perspective, parasites that fed on Spanish commerce and coastal settlements (Arenal and Bunes 1992, 203). Pirates and privateers became mere agents of forcible exchange throughout the Mediterranean. And in the early modern world this type of exchange bordered on legitimate commerce (Nadal 2001), as it did not deviate considerably from what were considered to be legitimate reasons for transborder violence (sovereignty), nor was it considerably deviant from the laws of war in that period.

In other words, at a time when Spain and its enemies planned or feared mutual subjugation, the harm inflicted by the corsairs was interpreted from the perspective of a general lack of authority among the major military powers. Between 1516 and 1571, Spain perceived the Barbary corsairs in direct relation to the Ottoman expansionist threat in the Mediterranean (Launder 1921, 20–21; Preto 2001). During this time, the raids of the Barbary corsairs were "operations of war conducted by entire fleets as part of a comprehensive strategy, for the Ottomans were contemplating conquering the Mediterranean and even invading Italy. The Barbary corsairs were no longer mere pirates, but were squadron commanders or admirals in a total war against Christendom, one waged by land and by sea" (Heers 2003, 31–32). But in the last quarter of the sixteenth century, the threat of Ottoman expansion considerably subsided and the Barbary corsairs as such posed no such territorial threat to Spain.

No definitive estimation exists as to the size of the corsair navy in the late sixteenth and early seventeenth centuries. Nonetheless, it seems that at the beginning of the seventeenth century—the heyday of Barbary corsairing—Algiers's fleet (the largest among the Barbary regencies') consisted of about seventy-five ships. It is clear, however, that the armament of the corsair vessels was rather weak (although they carried large numbers of men—300 to 450). The Algerian corsair fleet "was built for commerce raiding rather than for confrontation with other warships" (Wolf 1977, 139). Guns were sacrificed to speed (Braudel 1973, 886). G. N. Clark might have underestimated the North African corsair communities when he claimed that "indeed they had no serious 'war potential' at all" (1944, 24). But the corsairs obviously ceased to be a strategic threat to Spain once the Ottoman Empire disengaged itself from the western Mediterranean. During the westward march of the Ottoman frontier, the Algerian corsairs under Barbarosa and his successors had been key players in the struggle against Spain and were even integrated into the Turkish naval establishment. After Lepanto, however, Spain's struggle with the Ottomans was revealed for what it truly was: "a ritualized confrontation of two ideological hostile super-powers separated by two thousands miles of sea, hissing and posturing on the perimeter of their territories, neither able to inflict mortal hurt" (Thompson 1976, 26).

Once both Spain and the Ottomans realized that they had arrived at a strategic deadlock, the depredations of the Barbary corsairs lost their interpower enmity status: they became mere frontier raids and border brigandage. The Ottomans were not completely defeated in Lepanto, but the balance of power in the Mediterranean after Lepanto expressly favored Spain. And even though the Ottomans quickly rebuilt most of their navy, they were not willing to risk it again in a frontal collision with the Spanish navy. Furthermore, after Lepanto the center of Ottoman military policy shifted to the confrontation with Persia. The corsairs, who had previously been considered by Spain to be the sultan's proxies, were perceived with the demise of their eastern patron as no more than a nuisance, and as such they ceased influencing important policy decisions in Spain (Davies 1964, 175). They lapsed into the background of Spanish politics, "annoying as insects whose bites are certainly harmful, but cannot reach vital organs" (Amoraga 1999, 170). Even though the corsairs continued to vigorously raid Spanish shores and shipping, they could not succeed in dislocating the structure of Spanish imperialism in the Mediterranean without the support and involvement of the Ottoman Empire. "Consequently, the financial requirements of a Mediterranean [security] reform were unable to resist the new set of priorities that were now being imposed in the west. Wherever possible the [Spanish] king tried to pass the cost [of counter-corsair defense] on to the country" (Thompson 1976, 26). In the wake of the Ottoman-Spanish Mediterranean wars, the corsairs thus operated as robber merchants on the edge of the Ottoman Empire, or as "parasites whose hosts were the declining trade of the Mediterranean and the booming economy of the Atlantic" (Hess 1978, 124).

Being comfortably established in their institutionalized system of sea predation, slavery, and ransom, the corsairs perhaps never aimed to any higher goal than harassing Spain (Arenal and Bunes 1992, 111, 165). From the late sixteenth century, the whole economy of the Barbary regencies became dependent on corsair depredations. Thus, the European states considered the Barbary corsairs and their regencies as mere thieves and pests.[11] Spanish sources from the late sixteenth century also deem the Barbary corsairs as inevitable "pests" and "plague" (Temprano 1989, 215). Friar Diego Haedo, the important early seventeenth-century Spanish chronicler who was considered then in Spain as an authoritative source on Algiers, observed: "If it were not for the rapacity of the corsairs, the Algerian citizens would have died of hunger. Because of the work of these barbarians that are stealing from all the lands and coasts of the states in Christendom, and like some infernal harpies, they live off the continuous prey; so if they rest for two months and will not go corsairing, the residents of this house of thieves will die of hunger and misery" (quoted in ibid., 70). Similarly, in his *Cautivos de Argel* the great Spanish playwright of the Golden Age, Lope de Vega, referred to Algiers as a "fierce cave of thieves" (ibid., 71). Miguel de Cervantes defines Algiers in *Los tratos de Argel* as "the most insatiable glutton of all the Mediterranean shores, a universal haven for pirates and refuge for thieves," and he highlights the economic nature of the corsair threat by describing it—through the mouth of Hasan Pasha, the ruler of Algiers—as "a game of loss and gain" (quoted in Garcés 2002, 129, 136). The Spanish Crown also framed the corsairs as such a problem: "The corsairs may have terrified most Spaniards, but to the crown they were little more than a nuisance"

(Friedman 1983, 51). A privateering permit granted by Philip IV to one captain Juan de Amezqueta describes the problem of the corsairs not as a security threat to the monarchy but rather as *"grandes inconvenientes"* (great inconveniences) to its individual subjects (Lana 1999, 172). Thus, according to Maria Garcés, the politics of the Spanish Crown *permitted* the existence of Algiers and its sea predation (2002, 176). This was because the corsairs were seen by the Spanish state as nothing more than raiders who essentially sought booty, especially slaves, and not territory. Their commerce raids and coastal predations were believed to represent an unavoidable hazard of seaborne trade and not necessarily evidence of a state of war between nations, states, or creeds (Black 1998, 52).

The instability of the early modern period's territorial order was decisive not only in relegating the corsair problem to a parasitic threat but also in making international cooperation against the pirates difficult to achieve. The low level of authority among the dominant powers and the intense security dilemma they faced deeply affected the issue of international anticorsair cooperation. Thus, the Dutch competitive conduct with regard to cooperation against the pirates was largely motivated by a political calculation that considered Barbary piracy's benefits greater than its costs, due to the damages that the corsairs inflicted on Spain (Hebb 1994, 51). An international repression of the Barbary pirates could have alleviated Spain's need to protect its Mediterranean supply lines and enabled it to turn these resources against the Dutch. The allocation of naval forces to defend the Mediterranean part of the Spanish Road from corsair attacks was a great concern for the Spaniards and therefore beneficial to the Dutch. We must remember that the Spanish Road was the major route for Spanish troop transportation into the Spanish Netherlands and Germany, where they directly threatened Dutch sovereignty.

While Dutch expansionism prescribed competition with Spain with regard to the pirates and motivated mutual Spanish and Dutch objections to the other's participation in the antipirate enterprise, England's more status quo inclinations fostered guarded cooperation with Spain. Despite the existence of anti-Spanish and revisionist forces in England, the general direction of English foreign policy under James I was to avoid direct confrontation with Spain in the New World. In general, although he allowed English penetration into areas in which Spain did not wield effective control (such as North America and the East Indies), James respected Spanish claims and possessions overseas (Andrews 1984, 13, 298). But Spanish mistrust of England was deep-seated, going back to the

Armada War and Francis Drake's incursions into Spanish America and Spain's Iberian ports. Thus, in July 1617 Gondomar (Spain's ambassador in England) warned his government that the proposed league against the pirates was actually a cover for aggressive English schemes against Spanish interests in Italy (Hebb 1994, 61). Although Gondomar's report ran against the main thrust of English foreign policy at that time—which was rapprochement with Spain and countering the rising power of the Dutch—it could not have been overlooked by the Spanish government.

> [T]here was never any certainty in Spanish minds that the English raids of the previous reign [of Elizabeth] would not be repeated, and there was increasing suspicion that the English planned sometime to fall on the Flemish coast in conjunction with the French to recover the County of Atrois: the Spanish Habsburgs watched the warlike naval preparations against (the English said) the Turkish pirates as carefully as the latter did the preparations for an actual attack on Cadiz. (Carter 1964, 97)

In particular, the relative naval weakness of Spain in the 1610s raised concerns about the proposed antipirate cooperation with the English. "Spanish naval weakness meant that no Spanish statesman could in good conscience encourage the presence of a powerful and potentially dangerous fleet on the coasts of Spain. Even if friendly when it set out, an English fleet might become hostile. . . . Until Spanish naval forces were sufficiently strong, the presence of a foreign naval force on the coast of Spain was to be discouraged" (Hebb 1994, 66). We will see that such considerations and fears were almost absent in Russia's support of the American War on Terror in 2001–2. The Russians granted the Americans flying rights over their territory and encouraged Uzbekistan, a former Soviet republic bordering now on Russia, to allow American military basing in its territory. This despite (or, realists would say, because of) the relative weakness of Russia vis-à-vis the United States. The concept of systemic conservatism will be helpful in explaining this Russian cooperation in America's War on Terror. Yet systemic conservatism was barely relevant in the early seventeenth century. Thus, the revival of Spanish naval power in 1618–19, on its part, made the English uneasy: the true purpose of this buildup was very unclear, and the general conviction attributed it to preparations against Venice and Savoy. Accordingly, "the suppressing of the pirates, and the preventing of any unfitting attempt which might be made by the Spanish fleet were jointly in consultation" (ibid., 69). Thus, we can see how mutual fear motivated both English and Spanish decisions. Furthermore, the English, like the Dutch, also saw some advantages in the pirates, as evidenced by the vice chamberlain Sir John Digby's letter to the Lord High Admiral: "[I]t is certain that there is no nation so much annoyed & infested with the pirates as the dominions of the king of Spain . . . so that it may be considerable, whether we should make too much haste to pull the thorn out of the king of Spain's foot or not" (quoted in ibid., 71).

To sum up this discussion, then, because Spain and the other major powers of the sixteenth and early seventeenth centuries lacked authority (as it is defined in this book), the issue of the Barbary corsairs was framed within the broader intensive power rivalries and enmities of the period. Few normative rules existed to limit territorial expansion, and therefore it was the Ottoman imperialist threat in the western Mediterranean that primarily drove the high-intensity Spanish efforts against the corsairs during the first three-quarters of the sixteenth century. When the Ottomans disengaged from the western Mediterranean, the territorial threat that had been embodied by the cooperation between the corsairs and the Ottoman naval establishment dissipated—the corsair depredations were relegated to mere frontier warfare and commerce raiding. Spain was also distracted by the threat to Spanish imperial integrity in Europe and in the New World, especially after the outbreak of the Dutch rebellion and in light of Dutch expansionism in the early 1600s, and this rendered the Mediterranean corsair issue a lesser priority.

Turning now to explain why territorial and imperial motives and threats were so central in Spain's decision to use transborder force, I will examine how they combined with other reasons—such as the pursuit of glory and the advancement of "true" religious beliefs—to marginalize the corsair issue.

Reasons to employ transborder force. As late as 1625 Grotius noted that in his time "recourse was had to arms for slight reasons, or for no reason" (quoted in Howard 1976, 24). Jeremy Black's discussion of violence in early modern Europe elaborates this observation: "Violence was endemic. It was a common means of settling disputes between individuals, groups, polities and people, and dealing with outsiders. . . . War appeared natural, necessary and inevitable, part of the divine order, the scourge of divine wrath and the counterpart of violence in the elements, as well as the correct, honorable and right way to adjudicate disputes" (1998, 47). Moreover, the pursuit of personal prowess, reputation, prestige, and honor—*gloire*—often coincided with conflicts over inheritance and territory and produced war. It is no wonder that during the sixteenth century rulers waged "their" wars in person, acting as warrior kings. As late as 1688 France's Louis XIV referred to territorial aggrandizement through war in *gloire* terms: it was, according to the Sun King, the "most fitting and most pleasing occupation of a king" (quoted in Tallet 1992, 20). Rulers were extremely sensitive to dynastic territorial rights, and preservation or acquisition of these was the motivation behind many wars (Hale 1985, 22).

Losing reputation, whether by failing to make good a territorial claim or by making nonreciprocal concessions, was directly linked to perceptions of material power. In this sense, prestige and reputation in this era literally were, as Robert Gilpin considers them, the "everyday currency" of international relations; they actually mirrored power relations and potential for strength in war (Gillpin 1981, 30–33; Elliott 1983). During this era, a state's territorial sovereignty was almost always at stake (through the possibility of full conquest or major encroachments), the person of the sovereign was constantly threatened by external and internal enemies (see later discussion on the laws of war and international assassination), and war could be waged for almost any reason. As a result, reputation, glory, and prestige were rightly seen by statesmen and rulers as existential interests. This might explain why rulers were ready to defend their dynastic claims in remote regions or countries, in spite of the practical difficulties of asserting them: failure to do so would have been interpreted as a sign of weakness and an invitation to further attacks. Rulers also continued to claim territories that were not under their effective control but were allegedly their dynastic inheritance (Hale 1985, 23). Charles V's "political testament," written in 1548 to advise his son Philip how to govern after the emperor's death, insisted in this manner that no conquest should ever be returned: "And if you should show weakness in any part of this [inheritance], it will open the door to bringing everything back into question. . . . It will be better to hold on to everything than to let yourself be forced later to defend the rest, and run the risk of losing it" (quoted in Parker 2000, 13). Accordingly, in the early modern period dynasticism and *gloire* fused, encouraging a resort to violence in the pursuit of personal and monarchical interests and claims (Black 1998, 65; Sturdy 2002, 10). Although rulers proclaimed their love of peace, they showed few qualms in initiating war, since war remained the major path of attaining glory (Tallet 1992, 243).

Personal reasons for employing cross-border force were augmented by religious motives (Gunn 2001, 124). Emperor Charles V called himself

"God's standard bearer," and his religious aims fused with his political ends. He considered his main responsibility to be the protection of Christendom from external enemies—the Turk—and from internal enemies—Lutheran heresy. But while the crusade against the "infidel" was a strong motive for the wars of Charles V, Protestant "heresy" seemed more threatening to Charles's son Philip II because of its potential to undermine the domestic basis of monarchical legitimacy and to disintegrate the unity of the Spanish empire, which was founded on the Catholic religion. From the late 1560s, the struggle against "heresy" and rebellion in Holland thus became a central reason for Spanish use of force. Both the effort to subdue the Dutch revolt and the war with England (1585–1603) were imbued with religious motives on the part of Spain, as well as of England and Holland. During the 1590s, Spain also coerced Henry of Navarre, who later became the French king Henry IV, to convert to Catholicism. In 1590 and 1591, the Spanish invaded France in Brittany, Provence, and the Isle de France. Henry's epigram, "Paris is worth a mass," was not unrelated to this threat.

Religious animosity notwithstanding, the lack of almost any normative limits on territorial expansion[12] forced states in the sixteenth and early seventeenth centuries to ally themselves even with "heretic" and "infidel" states: the Catholic French king Francois I and the Ottomans in the 1540s, for example, or Louis XIII and the Protestant German states and Sweden in the Thirty Years' War. The reasons for such behavior are closely related to the extreme security dilemma faced by early modern states. As we have seen, this dilemma stemmed mainly from the fact that the institution of sovereignty did not guarantee the existence of states; the balance of power therefore was always precarious and at times had to be maintained by unholy alliances. Precisely because there were very few normative limits on transborder violence in terms of territoriality and rationale—religious, economic, and personal motives were deemed legitimate reasons for war of conquest or preemption—extreme realpolitik was the outcome.

Waging transborder force in order to provide distraction from domestic problems was also a common motive for war; as we have seen, the Spanish expulsion of the Moriscos in 1609 was such a diversionary tactic. During the sixteenth and early seventeenth centuries, many advocated diversionary wars (Hale 1985, 40). Intellectuals and statesmen alike openly considered diversionary wars as legitimate reason for wielding transborder force. International war was seen as a means to keep the population at bay; conflict with external enemies diverted their ("natural") tendency to rebellion and civil war. Richelieu wrote that war purged the state of "bad humors," and others claimed that war was an expedient way for the state to rid itself of riffraff and the lowest orders of society, which supposedly deserved this divine punishment. In this sense, Bodin dubbed war *"une medicine purgative."* Even Luther wrote that, while war is a plague, people should see how great the plague it prevents (Tallett 1992, 240n280).

How do these issues relate to the Spanish counter-corsair policy? During the reigns of Philip II and his son, Philip III, religion and the Counter-Reformation were considered the most important reasons for war, as Catholicism was the hub of the absolutist order and structure of the regime and empire. So central was religion to Philip II's war policies that he was said to be driven by a messianic vision: the opening speeches in his name to the Cortes of Castile normally began by stating that his government worked "first and foremost for the things that concern the service of God, Our Lord, and the defense and conservation of His Holy faith and the Catholic religion" (quoted in Parker 2000, 30). Even in the 1590s—when he knew that he could not win the wars with France, England, and the Dutch—Philip's religious dogmatism remained undiminished. He regretted the debts he had incurred in "the defense of our holy faith and the conservation of my kingdoms and lordships" but nonetheless warned his subjects that heavy tax increases should be expected: "I could not—and cannot—neglect the war with England and the events in France [the Spanish intervention in the French wars of religion], because I have such a special obligation to God and the world to deal with them. Also, if the heretics prevail (which I hope God will not permit), it might open the door to worse damage and danger, and we shall have war at home." When a close adviser questioned the need to devote so many resources to these wars, Philip replied decisively, "We cannot abandon these matters because they involve the cause of religion, *which must take precedence over everything*" (quoted in ibid.; emphasis added).

Religious matters continued to mar Spanish-English relations even after formal peace was concluded between the two monarchies in 1604. Despite the peace and King James's Hispanophile foreign policy, religious antagonism was ever present in the unstable relations between the two powers. Upon his ascension to the throne, James publicly announced his "utter detestation" of the Papist religion, which he condemned as "superstitious"; he ordered all Jesuits and Catholic priests out of the country and once again imposed fines for recusancy (Fraser 1996, 85).

The king was unequivocal in his opposition to Catholicism, and all hopes for toleration vanished. This worried many in Spain. The strong Protestant inclination of England was one of the underlying reasons for Spain's deep-seated mistrust toward the English; a 1611 missive of John Digby, then England's ambassador to Spain, revealed that

> the general opinion [in Spain] is that more respect and fayth is to be held with the Turkes then with us, whom they stile Lutherans. And this is an ordinary doctrine in their Pulpitts, where nothing is so frequent as the animating and invyting of the people to the hatred and detestation of us, though not *eo nomine* but under the name of Hereticks. . . . *it was the general opinion here in Spaine that they might better allie and have amitie with Turkes and Moors than with Hereticks, because the one knows not the truth and the other apostated from it.* (quoted in Hillgarth 2000, 456; emphasis added)

Indeed, evidence exists that collaboration with the "Moors" of Barbary against the Dutch "heretics" was seriously contemplated in the Spanish Council of State in 1633 (Lana 1999, 205).

In this context, it is important to note that the corsair communities were not seen in Spain as a serious religious threat. In fact, Spanish captives in Barbary were not only allowed to maintain their Catholic religion, but they were encouraged to continue to practice it. The Barbary slaveholders knew very well that captives who converted to Islam could not be ransomed by the Spanish redemptionist orders because the Spanish Inquisition strictly forbade this (and as the conversion to Islam requires circumcision, converters could not hide or deny their act). Questions of religious identity were so important to Spain that the Crown ordered the redemptionists to take special care to "watch with great vigilance that the captives you redeem are not Moriscos expelled from this kingdom" (Friedman 1983, 147). Many Christian captives saw conversion to Islam as an escape from the harsh fate of a galley slave, as Muslims were forbidden to serve as galley slaves in the corsair fleets. But the fact that such renegade Christians commanded zero ransom was a strong incentive to Barbary slaveholders and captive holders to prevent this conversion: "Conversions to Islam were accordingly few" (Bennett 1960, 80).

Moreover, in Algiers and the other Barbary regencies, churches were erected in which the captives and slaves held weekly mass and other religious rituals. The government of Algiers paid for the operation of these chapels, and slave owners often made generous gifts to them. There was never a shortage of priests, since many of them were also taken captive—sometimes intentionally.

> Many Spaniards who wrote about Algiers in the sixteenth and seventeenth centuries remarked that the regular religious services available to the captives compared favorably with those in Spain. The numerous Catholic holy days throughout the year, they pointed out, were celebrated with the same pomp and solemnity as in Christian nations. . . . A seventeenth-century Franciscan remarked that the adornment of the churches with silks and wax and oil lamps was so extensive "that it is no greater in any city in Spain." (Friedman 1975, 26–27)

By the early seventeenth century, all the major slave *bagños* in Algiers had churches, with Trinitarian and Franciscan friars assigned to them. In Tunis, as well, similar religious policies were introduced (Bennett 1960, 82). Beyond the need to maintain the Christianity of the captives for ransoming purposes, the Muslims also believed that devout captives made the best slaves. "The governor of Tunis once remarked that he would not give up Friar Gracián for any amount of money because 'he makes my Christians obedient'" (Friedman 1975, 32).

In other words, by discouraging apostasy and encouraging Catholic practice, the Barbary regencies were actually working to retain the economic value of their captives. "These faithless dogs," exclaimed Cervantes after being ransomed from five years of captivity in Algiers, "let us keep our religion" (quoted in Sola and de la Peña 1996, 202). This policy was perceived in Spain as highly parasitic in nature: the Barbary communities endeavored to preserve the religious rights of the captives not because of a moral obligation to guarantee these rights as such but rather to exploit these Christians. Obviously, the Spanish Crown was aware of these realities; the redemptionist orders were in constant communication with the captives in Barbary, and many captives eventually returned to Spain to tell their stories. For pious monarchs such as Philip II and Philip III, Dutch and English heresy thus represented a much more serious and predatory threat to religion—the foundation of the state—than the North African Muslim corsair communities (Lynch 1992, 57). English and Dutch imperial expansion was perceived as doubly threatening because Spain considered itself the inheritor of Rome's universal empire with a mission to extend the true faith into the New World (Fuchs 2001, 143). In this context, Muslim pirate attacks against Spain were understood in Spain as a heavenly scourge visited upon the country to be endured (de Gomara 1989, 15). This was part of the general perception of "decline" in early seventeenth-century Spain, a decline that was attributed by many intellectuals, advisers, and writers—the *arbitristas*—to divine wrath over Spain's moral degeneration (sexual permissiveness, decadence, idleness, and court corruption) (Elliott 1977).

Although protecting the religious integrity of their subjects and states was an important reason for war, early modern conceptions of sovereignty did not necessarily consider the protection of civilian subjects from extraterritorial violent harms to be the unequivocal commitment or first priority of the state. Monarchs did think of themselves as obliged to maintain social harmony, to promote trade and the economy, and to see to the welfare of their subjects; however, "their chief concern was with the pursuit of *gloire*" (Tallett 1992, 188). *Gloire* consisted mainly of acquiring new territories and insisting on dynastic and hereditary territorial rights already possessed. For Spain, with its extensive empire in Europe and the New World, the challenge was a serious one.

The rebellion of the Dutch was of special concern here. In 1589, a councillor to Philip II maintained that even though "to attempt to conquer the rebellious [Dutch] provinces by force is to speak of war without end, Christian obligation requires the preservation of one's reputation inviolate" (Parker 1998, 89). Philip, echoing his father's warning, was also extremely concerned that "if the Low Countries are lost, the rest [of the monarchy] will not last long" (ibid., 90). After Philip III's ascension, the Council of State advised him that "the security of the rest of your Majesty's kingdoms depends in large measure upon the conservation of the 'obedient provinces' [in the Netherlands] and the recovery of those that have rebelled" (ibid.).

Spanish statesmen during the reigns of Philip II and Philip III were very much engaged in debates about their country's international *reputación*, but they mainly understood this concept in the context of the credibility of Spain's military power. The purpose of this power was to preserve or obtain new territorial possessions for the Spanish Crown, to aid the Austrian branch of the House of Habsburg against Protestant heresy in Germany and Ottoman expansion in central Europe, and to secure and advance the cause of Catholicism in Europe in general (Elliott 1986, 55–65). Thus, in 1618, when the Duke of Lerma, Philip III's prime minister, proposed a major expedition against Algiers, the king eventually decided that the Algerian campaign would have to be abandoned in favor of sending aid to the Austrian Habsburgs in the Bohemian crisis. He wrote: "because it would be impossible to commit ourselves to both enterprises, and because of the risks involved if the aid to Bohemia is delayed . . . it seems unavoidable that we must see to the latter" (Parker 1997, 45). Such inevitability was the king of Spain's right and duty, which he could not "evade without grave offense to God and betrayal of His cause" (Elliott 1986, 64).

The threat of the Barbary corsairs was given lower priority because in the eyes of the Spanish Crown they were not aiming to destroy (nor were they capable of doing so) the domestic and international order the Spanish empire was pursuing. They were indeed perceived as a "thorn in Spain's side" (Parker 1997, 44; Lane 1998, 16)—they infringed on Spain's possessions and harmed thousands of Spanish nationals. But harm to civilians as such was not a reason for retaliatory violent measures in early modern Europe. Thus, the Spanish Crown did not perceive the problem of the Spanish captives in Barbary to be a security predicament (Friedman 1983, 51). In spite of the corsairs being "infidels" or "renegades," the religious threat embodied in their practice was, as seen previously, relatively low. The attacks of the corsairs "were a threat to the security of individuals and local communities, never to the security of the state [i.e., the territorial integrity of the state]. So other struggles took precedence over this one. The low priority given this problem may also have reflected the crown's geographical orientation. The principal victims of the corsairs were the inhabitants of coastal regions—the periphery and not the center" (ibid.).

In this context, we should note that while early modern rulers were expected to consult their subjects on decisions of peace and war—especially on the issue of financing war—these subjects were usually the nobility and high orders of society. The lower orders of society were often left out of such considerations (Kiernan 1980, 29). Rulers provided protection and security to their subjects mainly according to the contribution the latter made to the general war-making capabilities of the state (Hoffman 1980). Furthermore, war continued to be seen as having specific individual beneficiaries and victims rather than as a phenomenon that served or injured the state in its entirety. The differences between public and private benefits or costs resulting from violent conflicts were not clearly conceptualized yet. Governments believed that those who received the financial benefits or suffered from a given conflict should also sustain its "charges." "It was a view that emphasized the private nature of society and warfare rather any larger public purpose" (Drew

2002, 13). Not surprisingly, private reprisals were seen in this period as normal and were often encouraged by states, which saw no need to supplant them with public reprisals (Colbert 1948, 57–59).

Thus, the concept of the "state" in early modern Spanish legal and theological thought remained quite vague. Terms such as *respublica* and *civitas* made a distinction between the citizenry and the prince (Nussbaum 1954, 72). In general, early modern sovereignty was based on a concept of proprietary kingship, which "meant that public policy and, a fortiori, foreign policy were not conducted in the name of *raison d'état* or the national interest, but in the name of dynastic interests. . . . Since public political power was still personalized, European politics cannot be deemed to be the affairs of states, but was the affairs of its ruling families" (Teschke 2002, 13–14). This concept stood behind the differential and privatized protection provided by the Spanish Crown to its subjects. In general, the Spanish Crown had to be persuaded by its subjects that they warranted protection or that protecting them would serve the interest of the Crown (Hoffman 1980). The representatives of the Mediterranean provinces of Spain found it increasingly difficult to sway the monarchy to their side as the importance of the American empire grew. This was compounded by the fact that the majority of the Spanish subjects taken in corsair raids on coastal villages were often weaker members of society—and, as such, the interest of the state in them was low from the outset (Joaquinet 2002, 21). Indeed, the interest of the Crown in the captives was itself of relative proportion to their status: thus, for example, in 1582 Philip II donated three thousand ducats for ransoming captives from North Africa, but he stressed that the money should be used to ransom the "most able-bodied" captives (Friedman 1983, 116; see also Garcés 2002, 107)—obviously those who would be useful in the king's military service.

The growing importance of the American empire was due to the supply of silver from the New World, which was essential for the Crown's credit in Europe and the payment of its mercenary armies. Silver, along with Castilian land and agriculture, was the foundation of the Spanish economy (Lynch 1992, 1). Silver bought Spain's formidable military power in Europe and paid for its huge armies. After 1570, the output of silver from Peru and Mexico grew steadily, peaking between 1580 and 1630. The share of American silver in the Crown's income rose from 10 percent in the mid-sixteenth century to 25 percent in the 1590s (Parry 1966, 244). The American silver represented a direct income for the Crown—its yielding did not require lengthy negotiations with the Cortes.

And, furthermore, because it was brought as bullion, it had immediate purchasing power. Any hindering or delay in the silver shipments injured Spain's credit in Italy and Switzerland. The crucial importance of the American shipments made their protection the number one naval priority of the Crown, especially after the successful attack of Francis Drake on the silver caravan in Nombre de Dios in Panama in 1573. Twice a year, the precious metals were transported in heavily armed convoys, and when they approached Spanish shores the Crown intensified its maritime policing. A 1583 letter from the king to one of his naval commanders is illustrative: "I have received word from the Governor of Santa Cruz that in the middle of July the galleys from New Spain are arriving, so I request from you to clean Andalusia's shore from pirates and corsairs" (Launder 1921, 197). Indeed, English and French privateers and pirates (the Spaniards considered them all pirates) worried Spain in this period much more than the Barbary corsairs, because in addition to threatening the supply of precious metals from New Spain they were seen as the vanguard of Protestant heresy. Thus, in a tract titled *To Defend Your Empire and Faith* handed to King Philip circa 1590, the author, Manoel de Andrada, barely mentions the Barbary corsairs and instead deals extensively with the threat of English and other "Lutheran" pirates in America and in West Africa. He considers this menace to encompass religion, politics, and commerce, whereby the English pirates increase the power of their heretic queen through their plundering of the Iberian empire. According to P. E. H. Hair, this tract "can be taken to represent what there was, in that age and society, of 'public opinion', that is, specifically, of concern among literate citizens . . . regarding national and even international affairs" (1990, 8).

The discussion so far points to the fact that the Barbary corsairs were not perceived to significantly challenge the structure of rights and duties of the Spanish monarchy and its international position. I now turn to discuss the compatibility of the corsairs' practice with the second institution of violence—the laws of war.

ii. The Laws of War

Jus ad bellum. By the sixteenth century, the definition of what made just cause for war became so all-embracing as to be meaningless (Tallett 1992, 238–39). According to sixteenth-century political thought, war was just when it was necessary, and no one but the prince himself could decide when it was necessary. Machiavelli's dictum, *salus principis suprema lex,* was eventually endorsed by all the leading European jurists and political thinkers—Bodin in France, Gentili in Italy, and Vitoria in Spain. Francisco Suarez, one of the founders of international law in Spain, observed that the belligerent act of a prince is like a decree of the court of law. "The obvious objection that the plaintiff cannot be a judge at the same time is answered elusively by the observation that war, as an act of vindictive justice, is indispensable to mankind, and that no better method has been found" (quoted in Nussbaum 1954, 90). Similarly, Gentili contended that war could be just on both sides and not only because of excusable ignorance.

Because religion was a leading motive for war, defending "true" faith was a particularly strong justification for war. Protestant and Calvinist writers especially asserted the case for an offensive war in the cause of religion. On the Catholic side, because church and state often had a symbiotic relationship, Catholic theologians rarely denounced their rulers' proclaimed justifications for war. The Reformation added another cause for the Catholic tradition of just war: defense of the true faith. State rulers were not only entitled to respond to Protestant attacks but also expected to actively suppress Protestantism abroad.

Jus in bellum. Violence—transborder and domestic—during the sixteenth and early seventeenth centuries was highly indiscriminate in nature, and its formal and customary restraints had little regularization (Ferguson and Mansbach 2005). Mercy was granted through grace rather than through any sense of obligation—moral or legal (Hale 1968, 503). This was a world that took for granted cruel means of death. Grotius acknowledged the brute nature of warfare in his time when he commented in 1625 that "when arms were once taken up, all reverence for divine and human law was thrown away; just as men were thenceforth authorized to commit all crimes without restraint" (quoted in Howard 1976, 24). Brutality toward civilians especially was a practice shared by all violence-wielding actors in the period. Thus, for example, J. A. Lynn claims that "[a]buse [of civilians] did not simply undermine the system; abuse was the system" (1993, 290). The violent treatment of civilians was often the result of the difficulties of supplying and paying armies. Because most armed forces of the time were made up of mercenary units, payment to soldiers put a heavy toll on governments. Supplying the growing armies also posed a significant outlay. Thus, governments resorted to a "tax of violence" system, wherein armies preyed on the country—the enemy's or their own—for subsistence. "The fact that officials regarded the tax of violence practically as a given should come as no surprise, since it was extorted during an era that considered brutal

requisitions as standard. Even normal taxes were collected at gunpoint"
(ibid., 292).

But the tax of violence was not always, or even usually, the outcome of
insufficient resources for the soldiers or a lack of discipline on their part.
The plundering, raping, and killing of civilians—enemies and allies
alike—was supported by the traditional notions of what constituted legitimate warfare as such (Asch 2000, 297). Even jurists and writers who
wanted to introduce some restraints had to accept the soldier's *right* to
plunder the property of enemies. Whether or not soldiers were entitled to
plunder civilians in friendly provinces was debated, but this treatment of
civilians in conquered provinces was widely accepted. The early seventeenth-century laws of war were still very similar to those that governed
sixteenth-century conflict. In the first half of the sixteenth century, Francisco Vitoria, one of the Spanish founders of international law, stated that
the appropriation or plunder of property in enemy territory was quite
legitimate if this was the only, or at least the most promising, way to win
a war. When it was essential for victory, it was lawful to kill the innocent
too. He also stated that Muslim prisoners of war could be killed indis-
criminately and their wives and children enslaved (Nussbaum 1954, 82).
Luis de Molina, another Spanish jurist, wrote in the late sixteenth century
that women who march with the army are as a rule helping the enemy and
should not be spared. Such statements revealed the opinion that anyone
who was not for you was potentially against you (Hale 1985, 186–87). Similarly, in the 1590s Alberico Gentili (the Italian jurist living and teaching
civil law in England who tried to humanize the rules of warfare) acknowledged the victor's right to take away the enemy's property (ibid., 298–99).

Because the enemy was perceived to include not only the opposing
army and government but the civilian subjects of the opponent as well,
destruction of civilian property was considered to be a legitimate act of
war. Systematically destroying crops, livestock, and towns crippled the
enemy's war-making capabilities. Besieging commanders called upon
civilians in the town to surrender, and if they failed to comply they were
treated as enemies when the city fell. This practice was acknowledged by
Gentili as acceptable and legitimate: he left no doubt that in such cases
almost anything was permitted (Asch 2000, 299). Molina as well found
that although sacking and looting were morally deplorable they were not
in themselves unlawful actions. Molina's and Gentili's ideas recognized
the practice of war in their time (Hale 1985, 195).

Although, or perhaps because, the laws of war were far from codified,
blaming the victims for the cruelties their enemies were allegedly forced

to commit against them was common. Accordingly, although some minimal customary restraints on violence in war did exist, "for nearly every military 'crime' against enemies or civilians, there was a situation in which otherwise prohibited behavior became permissible or excesses became excusable. . . . Reprisal offered a particularly useful justification for appalling actions, matching atrocity for atrocity" (Donagan 1994, 1144; see also Swart 1971, 51). Thus, in an effort to suppress the Dutch revolt, the Duke of Alba began a major counteroffensive in Flanders in 1572–73, marked by some of the worst planned atrocities of sixteenth-century western European wars. "By official policy whole populations of towns were slaughtered, and thousands of civilians perished. . . . Yet it should be kept in mind that the Spanish outrages were no greater than those committed in certain other parts of continental Europe" (Payne 1973, 260). Later, when the Spanish army captured the city of Maastricht in the Dutch Republic in 1579, about a third of the civilian population died in its sacking. In 1631, when the Protestant city Magdeburg fell to imperial forces, about twenty-five thousand civilians, or 85 percent of the city's population, perished amid flames and pillage (Ruff 2001, 56).

The noncodified and minimal restraints on violence in war, coupled with the all-embracing reasons for war (embedded in sovereignty), enabled and reproduced the tendency of states and rulers to justify their harsh use of violence against civilians. When struggling to crush the Dutch revolt in the 1570s, Spanish king Philip II "made it clear that, under the prevailing laws of war, he would be justified in annihilating the rebellious provinces, which were guilty of two of the most heinous crimes, rebellion and heresy" (Waxman 1997, 339). In order to annihilate the "rebellion," Philip even considered using a sixteenth-century weapon of mass destruction: exploding the dikes of Holland and flooding the province and the rebellious inhabitants. Although Philip eventually opted for a policy of "strategic terror" by torching villages and towns instead of flooding the whole province—and while some moral considerations did play a part in his decision (he feared "a certain reputation for cruelty")—it is important to note that he actually preferred torching to flooding for instrumental reasons (see ibid., 345). Philip's rejection of the idea of mass flooding was not chiefly due to normative and moral restraints but because he feared that the flooding would get out of control. Proposals for flooding were raised again in 1602, although the act itself was avoided this time due to a mutiny in the Army of Flanders (ibid., 343). An earlier case is the 1550 Spanish occupation of Mahdiya on the Barbary Coast—a town that had previously been conquered by the corsair Dragut and his men. The inhabitants of Mahdiya had not welcomed Dragut and his corsairs in the first place, but when Emperor Charles V's forces took it from the corsairs, he and his Spanish council decided that the city would be too expensive to garrison and decided to tear it down. The walls, houses, and mosques were systematically blown up and the town's people expelled or enslaved (Wolf 1977, 35). Obviously, the "Black Legend" of Spanish cruelty was not completely without foundation (Maltby 1971).

But the Spanish were not much different from their contemporaries in this respect. In fact, killing enemy civilians and taking booty were seen as not merely necessary or inevitable acts of war but positive and even beneficial practices—when (of course) suffered by one's enemies. Thus, according to a report of the Venetian ambassador in England, when King James I—allegedly sympathetic to Spain in this period—heard that the Dutch "Prince of Nassau has withdrawn with 422 prisoners besides enormous booty taken in his raids, in which his men slew more than 1,000 of the country people of Brabant [a Spanish-ruled town], who were all laid under contribution [war tax] . . . . His Majesty [James I] has rejoiced greatly at these events."[13] The Venetian ambassador further reported that "the [Algerian] pirates and [the] Dutch think of sending a large number of Moors to Spain with arms and encouragement. . . . If this takes place it will undoubtedly please His Majesty [James] highly."[14] If indeed true, it seems that James's hatred of pirates was not absolute but rather restricted to piracy against his own subjects.

The enslaving of captives of war was also not a practice unique to the Barbary corsairs. Spain, as well as France and Venice, put captives and prisoners of war to row in its galleys along with Spanish criminals and vagabonds condemned to these floating penal institutions (Pike 1983, chap. 1). As late as the 1690s, Spanish authorities bought slaves from Spanish corsairs (Storrs 1998, 9). Dutch and English Protestants who fell into the hands of Spanish privateers and pirates during the late sixteenth century were often put to the oar as well. Spaniards—both privateers or pirates and navy ships—plundered ships of European states that were not at war with Spain and forced their crews into labor (Tenenti 1967, 45).

The indiscriminate nature of the laws of war in the early modern period also affected state rulers. In the sixteenth century, "if one did win some great victory, it was rarely decisive unless the opposing ruler was killed or captured" (Gunn 2001, 112). Thus, as Thomas Ward (2000) has shown, international assassination of heads of states was a common practice until the early seventeenth century. Philip II and Elizabeth I engaged in many attempts on each other's lives, and Philip openly promised twenty-five thousand gold crowns and the grant of nobility to anyone who would murder William of Orange, the leader of the Dutch rebels (Nussbaum 1954, 93). Earlier in the sixteenth century, Charles V challenged Francois I to a duel (Howard 1976, 21).

In such a brutal environment, the Barbary corsairs' deviation from the laws of war was obscure. Although in his *de jure belli* in 1598 Gentili declared piracy to be a violation of the law of nations, against which war can be made by every man, in his later *Hispanicae Advocationis Libri Dvo* he argued that "a pirate commits a less serious crime if he commits it on the high seas *which are under no law*" (1921, 111; emphasis added). And furthermore, for Gentili there seemed to be no universal criterion to establish the degree of piracy's lawlessness. Thus, when he acted as an advocate for Englishmen who bought Venetian-plundered goods in Tunis, he maintained that his clients could acquire a legal title in these goods because "while [the Barbary pirates] are infidels they are likewise enemies and, therefore, what has been captured by them has thereby become their property, and further, so true is that the citizen who buys the property back makes it his own; and further, that any of the original owners who may chance to have bought it holds it now by a different right" (ibid., 112). On the other hand, when Gentili was the Spanish advocate in Britain (1605–8), he held that English merchants who bought Spanish-plundered goods from the pirates in Tunis were obliged to surrender the goods back to the Spaniards, his clients (ibid., 54–57). This was despite the fact that Gentili admitted the Moors to be the enemies of the Spaniards, which would mean that according to his own reasoning in the Venetian case their plunder "belong[s] to unrestricted commerce" (ibid., 111).

These examples, and their historical context, help us to understand why Spain could not have "known" the Barbary pirates as predators of its authority; authority in the sense of legitimate versus illegitimate power barely existed or was very vague. The facts that Spain and its enemies had similar practices of war and that no clear laws of war existed rendered the corsairs, at the worst, merely parasitic actors abusing the minimal protections that did exist. They sacked Spanish settlements without formally offering them a chance to surrender, and they enslaved Spaniards and raided Spanish commerce at a time when Spain maintained a truce with Turkey—their nominal sovereign. But their actual practices did not differ considerably from those of Spain or the other European powers. "These corsairs lived in a world in which Christians and Muslims were bitter enemies, each seizing plunder, killing and carrying off slaves from the other" (Heers 2003, 22). Furthermore, and here we come to the issue of actorhood, their depredations were construed in Spain as part of a "little war" *(pequeña guerra)* or a private war between subjects and not states (Fernandez 2000, 9).

iii. Actorhood

Two questions should be distinguished when speaking of actorhood in the sphere of transborder violence: first, which actors possess the legitimate right to decide on the use of transborder force; and, second, which actors are legitimately entitled to wage transborder force? With regard to the first question, early modern monarchs, political theorists, and jurists generally accepted that only sovereigns had this right. This monarchial monopoly did not exist in the Middle Ages, when the nobility also had a right to resort to transborder force through the institution of the feud, which served as a means to avenge "private" wrongs even across feudal borders (Cowdrey 1970, 42–67; Carroll 2003, 74–115). The Church at this time, although not possessing armed forces, also considered itself and was acknowledged by others to have a right to issue orders to engage in transborder force—the Crusades being a prime example (Hall 1997). But after the late Middle Ages and the Renaissance, state rulers worked to establish a monopolistic right to authorize transborder violence (Thomson 1994). Monarchs and sovereigns began to prohibit unauthorized "private" warfare of their subjects, within the realms of the state and outside of them, and, further, refused to consider the orders of the popes as authoritative. Indeed, private and nonstate actors did not disappear from the realm of transborder violence in the sixteenth and early seventeenth centuries—on the contrary; but sovereigns tried to control their practices through authorization. Thus, for example, sovereigns issued letters of marque and letters of reprisal that permitted private individuals to avenge in the high seas wrongs done to them by nationals of other states. The authorization of transborder private violence, especially at sea, reflected states' material inability to construct and maintain capital-intensive war-making capabilities (such as permanent navies) and their corresponding need (due to intensifying international rivalries and rising costs of warfare) to tap into existing private war-making capabilities. But it also reflected a conception of the state as representing the interests of certain coalitions and groups, unlike its modern sense as an embodiment of national interests. As such, "[m]any rulers had no ambition to exercise an efficient monopoly on violence at sea and to deny their subjects the right to fight for their private interests at sea" (Glete 2000, 60). In other words, although state rulers wanted to monopolize the right to authorize private transborder force, they could not refuse the right of their subjects to engage in such authorized practices because they relied on societies' war-making capabilities (Thomson 1994). Moreover, and as discussed previously, early modern patrimonial and dynastic sovereigns sold or granted societal protection not as an unequivocal obligation but when it benefited their interests (Glete 2002).

The process of monopolizing the right to decide or authorize the use of transborder force conformed to the teachings of international jurists such as Vitoria, Ayala, Suarez, Molina (Spanish scholars), and Gentili (Italian), who argued that only sovereigns possessed a right to wage *offensive* war (in other words, to initiate a war). Sovereigns could go to war for defensive reasons as well, but international law did not exclude private individuals from defensive acts of violence (Ballis 1973, 83–95). Thus, for example, Grotius distinguished between sovereign (public) and nonsovereign (private) use of force. He defined war as "the condition of those contending by force" and noted that private war "is more ancient than public war, and has, incontestably, the same nature as public war; wherefore both should be designated by one and the same term" (quoted in Watkin 2004, 6n 37). But he maintained that the power to decide on "external war" should be reserved for the king (Baumgold 1993, 9). In his *De Indis* (1604–5), however, Grotius also reasoned that private trading companies were entitled to make war, as were the sovereigns of Europe— on the condition that their use of force was defensive and not aimed at taking the possessions of others (Tuck 1998, 85).

Accordingly, even though some agreement existed among international jurists and among sovereigns that only states have the right to authorize offensive wars, individual self-help across state borders was not unacceptable in the sixteenth and early seventeenth centuries—in legal terms or in practice. This caused many complications and blurrings. For instance, peace and war were not always distinguishable. Governments could be at peace while at the same time their subjects engaged in unauthorized violent conflict for reasons of "self-defense." In addition, because "states" were inchoate domestically, their subjects did not always perceive them a priori as enjoying the right to monopolize warfare and legitimate conflict (Black 1998, 53). This was evident in the difficulties monarchs had in recruiting armies: although the period was very violent, people were often reluctant to channel their violence into army service. Many reasons existed for this (Mackay 1999)—the harsh treatment of soldiers by their superiors being a major one—but it was also related to the fact that acceptance of the state as a corporate entity with a life of its own (in other words, sovereignty) was still lacking. Societies considered the individual right to avoid response for recruitment as valid. Kings were recognized to have the right to call even spirits from the vasty deep for military service in war, but this was accompanied by the mocking question, "[B]ut will they come when you do call for them?" (Hale 1985, 93).

Moreover, because sovereigns could not always reach a consensus among themselves as to who was to be recognized as legitimate sovereign from the outset, they often did not acknowledge each other's authority to decide on external war; Gentili claimed that a sovereign prince could revoke his recognition of another prince's sovereignty—and consequently of his war-making authority—pending his interests (Rubin 1998, 34). This low level of authority among sovereigns led to situations in which privateers authorized by one sovereign (such as Elizabeth of England) were considered to be nothing more than pirates by another sovereign (Philip II of Spain). Similarly, the Ottomans construed the Maltese knights of St John as pirates, even though they were authorized by Spain to act as privateers against the Muslims.

The lack of clear-cut definitions of war and of which actors possessed the legal right to declare it led to some strange outcomes. Some violent conflicts were dubbed rebellions—for example, the Dutch revolt. But other similar conflicts were regarded as "war"—for example, the violent response to Protestantism in Ireland between 1595 and 1603 (in spite of the fact that the Dublin Parliament of 1541 recognized Henry VIII and his successors as kings), which the English referred to as the Nine Years' War. The problem of legitimate actorhood was also evident in the Holy Roman Empire; because the conflicts between powerful "estates" of the empire were not clearly characterized, it is not obvious when exactly the Thirty Years' War became a "war." Furthermore, there was no consensus on whether princes of the empire had a right to wage war and enter into alliances with foreign powers, despite the empire's long history of military alliances between territories (Black 1998, 73). And sovereigns were not the only entities in the empire who could wage war. The Hanseatic League of merchant cities in northern Germany, for example, raised armies and fought wars within the empire as well as wars against external states: Sweden (1567–70), England (1470–74), and Denmark (1616). The Hansa also policed the Baltic Sea against pirates and used naval forces to blockade mercantile rivals

(Spruyt 1994, 126–27). In addition, city-states, especially in Italy, claimed a right to transborder force (ibid., chap. 7). Thus, despite a process of statist monopolization of the right to war-making decisions, the international system in our research period was still decentralized in this aspect, and more than one type of actor claimed a right to decide on transborder violence (Thomson 1994).

Leaving aside the question of who has the authority to decide on war, I come now to the right to participate in war. In this sense, this time period made much room for private enterprise. Thus, in 1589 Drake and Norris raided Spain and Portugal's Atlantic ports in the context of the Anglo-Spanish war. Drake and Norris's armada "was the most formidable armament that assembled at Plymouth in the reign of Elizabeth; but in actual fact it was more a joint-stock piratical enterprise than a properly equipped government undertaking" (Black 1959, 411). In fact, states were often eager to shift the burdens of war onto the shoulders of private individuals and were not much concerned about the resulting loss of control (Hale 1968, 201).

In the Mediterranean region, the two questions of actorhood in transborder violence—who had authority and who could participate—were often not clearly distinguished by contemporaries. "Marauding was open to all," writes Braudel.

> [P]rivateering, bordering on piracy, was part of the tradition of the sea, *l'usanza del mare*. The official navies of Mediterranean states harbored privateers, made a living from privateering, and sometimes owed their origin to it. . . . Privateering—perhaps one should say "true" privateering—was usually instigated by a city acting on its own authority or at any rate only marginally attached to a large state. This was true in the age of Louis XIV as it was true in the sixteenth century. (1973, 869)

The loose nature of the concept of actorhood in transborder force is evident in Spain's policy toward the Barbary corsairs. Even Charles V's decisive campaigns against Barbarosa were marred by his offers to the corsair to change allegiance and serve the Habsburgs: before embarking on Tunis in 1535 and again on the eve of the Algiers expedition in 1541, Charles offered that Barbarosa join his side in return for becoming a Spanish vassal. According to Abun-Nasr, the emperor offered the corsair kingship of the Maghrib from Algiers to Tripoli under Spanish suzerainty. But mutual mistrust foiled the negotiations. The exact details of the Spanish offer and Barbarosa's demands are not clear, but the fact that Kheir el-din avoided engaging Spanish naval forces in 1538 (despite favorable tactical conditions) suggests that he considered the emperor's offer seriously (Abun-Nasr 1987, 151; Fisher 1957, 71).

We should not wonder at the Spanish efforts to detach Kheir el-din from his allegiance to the sultan. After all, Emperor Charles had outbid the French king Francois I for the allegiance of Andrea Doria and his private fleet only a few years earlier. Similarly, in the 1560s Philip II tried to outbid the *reis* Dragut to change his loyalty from the sultan to the Spanish king; but Dragut's innate hatred of Spain and his memories of slavery on a Spanish galley forestalled this move. It is also a fact that Philip maintained a net of spies and secret agents in North Africa with the aim of not only gathering intelligence but moving prominent corsairs and Turkish military commanders to Spain's side (Floristan 1988, 579).

The lack of clear-cut criteria for actorhood in cross-border violence at that time seems to have enabled a Spanish perception of the corsairs as licensed thieves (*ladrones con patente*) (de Ibarra Bunes 1998, 99–100), a perception that embodied the parasitic status of these actors and made possible such policies as courting them. Because an enemy polity licensed them, they could be recognized—if Spanish self-interest benefited—as legal enemies (see Gentili's discussion of pirates and sovereign recognition discussed earlier), and, as such, the Spanish king could suggest they shift allegiance to him. On the other hand, when Spanish self-interests required it, the corsairs could be considered criminal robbers. In other words, they had no definitive status in the eyes of the Spaniards. In a similar manner, King James of England was willing to pardon certain English pirates who served with the Barbary corsairs upon their return to England—it was in his interest to do so. Thus, two notable English pirates in Barbary—Mainwaring and Walsingham—were not only pardoned by James in 1621, but they became officers in the British navy (Matar 1999, 61).

Spain was a victim of corsairs, but at the same time it operated against them through corsairs. The Spanish Crown not only used non-Spanish corsairs against the Barbary corsairs, but it authorized the operations of Spanish privateers in the Mediterranean against practically all targets. "The Spanish corsairs, overshadowed by their English, Dutch, French, and Barbary counterparts, remain very much unknown quantities; nevertheless, they continued to be active during the seventeenth century, certainly in time of war, both in the Atlantic and in the Mediterranean, and they were by no means unsuccessful. In any assessment of the importance of private participation in war they should not be forgotten" (Thompson 1976, 194).[15] One of the major targets of Spanish piracy and privateering was Venice, especially after 1585. Alberto Tenenti argues that in Naples and Sicily the Spanish viceroys—whose wives seem to have been involved in the plan as well—collaborated with privateers from Malta against Venice. Ships of the Spanish king ventured into Venetian ports as friends and then plundered them (Tenenti 1967, 47–48).

Between 1595 and 1604, privateering and piracy against Venice, under Spanish auspices, reached its peak. In Iberian waters, Venetian ships or English and Dutch ships that carried cargo from and to Venice were often raided—with the encouragement of the Spanish Crown—by Spanish pirates and privateers. For Spain, attacking the commerce of Venice in this way served a double purpose: first, it damaged Venice itself, and, second, it harmed its trade partners, which were also enemies of Spain. When the Venetians managed to catch Spanish pirates and privateers, they usually refrained from punishing them harshly out of fear of Spanish retaliation. And when in 1587 the pope ordered the Knights of Malta—Christian privateers who operated under the auspices of Spain— to cease their raids on Venetian shipping, the latter simply disregarded the papal demand, and Spain did not pressure them to abide by it (Tenenti 1967, chap. 3, 35).[16]

Privateering was also authorized by Spain against the Barbary communities. In 1601 the Council of State in Madrid decided to license Spanish corsairs to operate against the Turks and Moors. Ignoring the threat to commerce embedded in this stimulation of the "little war," the king's advisers considered that "[b]ecause the Turkish and Moorish privateers against whom the crown wished to direct its naval effort were not public enemies, they could be attacked privately" (Hess 1978, 125). The Crown *hoped* (but did not insist) that the Spanish licensed corsairs would avoid attacking friendly ships. Andrew Hess argues that this leniency stemmed in part from the fact that "the corsairs accomplished what both Habsburg and Ottoman empires required of their frontiersmen in a period of disengagement. Despite a vigorous commerce in prisoners and captured goods, the privateers turned Mediterranean coastal waters into a no-man's-land that, although full of passageways, nevertheless kept the populations of each civilization within the boundaries of their lands" (ibid.).

In other words, "private" warfare was tolerated because it substituted for "public" warfare, and at the same time it did not culminate in "public" warfare in the sense of involving aspirations for acquiring territorial metapolitical authority. But because "public" authority in the early mod-

ern period, especially in Spain and the Ottoman Empire, was to a large
extent personalized by the monarch, who regarded the realm as his patrimonial property (Teschke 2002, 9), "public" enemies were actually
often personal enemies of the monarch who presented a challenge to his
dynastic territorial rights, whereas "private" enemies in fact threatened
society as a whole (Hale 1985, 31). In the case of the Mediterranean corsairs and privateers, because their limited material resources prevented
them from posing a threat to dynastic territorial claims and "public"
authority by way of conquest, neither the Spanish nor the Ottomans
viewed them as a threat to their authority; in fact, the corsairs would
most likely not have pursued such conquest since they benefited from the
existing system of forcible exchange. Piracy was a system of violence that
did not match any sense of war understood by contemporary sovereigns.
It was parasitic in that it was an unauthorized or semiauthorized practice
that preyed on commerce and on coastal life, but it did not threaten religious, dynastical, or territorial interests of sovereigns.

It should be noted that once the Spanish Crown also opted for the
encouragement of privateering, it knowingly endorsed an all-out free-
booting campaign against Spain's enemies and embraced the piratical
logic of maritime warfare (Stradling 1992, 48). As a consequence, an age
of "Spanish Vikings" opened: "a scourge to make the lands of the Barbary rovers seem like the carnival visit of the ship of fools" (ibid., 50).
The endorsement of privateering and piracy by the Spanish Crown also
reflected the principle accepted by its contemporaries that maritime war
involved fighting piracy with piracy (Stradling 1992, 124; Arenal and
Bunes 1992, 171).

III. Conclusions

The nature of the institutions of violence in the early modern period only
negligibly supported the notion of Great Power authority. For authority
to emerge, brute force has to be converted into legitimized power. Rudimentary norms and notions of legitimized transborder power did exist in
the sixteenth and early seventeenth centuries, but in terms of the three
institutions of violence I discuss in this book—sovereignty, laws of war,
and actorhood—violence was barely tamed. Although Spain as the most
powerful state of the time aspired toward authority—even "universal"
authority—the policies adopted in order to achieve this goal often
ignored the minimal rights of other powers and states. Authority has to
be given, not only claimed; but the nascent structure of the institutions of

violence in that time precluded this voluntary element in authority. Because Spain and the other dominant military and naval powers perceived each other as highly threatening, they were locked in intense security dilemmas. The other powers were unwilling to grant Spain the authority it claimed, attempting even to achieve "universal" empires of their own (as in the cases of Ottoman expansionism or Dutch imperialism). The Spanish Crown thus had to prioritize threats according to their potential to undermine what it perceived to be its most important interests and identities—maintaining the territorial integrity of the Spanish empire in Europe and in the New World and thwarting "heretics" or "infidels" that menaced the "true religion."

In this bellicose and poorly institutionalized international system, the Spanish Crown could not have recognized the Barbary corsairs as anything more than a parasitic threat. Despite the intense material harm the rovers inflicted on Spanish nationals and commerce, they still fit into the world of the early modern period. They posed no *unique* threat to Spain. During the first three-quarters of the century, the corsairs were intensively attacked by Spain, but this was within the context of the overall Spanish-Ottoman enmity—when the corsairs were allies of the sultan. Once this enmity settled into a truce in the third quarter of the sixteenth century, the corsairs were seen at worst as abusing Spain. They did not pose a higher challenge to its claims for authority. Qualitatively, the corsairs' transborder practices and interactions were not much different from those of Spain. Quantitatively, they did not represent as urgent a challenge as other actors of the time.

Therefore, the corsairs were the lesser threat within the heterogeneous, decentralized, and extensive system of violence during that age. Their intensive use of violence against Christian societies and the harm they inflicted on individuals notwithstanding, they were still construed by states as nothing more than pests. It is hardly conceivable that similar piratical attacks against the present-day leading powers would go so unanswered. Can we reasonably envisage today, or even during the Cold War, a situation in which thousands of the nationals of the Great Powers are killed or merely kidnapped for ransom and slavery by nonstate actors such as pirates, and yet these powers are more concerned with the relative losses each of them suffers and give less attention to the effect of this practice on their international status and the welfare of their nationals? Would the present-day Great Powers routinely endure violent raids of pirates on their homelands for *any* reason? I doubt it. Such raids would certainly diminish the authority and prestige of the target states, which conceivably would cooperate with each other against the source of the threat in efforts to assert their authority and status. In the early seventeenth century, however, there was very little notion of authority for the pirates to have undermined in the decentralized and extremely violent system of the time.

◄ FOUR ►

"We May Defy Moral Criticism If Our Execution Shall Correspond to the Principles We Profess"

British Moral Authority and the Barbary Pirates

Barbary corsairing reached its zenith in the early seventeenth century, and from the middle of that century onward, its impact on the major European powers diminished. The growing naval strength of states such as Britain and France deterred the corsairs from attacking these nations' vessels. Merchant vessels as well grew in size and armament and thus became a less attractive target for the pirates. Moreover, the institution of sovereignty changed during the seventeenth and eighteenth centuries: protecting the lives and commerce of civilian subjects became a more prominent commitment of state rulers and therefore a stronger reason for wielding transborder force. Consequently, the European powers increasingly sent their navies to bombard the Barbary ports in response to the piracies of their corsairs.

These remained fitful efforts, however, and the European maritime powers actually encouraged Barbary piracy at the same time that they operated against it. While European powers tried to deter the corsairs from attacking their own vessels and coasts, they also worked to maintain good relations with the Barbary regencies, often in order to channel the aggression of the corsairs toward other European states in a beggar-thy-neighbor pattern. Thus, for example, the Dutch concluded a peace with Algiers in 1668, exempting their vessels from corsair attacks. But this peace was kept not only due to Dutch supreme naval power but also because of "presents" annually sent by the Dutch to the Algerians to ensure the immunity of their commerce: "In effect, the Dutch were supplying the Algerians with war materials to attack the commerce of other nations, for masts, guns, sails, powder, and shot were always part of the 'tribute'" (Wolf 1979, 224). Supplying war materials was also a part of the Algerine-Spanish peace treaty of 1788 (Lewis 1982, 46), as well as that of the U.S.-Algiers treaty of 1795, whereby the young American republic was to pay Algiers an annual sum of $21,600 in naval supplies on top of $60,000 worth of such supplies at the signature of the "peace" between the two polities (Irwin 1970, 70–77). Effectively, the Barbary corsair communities "established a protection racket to supplement their piratical income" (Woodward 2004, 600). Such racketeering was all the more characteristic of the Algerian corsair community's relations with the weaker states of Europe. Thus, when the Ottoman ambassador in Madrid asked an Algerian emissary to Spain in 1788, "Why do you [Algiers] make peace with them [Spain] when you are profiting from them so much?" the Algerian replied, "Our profits are indeed enormous. This peace will last at most three years, during which we retain our previous gains. As for now, we are collecting enough for two or three years, and we suffer no loss." The Ottoman ambassador concluded that "[h]e meant by this that the peace is no more than writing on water" (Lewis 1982, 47). The ambassador's metaphor symbolized the freeloading nature of Algiers's interactions with the weaker states of Europe—interactions whose purpose and content almost entirely entailed the exploitation of these states.

But although the purchase of protection in this manner was supposed to give the paying country a measure of security, in many cases during the eighteenth century the corsair *reis* "sought every excuse to condemn as prize ships those of states technically at peace with the regency. For the petty state, indeed even for the [Holy Roman] Emperor as the ruler of the Austrian Netherlands, it was often impossible to get much redress" (Wolf 1979, 311). The precarious position of Algerian rulers (deys) vis-à-vis the powerful corsair *reis* and janissaries often made them "forget justice and violate the faith of treaties" (ibid., 316). The Algerian divan (the council of janissaries and *reis*) thus continued to make its own decisions on war and peace with European states, usually ignoring the wishes of Algiers's nominal sovereign, the Ottoman sultan (Le Gall 1997, 96). Therefore, the Algerian agents of transnational harm—the corsairs and the janissaries—retained a persistent and self-interested nature during the eighteenth and early nineteenth centuries too. They were willing to acknowledge the authority of the Algerian dey or that of the Ottoman sultan only when the wishes of their nominal superiors coincided with their self-interests. Their loyalty to the Algerian system of government was "bound up with the material advantages they drew from it" (Abun-Nasr 1987, 166). The rest of this chapter indeed focuses on Algiers, which remained the "capital and the main center of piracy" (ibid., 161) in North Africa during the eighteenth and early nineteenth centuries.

The fact that the stronger European powers did not demand an absolute abolition of corsairing and slavery was significant in the perpetuation of this harmful phenomenon. Even between 1801–5 and 1815, when the United States forced the three Barbary regencies to stop their depredations on American vessels, the agreements were bilateral ones and did not include the abolition of corsairing against other states. The early nineteenth-century American naval missions in Barbary deterred the corsairs from attacking U.S. vessels, but the Americans were concerned only with the security of their own nationals and commerce, not with the fate of others who continued to suffer at the hands of the pirates. Similarly, Spain started a war against Algiers in 1770 in order to release about ten thousand Spanish slaves held there but ignored the other eight thousand Europeans in slavery (Abun-Nasr 1987, 166). British and French naval expeditions against the Barbary corsair communities during the seventeenth and eighteenth centuries were equally only concerned with their respective civilians and not with attempting to put a total end to Barbary slavery.[1]

This state of affairs changed in 1816, when the British government sent a powerful expedition under the command of Lord Exmouth against Algiers and other major Barbary corsair ports with a demand to abolish Christian slave taking altogether. To my knowledge, this was the first naval mission that stipulated the unconditional release of *all* the slaves—regardless of their nationality—and an indiscriminate abolition of slave taking. Tunis and Tripoli yielded to the British admiral's demand without the latter resorting to actual force. But Algiers refused to accept the British terms and consequently was heavily bombarded into submission. As we shall see subsequently, this operation was considerably costly to Britain, both in human lives and in financial and political terms. The empirical puzzle here is the rationale behind Britain's actions. Unlike states that attacked Algiers and other Barbary ports for defensive reasons—due to harm done by the corsairs to their commerce or subjects—the British and their interests by the early nineteenth century were not threatened by the corsairs of Algiers. Britain was no longer, at that time, a target of piratical aggression. We have seen in the previous chapter that two centuries earlier the corsairs had indeed been a serious threat to British subjects. During the first half of the seventeenth century, the pirates went so far as to encroach upon the British Isles and kidnap thousands of British subjects into slavery. But from the 1690s onward, the British imposed a peace on Algiers that was kept by their naval supremacy and not by tribute. Hence, there is no evidence that from the early eighteenth century onward Algiers posed a threat of material harm to Britain's security or to its commercial interests (Anderson 1956, 87, 101–2). I have been unable to find any references to complaints of British merchants against the Barbary pirates or to demands that they eliminate their activity on commercial grounds. On the contrary, British shippers benefited from the corsairs' harassment of Britain's competitors in the Mediterranean, because many foreign merchants preferred to use Britain's secure maritime services (ibid., 101). But "[t]he victory of Lord Exmouth at Algiers, at the expence of British blood and treasure, unfortunately deprived the British ship owner of the advantages of the Mediterranean carrying trade" and instead increased Britain's competitors' share in this industry (Harding 2000, 42).[2]

In fact, prior to the 1816 expedition against Algiers, significant voices were heard in Britain objecting to the intervention against the pirates for precisely these reasons. The influential Tory-inclined journal *Quarterly Review* noted that, as far as the national interests are concerned, "it would be an act of madness" for Britain to intervene against the pirates. The *Quarterly* emphasized that "[i]f England is to be constituted piratetaker-general, she had better commence with the Malays and Ladrones of China, who plunder her ships and murder her subjects; the Barbary pirates do neither." In addition, it argued that Britain should not become the redeemer of foreign nationals: "The greatest number of slaves taken by the Barbary powers of late years, consists of Sardinians, Neapolitans and Sicilians. It is thus in the power of the government to which the unfortunate captives belong, or of their friends to procure their release. What has England to do with it, that she must stand foremost as the avenging power, and sacrifice her seamen to evince her humanity toward Sardinians, Sicilians and Neapolitans?" (*Quarterly Review* 1816, 142, 145, 147–48). The *Times* of London also highlighted the disinterest of Britain in suppressing the pirates and their slave trade and brought forward the issue of burden sharing: "Assuredly, Britain must and will defend the honour of her own flag. But it is quite a different question

whether we shall lavish our blood and treasure for Neapolitans, Sardinians, Romans, Spaniards or Portuguese. In the present state of our finance
we cannot afford mere Quixotism. If these powers, or any of them, are
incapable of defending themselves, let them pay us for the service"
(*Times,* June 29, 1816). In the end, of course, none of these states paid for
the British effort.

Not only did Algiers pose no material harmful threat to the national
security of Britain, but it was an ally—one that the British would lose
through its chastisement. Since the late eighteenth century Algiers had
become the central source of grain for the British garrison on Minorca
Island—a strategic location in the Balearic Islands. After the American
War of Independence, the British turned a blind eye toward Algerian corsair attacks against the commercial shipping of the young United States,
which had significant interests in the Mediterranean (Edwards 1968, 60).
Britain did not prevent the corsairs from crossing the Strait of Gibraltar
in order to intercept American ships in the Atlantic. As a result, dozens of
Americans fell into the hands of the corsairs as slaves and hostages, the
Mediterranean commerce of America was badly injured, and the dey
compelled the United States in 1795 to buy peace for a sum of $642,000
and to pay an annual tribute of $21,600—all this under tacit British per-
mission.

Nonetheless, the British were resolved to impose on Algiers an abolition of its corsairs' slave-trade and captive-taking depredations. The
argument of this chapter is that the British attack on Algiers should be
seen in the context of Britain's effort to terminate the Atlantic slave trade.
In this regard, I am not familiar with a more intensive single naval
engagement in the history of the suppression of the slave trade.[3] Algiers
was also an important maritime battle by the standards of the period.
Thus, except for the bombardment of Copenhagen in 1807, the Battle of
Algiers was most likely the largest cannonade dealt upon a littoral target
by a naval force during the Age of Sail (Clowes 1901, 228).

In the following sections, I first describe the details of the British 1816
expedition against Barbary corsairing and then examine it according to
the framework of Great Power authority and the institutions of violence.
I conclude that Barbary corsairing was construed by Britain in that time
as a phenomenon that undermined British moral authority over the European powers in the context of London's demand during the Congress of
Vienna that the other European powers abolish their Atlantic slave trade.
As such, Algiers was punished by Britain in order to restore its moral
authority as a Great Power.

I. The British Expedition against Algiers: Its Scale and Costs

In early 1816, the British admiral Lord Exmouth was ordered by his government to visit Tripoli, Tunis, and Algiers and negotiate the release of white slaves held there. Since his orders were secret and thus not recorded in history, it is unclear what freedom of action he was given (*Annual Register* 1816, 97; Perkins and Douglas-Morris 1982, 63, 73). In April 1816, Exmouth arrived at Barbary with five ships of the line and seven frigates and sloops. The admiral negotiated slave redemption treaties with the rulers of the regencies, and for the total sum of 490,000 Spanish dollars he bought the freedom of 1,475 Sardinians, Neapolitans, Genovese, and German nationals. Tunis and Tripoli, the weaker Barbary regencies, agreed to completely abolish the practice of kidnapping Europeans to slavery.[4] But the Algerian dey remained defiant and refused to consider such an obligation. Despite the British show of force, refusal was not irrational for the dey. On May 31, 1816, the *Times* reported that, when Exmouth landed in Algiers and presented to the dey and the divan his demand to abolish Christian slavery, "the indignation of the Divan and the Turkish militia [the janissaries], whom the Dey consulted successively, rose to the highest pitch. Lord Exmouth and his suite had great difficulty in getting through the crowd that collected, and reaching again the beach and their boats." So firm were the Algerians in rejecting the British demand that "the Turkish militia swore to bury themselves under the ruins, rather than suffer their dey to be reduced to depart from the laudable customs of their forefathers" (ibid.). In fact, accepting the British demand would have been a suicidal move on the part of the dey, since the corsairs and the janissaries of Algiers often murdered deys that failed to supply them with opportunities for sea predation (Irwin 1970, 61). Between 1805 and 1816, seven deys were assassinated by the corsairs and janissaries. In 1784, during the war with Spain, the janissaries allowed the Spanish navy, then blockading Algiers, to come close enough to the port to bombard the dey's palace after the latter decided to cut their battle premiums (Abun-Nasr 1987, 166). In light of this, it is no wonder that during the later part of the eighteenth century the dey was a "prisoner in his palace, always under threat of assassination." And indeed, in September 1816, after finally submitting to the British demands and formally announcing the abolition of the Christian slave trade in August, the dey, Omer Agha, was strangled (Wolf 1979, 291, 332).

Back in April 1816, with no clear orders, Exmouth headed back to Britain. But immediately upon his return to Britain, Exmouth was resent to Algiers, and this time he was clearly ordered to negotiate only through the mouth of the gun and render the pirates incapable of kidnapping Christians into slavery and raiding European vessels and shores. Thus, in July of that year a second fleet, larger than the previous[5] and commanded again by Exmouth, was dispatched for a punitive mission against Algiers. This second expedition was joined (by coincidence rather than design) by six Dutch frigates.

Exmouth's fleet was a relatively strong one compared to the number of British full commissioned vessels at the time, representing 16 percent of the navy's full commissioned ships of the line. But in relation to the overall maritime capabilities of Britain, Exmouth's fleet was modest (the navy had 30 full commissioned and 70 in ordinary ships of the line, in addition to 203 smaller vessels full commissioned and 134 kept in ordinary; Brown 1990, 26). The same can be said about the manpower of the fleet: the 5,100 men and officers of the squadron represented a fairly big force compared to the commissioned fighting manpower of the navy in that year (which numbered 39,000 men and officers; James [1827] 1902, 276), but this was a rather small number in relation to the complement of the navy in 1813 (which stood at a peak of 145,000).[6] Accordingly, in terms of size the Algerian fleet was a significant one by peacetime standards but small when compared with the overall naval potential of Britain.

While the April expedition did not involve the use of force, the August operation included a daylong bombardment of Algiers, the extent of which left the British and the Dutch almost without ammunition. "The expenditure of ammunition during the action was beyond all parallel. The fleet fired nearly 118 tons of powder; 50,000 shots weighing more than 500 tons; nearly 1,000 shells, besides rockets and carcasses" (Playfair 1884, 272).[7] During the battle, the British lost 128 men and 690 were wounded, and the Dutch lost 13 men and 52 were wounded. The Algerians suffered between 2,000 and 7,000 casualties, and their entire fleet was ruined, as were their coastal fortifications (Clowes 1901, 227). Under these circumstances, the dey finally yielded to the demand to completely abolish Christian slavery. A total of 1,528 white slaves were released, making the number of redeemed slaves in the two expeditions 3,003. Not one of these slaves was "a native of the British isles" (James [1827] 1902, 291).

Though the Algerians managed to reconstruct part of their naval power in the next few years, the problem of Christian slavery never again reached its previous dimensions, and thus Exmouth's operation achieved its main goal. Eventually, the 1830 French occupation terminated

Algiers's piracies. But how much exactly did the 1816 campaign cost Britain? Did Britain gain any material profit from it? Clarifying these points is an important step toward understanding the causes leading to Britain's action.

I find that, on the whole, this operation was a medium effort for Britain. Algiers was relatively weak and politically isolated, but it was still considered by Britain as a challenging target. The cost of suppressing the slave trade and sea predations of the corsairs was not even close to the British war effort against France in the previous years, yet it was significant enough for Britain to notice. It also brought no material gains to Britain. In the analysis that follows in the next sections I demonstrate these points.

A. The British Perception of Algiers's Strength Prior to the Expedition

Although the power of the pirates was not even the tenth strongest opposition compared with Britain's overall capabilities, they were nonetheless perceived by many Britons as tough and fierce warriors. The difficult topography of the port of Algiers, the "warlike city," and the strong fortifications protecting it were deemed by some British naval experts as unassailable. Algiers was strong enough even in 1775 to repel a Spanish invasion force of three hundred ships and twenty-two thousand men (Hess 1977, 83). The experience of the Spaniards in the sixteenth centuries (1541 and 1560) in assailing Algiers was also known to the British. Thus, Admiral Horatio Nelson estimated in 1799 that in order to subdue the Algerian corsairs a (very considerable) force of twenty-five ships of the line would be required (Osler 1835, 309). But Nelson's estimation was based on secondary sources rather than firsthand intelligence. In contrast, Exmouth had himself been to Algiers and had even conducted a meticulous survey of its defense. Consequently, Exmouth asked for only five ships of the line (with a large number of smaller vessels) to attack the pirates' port, even though the admiralty were willing to provide more ships of the line (ibid., 310).

We can infer more about the British confusion with regard to Algiers's strength from the public debates that preceded the operation. The expedition was openly debated, and opinions regarding it were divided. The House of Commons debated the issue on June 19, 1816, and the expedition was also discussed by the leading journals and newspapers of the time. At the parliamentary debate, member of Parliament (and the country's greatest living sea hero) Lord Cochrane contended from his own knowledge of Algiers that "two sail of the line would have been sufficient to compel the *dey* of Algiers to accede to any terms" (*Parliamentary Debates* 1816, 34:1149). In contrast to this minimizing view of Algiers, the *Quarterly Review* noted that

> we do not believe that Algiers is so defenceless, or the people in so ignorant a state, that the one might be destroyed and the other humbled by two sail-of-the-line, as Lord Cochrane is said to have asserted in the House of Commons. Whoever knows Algiers cannot be ignorant of the strength of it. The truth is, if well defended, it is almost impregnable; and the man who affects to speak lightly of bringing a squadron of line abreast of a connected series of works mounting more than 800 pieces of heavy cannon, and within a few hundred yards of them, is woefully ignorant, or willfully wishes to deceive. . . . we are generally too apt to hold cheap on untried enemy. (*Quarterly Review*, 1816, 149)

Similarly, the *Times* wrote on June 29, 1816, "There are persons who pretend to think that Lord Exmouth should have had [in April] his ships along the Algerine batteries and negotiated only at the mouth of the cannon. [But it] is not justice to the character of our navy to commit it rashly to unequal contests." Lord Castelreagh, the foreign minister, seemed to summarize the debate on Algiers's strength in his words on a special parliamentary Vote of Thanks to Lord Exmouth for the attack on Algiers (February 3, 1817):

> [T]he enemy might be inferior in scientific excellence and in the knowledge of modern warfare, yet sufficient proof was given during the battle that the arm of this country was never turned against a foe more capable of opposing an obstinate and fierce resistance. That fact was proved by the loss we sustained, which compared with the force employed, exceeded the proportion that of the greatest victories this country had achieved. [Prior to the attack] some persons of scientific authority had stated that even a single line of battle ship would be sufficient. Other authorities, equally entitled to respect, declared that it would not only be difficult, but so difficult, as to make it a matter of prudent consideration whether anything should be undertaken against such formidable batteries. Lord Exmouth steered a middle course between the two

extreme points. He said he considered it a service which would be attended with a considerable degree of risk and loss, but he felt confident he could perform it. (*Parliamentary Debates* 1817, 36:178)

Hence, I conclude that Algiers was perceived as a worthy adversary, but surely not as unbeatable by a medium British force.

B. The Human Cost of the Expedition

As Castelreagh noted, the proportion of British casualties (and dead) was high: of those engaged in the battle, 16 percent were wounded or killed. This can be compared to 11 percent in the Battle of the Nile (1798) and 9 percent at Trafalgar (1805) (Parkinson 1934, 469). In absolute numbers of casualties, the Battle of Algiers was comparable to a medium-range naval engagement. For the sake of comparison, the number of British men killed in Algiers was 53 percent of the average number of British deaths in the six great naval battles of the Revolutionary and Napoleonic Wars and 97 percent of the average number of wounded (Lewis 1960, 362). In relation to squadronal actions (engaging only frigates and smaller vessels), Algiers's deaths were 213 percent higher than the average and the number of wounded was 383 percent higher than the average of four notable operations (ibid., 374). All this indicates that the human cost of the battle was medium in relation to the standards of the time. However, when comparing the human costs of the suppression of white slavery to those of the black slavery, I find that Algiers stands as one of the single cases in which a great number of British lives were lost in actual combat against slavers. During the suppression of the Atlantic slave trade (1807–67), the British lost some five thousand lives altogether, most of them from the navy (Kaufmann and Pape 1999, 635). Yet the vast majority of those losses were due to disease (malaria) and not to combat engagement (Lloyd 1968, xi).

C. The Financial Costs of the Expedition

According to Perkins and Douglas-Morris, the total cost of the expedition to Algiers was more than £1 million (1982, 152). However, my calculations reveal a figure of around £500,000—the total of the gratuity money paid to the participants of the battle, combat damages to ships, regular wear, cost of ammunition and victuals, promotions, compensations to the wounded and to widows, and so forth.[8] Further (indirect) monetary cost could have been related to losses to British Mediterranean commerce due to the suppression of Algerine piracy. The pirates were perceived by many in Europe and America, as well as in Britain itself, as instrumental to British commercial interests in the Mediterranean, since they avoided attacking British vessels and aimed instead at Britain's competitors. "Were the commerce of the Mediterranean perfectly free from the depredation of the Barbary states, the British would lose forever the commercial advantages they now possess in those waters," wrote the *Washington Whig* on November 4, 1816. In the same vein, the *Edinburgh Review,* a prominent (British) Whig-disposed magazine, wrote, "The true reason of [British] forbearance so long shown towards the Robbers, has been some pitiful shopkeeper's calculation, that their traffic might yield exclusive advantages" (1816, 26:450–51). Furthermore, British and East Indian goods were among the major imports in Algiers (Shaler 1823, 83). Thus, theoretically, the suppression of Algerian piracy and the damage wrecked on the city-state as a result should have increased Britain's competition in the Mediterranean and diminished its revenues there. However, it is very difficult to assess the exact figures of British losses or gains following the expedition because the available statistics relate only to larger geographical regions; in the few years after 1816, British exports to Africa, Asia, and southern Europe (exports that were partially transported through the Mediterranean) actually expanded (Mitchell 1988, 495). This growth in British exports was most likely influenced by the ensuing of peace between the Great Powers, but there is no real way to tell whether the growth of British trade would have been greater were the pirates not punished.

Bearing this in mind, we can now establish a contextual point of view as to the financial cost of the operation. To cite some economic indicators, in 1816, the budget of the Royal Navy totaled £9,500,000, the public income of the state was £75,500,000, and the service of the national debt amounted to £30,000,000.[9] The mid-decade average of British national income in the 1810s was £296 million (Williamson 1984, 695). Thus, the expedition to Barbary cost about 5 percent of the navy's (peacetime) annual budget, 1.66 percent of the yearly interest on the national debt, 0.65 percent of the year's public income, and 0.16 percent of the national income. At a time when the navy was under strong governmental and parliamentary pressure to economize (Bartlett 1963, 21–28), this would certainly not be considered a trivial expenditure. Indeed, according to Chaim Kaufmann and Robert Pape, the average annual cost of the abolition of the Atlantic slave trade, estimated at 1.8 percent of the national income between 1807 and 1867, was a costly moral effort (1999, 637). In light of this figure, Algiers was a relatively small operation. However, most of the costs incurred by the Atlantic abolition were related to economic self-concessions such as rising prices of sugar, increasing prices of labor, and reduced competitiveness of British planters versus Brazilian, Cuban, and French counterparts. Only 0.05 percent of the national income was allotted, on average, to the suppression effort itself—meaning diplomatic, legal, *and* naval costs (ibid.). Compared to this figure, the Barbary expedition was equivalent to the cost of more than three average years of the Atlantic naval suppression effort. Algiers's significance as an armed intervention is highlighted when we examine the British naval record in the Atlantic campaign. Until 1839, the British efforts to suppress the Atlantic slave trade were focused largely on diplomatic measures rather than armed ones (Mathieson 1929, 28). In the following years (1840–67), the West African and Brazilian squadrons of the Royal Navy were highly involved in the suppression of the slave trade, but these operations usually included destroying slave depots and slaver factories in Africa and chasing individual slavers (usually only lightly armed) on the high seas—missions that did not require an intensive and concentrated attack like the Battle of Algiers. This does not mean that the British were not persistent and consistent in their efforts to abolish the slave trade. They implemented economic and diplomatic sanctions and inducements and moralistic appeals to solicit concessions from other powers involved in the human traffic. But the suppression of white slavery on the Barbary Coast was rather a unique effort in that it involved a massive attack on probably the best-defended land base of slavers.

And while an argument could be raised that there was a territorial expansionist motive working in this attack, the evidence does not confirm such a claim. In fact, during the eighteenth century, Britain did not try to occupy territories in Barbary, despite several suggestions and appeals from the Barbary regencies to cooperate in conquering Spanish outposts on the North African coast (Anderson 1956, 99). Moreover, during the 1816 operation itself, no plans or attempts were made to conquer Algiers or neighboring territories, only to destroy its navy and release the white slaves. While Exmouth had a force of royal marines under his command, "he was not offered, nor did he request, any army units of sufficient strength to seize and exploit a bridgehead on an enemy coastline. From the outset this was to be a punitive expedition, not an attempt at conquest" (Perkins and Douglas-Morris 1982, 83). Thus, no territorial gain was made here. Furthermore, in the years following the expedition, the British did not make any efforts to conquer North African land, and they raised almost no objection to the French occupation of the region in 1830.[10]

Finally, asserting British capabilities in order to deter Russia—the other major European power in the aftermath of the Napoleonic Wars—from future encroachments on Britain's Mediterranean sphere of influence could also be argued as a motive in attacking Algiers, a way to demonstrate Britain's supremacy in the Mediterranean. But in the first years of the postwar order Russia could not compete with Britain; its economy was devastated, and it was plagued by peasant unrest, an expensive military establishment, discontented army officers, and troublesome new territories, especially Poland and Bessarabia. "The reforms the government attempted seldom worked and were usually soon abandoned, but affected Russian foreign policy by discouraging adventures and making Russia seek co-operation from other governments. Neither government [Britain's or Russia's] paid much attention to the alarmists within its camp or tried seriously to encroach on the other's sphere" (Schroeder 1994, 588–89).

To conclude, it seems that in the material cost-benefit balance, this operation incurred many costs and no benefits. The British lost lives, money, and instrumental allies. They gained no security dividend, as the pirates did not attack their shipping, and their naval prestige was already acknowledged. They also did not win any territorial prize nor a new sphere of influence. Furthermore, in spite of the fact that the punishment of the pirates was followed by an enlargement of British commerce in the Mediterranean, the expectation beforehand was that it would reduce it. Thus, even the hegemonic stability model does not explain this case, because it links hegemonic benevolence to some kind of material interest of the hegemon. With no such interest, it is very difficult to understand, from a realist perspective, why Britain was willing to bear noticeable costs in order to suppress the Barbary slave trade and piracy. In the next part of this chapter, I resolve this puzzle by showing how the pirates threatened Britain's authority as a Great Power.

II. Explaining the 1816 British Expedition against Algiers

A. Great Power Authority in the Congress of Vienna

The argument here is that during the Congress of Vienna, which preceded the British attack on Algiers, the authority of the Great Powers was augmented and even came to represent what Simpson denotes "legalized hegemony." At Vienna, the dominant military powers of Europe constructed for the first time a formal "directorate" of major powers and became Great Powers (Simpson 2004, chap. 4). "The Great Powers not only enforced their will on Europe but regarded themselves as possessing a right to do so. They not only instituted a new political order in European affairs but did so using legal techniques that sought to entrench this dominant position" (ibid., 105). Moreover, "these rights were not simply asserted by the Great Powers but also were conceded by most of the small powers. . . . the minor powers at Vienna were disappointed with certain outcomes and disliked the superior attitudes of the big powers but nonetheless did not question the preeminent role of the major states" (ibid., 107). Authority was not only claimed by the Great Powers but given to them by the weaker states in the system.

What enabled Great Power authority in Vienna? On one level, the fact that Britain, Prussia, Russia, and Austria defeated Napoleon and bore the overwhelming part of the costs of this victory put them in a position to institute the postwar world order (Nicholson 1970, 235). However, on a more fundamental level, the authority of the Great Powers in Vienna was made possible by the institutions of violence that were bequeathed to them from the eighteenth century and by the reformulation of some of these institutions in Vienna itself. I will subsequently discuss this process and then explain how Algiers's piracy and slave trade undermined British authority as a Great Power.

Great power authority is first and foremost grounded in the institution of sovereignty. Sovereignty, as an institution of transborder violence, is understood in this book to have two major meanings: territoriality and the reasons for war.

In terms of the territorial aspects of sovereignty, the five Great Powers of Vienna (France was added to the group of four after its Bourbon king was restored) generally avoided expansionist policies as such, thinking rather in terms of "just equilibrium" and systemic security. Although each power stressed its own territorial interests and pursued its security, this was usually done within the context of maximizing systemic stability, not for the purpose of "aggrandizement" (Osiander 1994, 171–86). The nature of the balance of power was such that "each of the winners managed to get some key lands that they desired by way of reward for their victory, without being so greedy as to incur the jealousy of the others or the wrath of France or the lesser states. France was barely punished and certainly there was no sense of revenge as it was even spared paying any compensation at this stage" (Chapman 1998, 42). In other words, the territorial claims of the powers were couched in a discourse of "equilibrium," "balance," and European stability. Certainly the Great Powers had no intention or wish to eliminate each other's sovereignty, as would have most likely been the case in the sixteenth and early seventeenth centuries. "Legitimacy, not force, was the centrepiece of the [1815] balance of power" (Nau 2001, 586).

This does not mean that territorial change, even change incurred through the use of force, was delegitimized in Vienna. On the contrary, the Right of Conquest continued to exist in international law until at least the early twentieth century (Korman 1996). Thus, during the Congress of Vienna, one of the justifications Russia gave for its annexation of Poland was that the country was conquered during the war. Furthermore, to a great extent the Great Powers in Vienna were preoccupied with redistributing large territories across Europe, which often resulted in dismembering sovereign states (the annexation of two-thirds of Saxony by Prussia is a prime example). As Simpson notes, in Vienna "[s]tates were divided, territories amputated and principalities confederated. In particular, a large part of Poland was incorporated into Russian territory and the 300 pre-war German principalities and kingdoms were merged into the 30-member German confederation." Ultimately, then, "the existence of states was insecure" (2004, 113, 114). However, the Great Powers tried to persuade each other and the smaller states of the necessity and justness of such territorial changes. As Castlereagh stated in October 1814, "The courts parties to the Treaty of Paris, by which the present congress has been set up, *hold themselves to be obliged* to submit for its consideration and approval the project of settlement which they judge to be most in accordance with the principles recognized as the necessary basis for the general system of Europe" (quoted in Osiander 1994, 235; emphasis in original).

Territory was considered the main source of power (Chapman 1998, 16), as it supplied war-making capabilities, wealth, and people and provided buffering zones between the powers. But territorial self-aggrandizement, especially at the expense of other Great Powers, was not the main motivation of the Great Powers at Vienna. As opposed to the pursuit of *gloire* that characterized territorial expansion in the sixteenth and seventeenth centuries, in Vienna territorial expansion and infringements on others' sovereignty had to be legitimated by communal principles and consensus. The negotiators shared the view that they had a common responsibility for the future destiny of Europe. They also knew that the destiny of each of the actors was intertwined with the destiny of the others and that whatever policy they adopted would have systemwide ramifications. Thus, they approached the congress with a high degree of system consciousness. According to Andreas Osiander, the word *system*—and the system-oriented approach it implied—had positive connotations of political credibility and therefore was repeatedly used (1994, 186–87).

Accordingly, the preservation of the balance of power (which was inherently linked to territorial possessions) became the principal reason for infringing on others' sovereignty. This infringement could be carried out through consensus but also through the threat of force. The notion of a need to actively maintain and manage the balance of power was not unique to Vienna (the concept of balance of power as a political goal could be traced back at least to the Peace of Utrecht in 1713). However, the concept of *just equilibrium* that dominated the Vienna discussions conferred authority on the Great Powers precisely because they represented themselves as guarantors of the territorial order in the aftermath of Napoleon—the greatest challenger of territorial sovereignty in modern Europe up to that time. "Despite the fact that their emerging privileged role generated some discontent, the great powers were, in a sense, mandated by the expectations placed in them" (Osiander 1994, 234).

Thus, the principle of just equilibrium usually succeeded in generating consensus among the Great Powers, who saw each other as capable of authority. Indeed, mutual distrust between the Great Powers did not vanish, and some territorial questions even raised the specter of renewal of the war, this time among the former allies that defeated Napoleon (Chapman 1998, 26). However, the powers also understood their mutual dependence. This eventually led them to consider each other as equals in terms of rights (Simpson 2004, 108). Of course, material imbalances existed between the Great Powers. Notably, the military power of Britain and Russia was considerably higher than that of Prussia, France, and Austria (Schroeder 1992, 686). Nonetheless, "[a]mong the Great Powers themselves, the question of legalized hierarchy did not appear to arise at all" (Simpson 2004, 108). Most important, the more powerful states among the Great Powers—Britain and Russia—restrained themselves vis-à-vis each other and the other powers and states. The Vienna settlement thus represented, according to Ikenberry, "an order that secured the 'balance of power' which in its specific context meant a just and mutually agreeable distribution of territory, rights and obligations" (2001, 96). It was understood that the Great Powers would have the right and the duty to make decisions on territorial disputes and that territorial expansion by a Great Power should take place only after the other Great Powers consented (ibid., 105).

Even though the Great Powers established in Vienna a regime of legalized hegemony and considered each other as equals and at the same time superior to smaller and weaker states (in terms of authority), they did consider to a certain degree the rights of the latter and did not treat them in a complete arbitrary manner. The sovereign rights of smaller states were seen mainly from the perspective of Great Power interest and diplomacy, but the congress mechanism was nonetheless an open invitation for weaker states to have their rights and territories claimed. At the same time, the Great Powers were not about to give the assembly of the entire states "the authority to rewrite the map of Europe and articulate the terms of peace. The final settlement would have looked as much as it did even if most of the officialdom that flocked to Vienna had not come at all. The Great Powers understood the congress to be essentially a way to put a legitimate stamp on the agreements and secret treaties that they worked out among themselves" (Ikenberry 2001, 114). In fact, the congress never met in full session, with all of the plenipotentiaries concerned, until the signing of the Final Act in June 1815. This was due to the fact that the four victorious powers, joined later by France, created a hierarchical system of committees. The Directing Committee, in which only the Great Powers participated, was thus the major decision-making forum of the congress. Spain, Portugal, and Sweden—minor powers that nonetheless contributed to the defeat of Napoleon—were allowed into other committees of the congress. However, and this is an important point, the Great Powers felt at least to a certain degree that they must show themselves duly considering the rights of the smaller states. Castlereagh noted on this, "The advantage of this mode of proceeding is that you treat the plenipotentiaries as a body with early and becoming respect. . . . You obtain a sort of sanction from [the small powers] for what you are determined at all events to do, which they cannot well withhold . . . and you entitle yourselves, without disrespect for them, to meet together for dispatch of business for an indefinite time to their exclusion" (quoted in Simpson 2004, 99).

This raises the following question: If "you are determined at all events to do" something, why treat the smaller states with "early and becoming respect" and obtain this sanction from them? It seems to me that the rationale behind Castlereagh's logic was that even the Great Powers have to legitimize their power in such a way that the other states will accept without too much opposition the order the powerful establish—or even impose. This brings me back to the argument from chapter 1: even the security of the most powerful depends, to a certain degree, on the acquiescence of the weak within the systemic order that the powerful actors establish. As we shall see later, the settlement of Vienna was concerned not solely with rearranging the map of Europe in territorial terms but also with reestablishing a social order within this territorial rearrangement—that of the "old regime." In this respect, even weak states (militarily) could have fomented significant threats to the territorial order and the interests of the Great Powers by harboring revolutionary and nationalist ideas and movements. One way to prevent this was to acknowledge the rights even of weak states (or, more accurately, of their monarchs and dynasts) and to treat them according to the principle of dynastic legitimacy. Accordingly, even if a weak state's territories were dismembered or amputated, the Great Powers insisted on receiving its approval of, or at least its tacit consent to, this action.

To conclude, although the territorial aspects of sovereignty were seen at Vienna through the perspective of the balance of power and political equilibrium mainly between the Great Powers, they were also linked, on another level, to concepts of rights, legitimacy, and the rule of law (Schroeder 1992). As I understand it, states accepted the fact that the most important task before them was not to gain more power but to restore order and stability in Europe. The principle of monarchical or dynastic legitimacy thus served as a reassurance for the stability of the balance of power system. The "dynastic legitimacy" principle so often discussed in Vienna was not about monarchism as such but about restoring and preserving a hierarchical societal order that monarchism symbolized (Osiander 1994, 222). Revolutionary forces—domestic and international—threatened this order. In fact, the Great Powers retained their wartime alliances for the preservation of the hierarchical domestic political system of authority that was reestablished in the wake of Napoleon and the Revolution. Revolutionary and national movements and governments—beyond threatening the domestic stability of multinational empires such as Austria and Russia—were also perceived in Vienna as incapable of living at peace with the rest of Europe (Schroeder 1994, 552). Thus, revolutionary and national reasons for war were clearly delegitimized in Vienna. Moreover, the preservation of dynastic hierarchical order became a legitimate reason for Great Power forceful infringement on other states' sovereignty after Vienna.

Algiers and the other Barbary corsair communities did not threaten the European balance of power. They posed no challenge to the authority of Britain or any other Great Power by undermining the territorial aspects of sovereignty. The corsair communities of North Africa were not part of the new territorial order in Vienna, nor did they possess war-making capabilities that could have undermined this order. The Algerians were also not considered to be a revolutionary threat, because they propagated no political ideology that competed with the principle of monarchical legitimacy. But the facts that the Great Powers established a system of authority in Vienna that was based on legalized hegemony and that their authority was formally acknowledged by each other and by the lesser states framed the issue of the Barbary corsairs in a new conceptual environment. One of the corollaries of Great Power authority was that the Great Powers had to consider not only their rights but their duties toward their peers *and* nonpeers. Authority—as legitimized power—means that the holder of power cannot simply demand others to obey commands but must convince them that these wishes are grounded in a structure of legitimacy. This means that moral consistency becomes essential for the reproduction of authority.

And, indeed, questions of moral consistency were a central issue in Vienna from the outset of the congress. Thus, for example, while the four Great Powers initially intended to exclude France from their deliberations, they eventually agreed to include it in their decision-making forum, not because of France's material power—which was in ebb at that time—but due to the arguments of Talleyrand, the chief French negotiator at Vienna, about moral inconsistency. He maintained that the Quadruple Alliance was no longer a legitimate decision-making body, because

> the principles of monarchical legitimacy on which the war had been fought would be fundamentally violated if France was not admitted as a full partner in negotiations: "The presence of a minister of Louis XVIII consecrates here the principle upon which all social order rests. The first need of Europe is . . . to cause the revival of that sacred principle of legitimacy from which all order and stability spring. To show today that France troubles your deliberations, would be to say that true principles are no longer the only ones that guide you, and that you are unwilling to be just." The representatives of the four Great Powers had no response to such arguments, choosing instead to withdraw the offending protocol. Friedrich von Gentz, who was the meeting's secretary,

recorded that Talleyrand "hopelessly upset our plans. It was a scene I shall never forget." (quoted in Reus-Smit 1999, 137–38)

Similarly, British moral credibility was at stake in the case of the Barbary pirates. The next section explores how this happened and interweaves the historical relation with a discussion of the two other institutions of violence: the laws of war and the principle of actorhood.

B. The Barbary Pirates and the Challenge to Britain's Authority

In this section, I argue that the Algerians' explicit refusal to abolish Christian slavery amounted to a severe challenge to Britain's authority as a Great Power in the post-Napoleonic world. By waging transborder violence mainly for the attainment of slaves and plunder—in spite of British demands to cease this practice—Algiers approached the predatory type of PATH, at least from Britain's perspective. But this perception ensued only once Britain abolished its slave trade (1807) and made the abolition of the slave trade an important foreign policy priority in the Congress of Vienna. One of the results of the congress was that the European powers, under British pressure, officially declared their abhorrence of the Atlantic slave trade and their intention to bring an end to it. At the same time, the issues of suppressing Algerian piracy and slave trade and the British pursuit for abolition of the Atlantic slave trade were tangled together, and the first became a test of the moral sincerity of the second.

Much has been written on how the abolition of the slave trade came to be a part of British identity and interests since the late eighteenth century. The effect of humanistic ideas and religious motives on Britain's decision in 1807 to abolish the slave trade in its empire has been extensively covered by other authors, and due to space limitations I will not repeat this discussion here. While some have argued that abolition was a result of economic factors (e.g., Ryden 2000), this alone cannot explain the British zeal and persistence to abolish the human traffic. Drescher (1986) and Walvin (1999), among many others, have made a strong argument about the influence of humanistic and religious ideas and notions on the British decision to abolish the black slave trade. However, as Kaufmann and Pape show, the main motive of the abolitionists was not to relieve the sufferings of the blacks (that was important, of course, but not their first priority) but rather to root out corruption and evil in British society, vices that were linked to the institution of slavery. The reformers believed that the continuance of slavery would not only subvert British morality and values but bring God's wrath on the nation for its sinful conduct. "The strongest of all the abolitionists' concerns was fear for the fate of their country. [They] believed in an activist God who rewarded and punished people and nations according to their merit" (Kaufmann and Pape 1999, 648).

The political appeal of abolitionism grew as British politicians realized it was the most popular reform movement. Due to their need for popular legitimacy in an era of limited political participation and growing calls for various political, social, economic, and religious reforms (Mori 2000, 62–65), British elites embraced the abolitionist agenda as a token of their responsiveness to public demands. Abolishing the slave trade was perceived by the elites as the less subversive of the reforms called for at the time. This convergence of political interests with ethical ambitions finally led to the 1807 abolition of the slave trade in the British empire. After this, abolitionist influence on the shaping of British identity and interests increased sharply.

These developments were the background to the attack on Algiers. But the direct causes were related to the British effort at the Congress of Vienna to secure an international abolition of the slave trade. Prior to the congress, the British public revealed its vehement desire that international abolition would be solicited at Vienna. Through parliamentary addresses and hundreds of public petitions, it became clear that the British constituency considered their country responsible for the human trade and wished to wash away this guilt—not only by abolishing the slave trade in the British empire but also by stopping other Christians from damning themselves due to previous British bad example. The strong popular appeal of the abolitionist movement is clearly revealed from Castlereagh's words (from August 1814): "The nation is bent [upon abolition]. I believe there is hardly a village that has not met and petitioned upon it; both houses of Parliament are pledged to press it, and the Ministers must make it the basis of their policy" (quoted in Allison 1861, 516). Furthermore, the "British realized that abolition could only be effective when the slaver no longer had the flag of foreign powers for his protection" (Nelson 1942, 192). Thus, the abolition of slavery was constructed as one of the nation's most important priorities in Vienna. In fact, the Duke of Wellington, about to go to Paris as the British ambassador, noted in July 1814 that the British people "think that it would suit the policy of the nation to go to war to put an end to that *abominable* traffic; and many wish that we should take the field on this new crusade.

All agree that no favour can be shown to a slave trading country" (quoted in Murray 1980, 52).

Yet the abolitionists paid little attention to white slavery on the Barbary Coast and Algiers (Crocker 1816, 3). They may have believed in a need for a gradual process—to end mass black slavery first and only afterward turn to the issue of less extensive white slavery. More likely, however, they perceived the two issues as separate ones; we have seen how the *Times* and the *Quarterly Review* stressed that it was the obligation of the origin states of the white slaves to redeem them. As mentioned before, the ransoming of Christian slaves from Barbary by their families and governments was a centuries-old practice, and the abolitionists probably saw the issue through this perspective. In contrast, the black slaves had no states that would have ransomed them. Also, and more important, the abolitionists probably did not think their country was responsible for the system of white slavery, as opposed to the guilt Britain bore with respect to the black slave trade. Consequently, the enslaving of white Christians in Barbary could have gone almost unnoticed had it not been for the activities of one man—the retired British admiral Sir William Sidney Smith—who changed this reality.

Admiral Smith was a well-known person in his time—his career spanned an attempt to burn Napoleon's fleet at Toulon harbor; a service to the king of Sweden against Russia; and the defense of Acre, which thwarted Napoleon's plan for the conquest of central Asia and India. During his years of service in the Mediterranean, Smith became devoted to the abolition of the white slave trade. When retired, Smith focused his efforts on (and gave a considerable portion of his fortune to) a transnational public relations campaign against white slavery. In 1814, he founded an organization called the Knights Liberator of the Slaves in Africa and launched a private battle against white slavery (Barrow 1848, 383). He sent numerous letters to all the governments and rulers of Europe and underlined the unbearable conditions of the Christian slaves while denouncing the inaction of the Europeans. Beyond urging a moral stance against white slavery, Smith also suggested that the pirates' harbors be blockaded by a supranational special naval force (Howard 1839, 201). In fact, Smith was nothing more than a transnational policy entrepreneur who put the issue of Barbary slavery on the European agenda with great vigor. He received numerous answers to his letters, all pledging support to his moral claims (including Austria's Metternich and France's Talleyrand), but none contained any practical promises. In

December 1814, he used his connections to appear before the Congress of Vienna and convinced the delegates to call for the abolition of slavery and piracy in Barbary, but this remained a symbolic gesture not backed by concrete plans. Smith also managed to solicit donations from the monarchs for a special charity fund to ransom Christian slaves (Spiel 1965, 110). But these were only their personal—not national—endowments, and thus only a few thousand Dutch gildens were collected. To a great extent, the whole issue was treated as good entertainment, not a serious problem (Nicholson 1970, 132). Certainly, there was no competition among the powers as to who would be the "pirate-taker-general" or the redeemer of the white slaves. Even the Russian czar Alexander I, who talked about a "holy alliance" in Europe based on the Christian gospels, did not signify he was willing to actively tackle (or was even capable of doing so) the problem of Barbary slavery.

But at the same time as Smith was lobbying for the Christian slaves, Castlereagh endeavored to convince the powers to abolish the Atlantic slave trade on grounds of its inhumanity and immorality. The latter viewed Castlereagh's efforts variously. The Spanish and the Portuguese—the major slave-trading nations—were convinced that the English aimed to prevent them from replenishing the supply of slaves to their colonies after the war, while the British colonies had already been stocked with large numbers of slaves before 1807. Thus, the British were suspected of trying to gain an advantage over the other colonial powers. The French, on their part, resented the British stipulation of returning their occupied colonies in exchange for an abolition of the black slave trade. On the other hand, the noncolonial powers—mainly Austria, Prussia, and Russia—had no embedded interests in the slave trade, and Castlereagh hoped to win their support for abolition and thus create a moral pressure on the Spanish, French, and Portuguese. The moral support of Russia, the preeminent continental power, was regarded by the British as highly important in this context.

The Austrians and Prussians were rather indifferent to Castlereagh's appeals, but the czar was more open to moralistic arguments and supportive of the cause of abolition (though he also hoped to win some concessions from Britain in Europe in return for his support for abolitionism). Already before the congress, the leader of British abolitionists, William Wilberforce, obtained the support of the czar (Reich 1968, 130), and during the congress Alexander reassured Castlereagh by promising him he would pressure the colonial powers to shorten the interim period (between five and eight years) that they demanded for the abolition of the slave trade (Webster 1921, 275). However, the czar also asked Castlereagh what Britain intended to do about white slavery. Thus, it happened that Smith's public relations campaign for freeing Christian slaves ran concurrent to and came into conflict with London's call for abolition. Soon, the representatives of Spain and Portugal realized that the issue of white slavery could be used to ease the British pressure on their countries to abolish their slave trade.

> Rightly or wrongly, the ministers of the Powers most nearly concerned saw in this proposal [to abolish the black slave trade] yet another instance of English hypocrisy. They scented sharp practice. When assured that the English attitude was purely philanthropic, they asked why English philanthropy only concerned itself with black slaves? They wished to know what the foremost naval power had done to abolish white slavery in North Africa. To these unkind questions Castlereagh had no immediate reply. But he was resolved that the questions should not be asked again when he next returned to the charge. (Parkinson 1934, 423–24)

Even after the closure of the Congress of Vienna, in March 1816, when the British renewed talks with the other powers on the abolition of the slave trade, Castlereagh was confronted again with "unkind" questions regarding the Barbary pirates' slave trade.[11] In particular, the czar raised the issue of Christian slavery in Barbary. Thus, "[u]nfortunately for Castlereagh, time-consuming, and ultimately futile talks about the pirates side-tracked the conferences" (Kielstra 2000, 64).

Back in Vienna, in February 1815, the British obtained a declaration against the slave trade from the other major participants in the congress: France, Spain, Russia, Portugal, Prussia, Austria, and Sweden. In this declaration, which was annexed to the official Final Act of the Congress of Vienna as Article XV, the powers denounced the slave trade and committed to abolish it. They declared the slave trade "repugnant to the principles of humanity and universal morality" and claimed that at last "the public voice, in all civilized countries, called aloud for its suppression." The powers maintained that it was their "duty and necessity" to abolish the slave trade, which they considered a "scourge which has so long desolated Africa, degraded Europe, and afflicted humanity."[12]

But the French, Spaniards, and Portuguese signed this declaration only half-heartedly. Their colonies in the West Indies and South America were highly dependent upon slave labor, and strong domestic interests in their countries objected to the abolition of human traffic (Murray 1980). Thus, the Congress of Vienna merely declared a general intention of the powers to abolish the slave trade. This declaration had important value for Britain, however, because it represented a framework in which future negotiations on the abolition of the slave trade would take place. But the British also painted themselves into a corner in this issue. By vehemently demanding that other states accept British moral principles, they had to take on the role of exacting costs from those who deviated from them.

Although the Atlantic slave trade was not considered by Britain to be a violation of the laws of war (the Africans kidnapped into slavery were not subjects of recognized states,[13] and hence these laws did not apply to them), Algiers's slave trade was eventually understood by Britain as a deviance from these laws. I shall further elaborate on this point later, but here it is important to note that taking slaves and captives for ransom purposes during war was gradually delegitimized in Europe in the eighteenth century. Moreover, targeting civilians in war was also increasingly delegitimized over that period. These two facts enabled the representatives of Spain and Portugal at the Congress of Vienna to turn the practice of the Barbary corsairs into an embarrassment for Britain and thus to compromise the British call for universal abolition of the slave trade. Consequently, for Britain to augment its moral authority, it had to exact the cost for deviance from Algiers—which persistently refused to abolish its enslaving of Europeans. In other words, while the Spanish and the Portuguese did not openly defy British authority—after all, they signed the declaration against the slave trade and were (although reluctantly) ready to negotiate its abolition—the Algerians completely defied Britain, and therefore they undermined Britain's authority over the European colonial powers.

As mentioned before, prior to the Congress of Vienna, the British did not consider the issue of Christian slavery in Barbary to be their problem. Moreover, Britain perceived Algiers, Tunis, and Tripoli as legitimate polities in international politics. It is important to note here that from the late seventeenth century, the British, and also other European powers, entered into international legal treaties with the Barbary regencies. Although the regencies were nominally known as vassals of the Ottoman sultan, the Europeans treated them as "states," "city-states," "famous cities," "warlike cities," "powers," and "kingdoms." Of course, there were two main reasons for entering into treaties with the Barbary polities: first, to exempt one's nationals and commerce from the corsairs' depredations, and, second, to divert the latter's violence to rival European states. This recognition in the Barbary communities also had the effect of legitimizing the corsairs as lawful actors in war—thus turning them into privateers. However, the problem was that the governments of the Barbary regencies or states were often too weak to discipline the corsairs, who, as we have seen, time and again disregarded the agreements and treaties that their nominal rulers signed with the Europeans.

In Europe during the late seventeenth and the eighteenth centuries, privateering increasingly became a practice regularized and supervised by the state. Although private men-of-war continued to play a significant role in maritime warfare and conflict, nonstate activity in this sphere came more and more under the control of the state (Thomson 1994; Ritchie 1997). Privateers had to provide securities for their good behavior and abide by growing lists of regulations. Admiralty and prize courts were established in each seafaring nation, and usually the application of international prize law was uniform. Established prize courts procedures usually guaranteed that privateers would not stray from their commissions. Only after a prize court decided that the privateer's seized vessel and goods were a legitimate prize could the privateer dispose of them and sell them at auction. "The privateer had a strong incentive to follow the rules and bring the prize before the court to be legally condemned. That gave the privateer legal title, without which the prize would have been stable only at a discount and the privateer legally defined as a pirate—a crime punishable by death" (Anderson and Gifford 1991, 110). In fact, European prize courts accepted each other's decisions as legitimate. Prize courts routinely released neutral ships captured illegally and also obliged privateers to compensate the owners of illegal prizes. Neutral rights were reasonably well protected, and the basic principles of prize law were accepted internationally (ibid., 112).

The Barbary regencies, on the other hand, were considered by many Europeans as piratical states precisely because of their "general lack of adherence to the niceties of prize courts and other aspects of Admiralty law" (Woodward 2004, 601). But the powerful maritime states, namely Britain and France, cared little about such infringements and deviations because they benefited from them and at this time did not claim a role of formal authority in the international system ("legalized hegemony"). Moreover, war was still endemic in the eighteenth century (Tilly 1990, 72), and European states often broke and violated peace treaties on various pretexts. Europeans continued to perceive war as a normal part of their lives (Anderson 1995, 212). And, finally, although the corsairs' practice of piracy and slave taking was increasingly denounced in Europe on moral grounds (Thomson 1987, 123–42), no strong social norms or binding legal concepts were in place yet against such conduct. The corsairs enslaved civilians (of weak European states), but that was still not in complete opposition to the prevailing norms and laws of war of the period: "Thus the immediate commercial interest of each state (and in particular the most powerful, namely the British, French, and Dutch) is stronger than their humanitarian feelings, and the English care little if the Spaniards are enslaved as long as their own shipping and profits are safe" (ibid., 128, citing d'Arvieux, an eighteenth-century writer). Therefore, throughout most of the eighteenth century, the corsairs were at most abusing the developing laws of war. In general, toward the end of the eighteenth century, "the Regency of Algiers, like the other Barbary states, floats somewhere, in the eyes of the Europeans, between barbarism and civilization" (ibid., 98). They were seen as "impolite" and "rude," but were not conceived as savages (ibid.). They were seen as thieves rather than violators of human rights.[14] This perception of the Barbary regencies seems to fit the parasitic category of PATH and hence may help to explain the fact that European states tried to buy the corsairs off (by treaties) or that at most sent limited naval expeditions against them.

The main rationale behind the wars declared and waged by the Barbary regencies was to take captives for slavery and ransom and, later, to extract tribute. We have seen how the Algerian emissary to Spain bragged about his regency's "enormous profits" from the Spanish. The words of the Tripolitan bashaw in 1801 to the American consul are also revealing in this context: "[A]ll nations pay me," he exaggerated, adding that he knew his "friends" (i.e., tributaries) by the value of their "presents" (U.S. Congress 1832, 350). On the other hand, in Europe in the eighteenth century, wars between European states assumed a "public" nature of raison d'état (Schroeder 1994, 8) and were not conducted for ransom or captive-taking ends nor for the enrichment of specific individuals as such. In this context, norms and legal codes on how to treat prisoners of war solidified. The idea developed that

> captivity was a device whereby the prisoner [of war] was to be prevented from returning to his own force and conducting the fight again. As a corollary to this idea it came to be accepted that the prisoner [of war] was not a criminal but a man pursuing an honorable calling who had had the misfortune to be captured. The practical implication of this was that the prisoner [of war] should

not be put in irons and thrown into a penal establishment with the local convicts. (Levie 1978, 101)

Ransoming prisoners of war continued in Europe until the late eighteenth century. The British and the French, for example, still ransomed prisoners of war from each other as late as 1780 (Anderson 1960). But this was due to the "strong moral duty of every State to provide for the release of such of its citizens and allies as have fallen into the hands of the enemy. . . . This is a care which the State owes to those who have exposed themselves in her defence" (Baker 1908, 28).

But the purpose or reason for taking prisoners of war was not the only distinction between the Europeans and the Algerians (obstructing the rival's war effort versus extracting ransom): the difference in the treatment of captives was also marked. Indeed, European armies had not always been humane toward their prisoners of war. In 1799, for example, Napoleon ordered the massacre of three thousand Ottoman prisoners of war in Jaffa. However, such cases increasingly became exceptional. In addition, European states and armies devised formal codes and agreements as to the treatment of prisoners of war. Thus, the first peacetime attempt to define the protection of prisoners of war—in the event that the then friendly relations between the two countries should be disturbed by war—was most likely the 1785 Prussia-U.S. Treaty of Amity and Commerce. The treaty provided an article (XXXIV) on how "to prevent the destruction of prisoners of war." Seven years later, in 1792, the French National Assembly enacted a decree that attempted unilaterally to establish a formal code of humanitarian rules governing the treatment of prisoners of war. This code declared prisoners of war to be under the safeguard and protection of the French nation. All cruel acts, violence, or insults committed against a prisoner of war were to be punished as if committed against a French citizen (Levie 1978, 101). Generally, by the late eighteenth century, the killing of prisoners of war became "obsolete among all civilized nations" and the practice of selling prisoners of wars into slavery had "fallen into disuse" (Baker 1908, 24, 26). At least among the colonial powers, which significantly increased their African slave trade during the eighteenth century, the role of developing norms and morals in this context cannot be disregarded; after all, the British and the French could have sent their captives to their colonies as slaves or indentured workers. The British did send convicts to penal colonies in Australia (since the 1780s), where they were condemned to unpaid hard work. On the other hand, prisoners of war were spared from such a fate.

Furthermore, not only were military prisoners of war treated in a more restrained manner and according to more formal and binding norms, but civilians as well received better treatment during the eighteenth and early nineteenth centuries. Because warfare in this time was that of movement, few sieges took place, which meant that civilians were less involved in combat. There is little evidence that soldiers attacked civilians: "For all their passion, the French revolutionary and Napoleonic Wars were in the context of modern warfare relatively civilized" (Browning 2002, 47). In addition, military planners and commanders during the eighteenth century seriously worked to keep civilian society from war's havoc. Fredrick the Great of Prussia believed that the civilian population should not even be aware when a state of war existed (Holsti 1991, 103). Plundering civilian property increasingly came to be regarded as a war crime (Baker 1908, 36–37). Eighteenth-century armies became much more disciplined and organized than their sixteenth- and seventeenth-century predecessors, a fact that significantly reduced the ravaging of civilians. War became more "scientific" and less arbitrary (Gat 1989), and while the French Revolutionary and Napoleonic regimes transformed war in important ways (socially, organizationally, and ideologically), even Napoleon's armies usually refrained from harassing and plundering civilians (Veale 1993, 115). Moreover, "[a]fter the Congress of Vienna . . . military dispositions tended to revert to pre-revolutionary patterns" (Holsti 1991, 156). Thus, a great deal of the "restoration" work of the Congress of Vienna actually dealt with reestablishing the principles of European laws of war (Schmitt 2004, 13).

In such an institutional environment, "enlightened" opinion considered the continued existence of the Barbary corsairs to be the fault of European governments' self-interests. "The usual corollary of this belief was that [the corsairs] could only be destroyed by the action of the same European governments" (Thomson 1987, 130–31). Now, even if Spain and Portugal did not share such enlightened principles and beliefs, they actually capitalized on them and thus embarrassed Britain, which portrayed itself as the most moral leader of Europe and demanded that the other Europeans accept British morality by virtue of Britain's position as a Great Power.

Turning back to the Congress of Vienna, Napoleon's escape from his prison in March 1815 and his usurpation of power in Paris diverted Europe's and Britain's attention from other issues, including that of the Barbary corsairs. The dramatic escape of Napoleon from his exile in Elba and the renewed revolutionary threat from France led Britain to focus on containing this threat. Though Napoleon was incapable of invading Britain in June 1815, it was clear that his return meant the shattering of the settlement of the Congress of Vienna and the resumption of war in Europe, as Russia, Prussia, and Spain were eager to revenge and abolish any chance of future French aggression. The whole order of Vienna could have collapsed, to the detriment of Britain (Schroeder 1994, 549–52). Napoleon had already shown his intentions and capabilities to turn Europe from a Lockean system into a Hobbesian one, and therefore he represented a predatory threat of the first degree that precluded any other armed efforts. The Barbary expedition had to be postponed until the pacification of Europe.

However, after Waterloo, Admiral Smith renewed his diplomatic campaign against the Barbary pirates. Again, he bombarded sovereigns and officials with letters calling them to act against white slavery in Algiers and Barbary. Once more, Castlereagh, ever soliciting for more concessions from the slave-trading powers and obtaining the czar's support, found himself dealing with the issue of Algiers. In a letter to Lord Cathcart, Britain's ambassador at St. Petersburg, he notes,

> Your lordship will perceive that it is only by making the Slave Trade and the question of the Barbary Powers go *pari passu,* that we can fully meet the wishes of the Emperor [the czar] and the other Powers, who press the latter point as one of universal interest. I think his Imperial Majesty will enter cordially into the views of the British Government upon thus combining them in one common cause, and I have no doubt, if we all draw heartily together, upon the broad ground of giving repose upon Christian principles to the human race, of whatever colour, and in every part of the globe, that we shall do ourselves credit, and render a lasting service to mankind. May 28th, 1816. (quoted in Vane 1851, 255)

Later on, in a letter to Count Capo d'Istrisa, a close adviser in foreign affairs to Czar Alexander, Castlereagh hints at the Spanish and Portuguese critique of the British so-called double standard with regards to black versus white slavery. He maintains that "we may defy moral criticism if our execution shall correspond to the principles we profess . . . the Prince Regent feels, as he doubts not the Emperor will feel, a moral obligation not to sacrifice a principle which he has professed in the face of Europe, even to those two [Spain and Portugal]; and his Royal Highness doubly feels this duty to be imperative upon him when he is associating himself in an alliance against the States of Africa [i.e., the Barbary Powers]" (quoted in Vane 1851, 301, 303).[15] This alliance was a British plan, dated from August 1816, for an international naval league with the dual purpose of suppressing the Barbary pirates and the slave trade. The marquis d'Osmond, the French representative at the antislave trade conferences of the Great Powers, believed that the British proposal was so unattainable that its real purpose was merely publicity (Kielstra 2000, 65). But, evidently, the British were serious in their intentions, as the August 27 bombardment of Algiers demonstrated. On September 20, 1816, the representatives of the five Great Powers drafted in London a treaty on the right of search on slave-carrying vessels and also called for a seven-year maritime alliance "with an international force and a joint commander-in-chief under a five power control commission, which would respond militarily to any outrage the Barbary corsairs committed" (ibid.). The antipirate league did not in the end materialize, mainly due to French objections to it. France saw the league as an "excess of humiliation," as it would expose its naval weakness, place French vessels under British command, and give the impression that Britain used its territory to exert maritime supremacy (ibid., 67).

It is evident that Britain was sensitive to other states' demands in return for the abolition of their slave trade and to the need to persuade foreign public opinion in British moral sincerity. In a letter from October 1815, titled "On Forcing Abolition of Foreign Powers," Castlereagh notes:

> The more I have occasion to observe the temper of Foreign Powers on the question of abolition, the more strongly impressed I am with the sense of prejudice that results, not only to the interests of the question itself but to our foreign relations generally, from the display of popular impatience which has excited and is kept alive in England on the subject. It is impossible to persuade foreign nations that this sentiment is unmixed with views of Colonial policy; and their cabinets that can better estimate the real and virtuous motives which guide us on this question, see in the very impatience of the Nation a powerful instrument through which they expect to force at a convenient moment the British Government upon some favorite object of policy. (quoted in Ward and Gooch 1922, 971)

Thus, the link between the issue of the Barbary pirates and the abolition of the Atlantic slave trade was eventually also understood by abolitionists and other reformers within Britain. While the most notable abolitionist, Wilberforce, ignored the subject even after Smith's direct appeals to him, others brought the problem before Parliament and the press. Through their narratives, we can trace the effect of foreign allusions to British moral inconsistency. It should be remembered that during the Congress of Vienna the British not only tried to obtain universal abolition of the Atlantic slave trade but also strove to persuade the other powers to define the slave trade as piracy (Allison 1861, 582). Hence, the continuation of Barbary piracy and slavery (which were virtually inseparable) became a test of British sincerity regarding the general issue of the slave trade. Members of Parliament Brougham, Acland, Smith, Cochrane, and Ward (three of them professed abolitionists) reproved the government for its toleration of the piracy and slave trade of Algiers, and, with regard to Exmouth's April ransoming of slaves from Algiers without securing a complete abolition of white slavery there, they noted that if Britain had sanctioned such agreements with pirates, "a great stain would be fixed on her character and consequence injuries to her reputations and honour could not fail to arise from such an arrangement [that] acknowledged the right of depredation exercised by the barbarians, by providing a ransom for the slaves whom they had made" (*Parliamentary Debates* 1816, 34:1147).

If the slave trade was branded by Britain as piracy, how could Britain ask other states to abolish their trade while allowing the Algerians, who increasingly were seen now in Europe as pirates (Thomson 1987, 130), to continue enslaving white Christians? How could Britain make treaties with pirates? Already seventeen years before these events, Nelson exclaimed, "My blood boils that I cannot chastise these pirates. They could not show themselves in the Mediterranean did not our country permit. Never let us talk of the cruelty of the African slave trade while we permit such a horrid war" (quoted in Perkins and Douglas-Morris 1982, 35). Now, in 1816, the *Edinburgh Review* noted that Exmouth's April ransoming of Christian slaves from Barbary "is a tacit permission given by England to whatever depredations the Barbarians may commit upon all the vessels and coasts not protected by these treaties. In what other light can the affair be viewed by the rest of Europe?" (1816, 455).

Europe probably viewed the issue as a test of British moralistic credibility and obligation as a Great Power. The *Annual Register* thus noted that "it has long been a topic of reproach, which foreigners have brought against the boasted maritime supremacy of England, that the piratical states of Barbary have been suffered to exercise their ferocious ravages upon all the inferior powers navigating the Mediterranean sea, without any attempt on the part of the mistress of the ocean to control them, *and reduce them within the limits prescribed by the laws of civilized nations*" (1816, 97; emphasis added). The *Times* (June 29, 1816) wrote, "The violences of the Barbary powers are the subject of much and just complaint throughout Europe; and as usual, when assistance is needed, England is looked up to for it. The inferior powers have been so long accustomed to our gratuitous exertions in their favour, that they seem to consider themselves entitled to demand them as a matter of right, and even to heap reproaches on us in case of delay." And the *Quarterly Review* complained against the "easy complacency the grandees and ministers of foreign powers impose this quixotic enterprize on England, who of all nations in the western hemisphere should be the last to trouble herself about it [i.e., in material harms terms]." Resenting public opinion in Europe, the *Quarterly* mentioned that the *Frankfurt Gazette* considered Britain responsible for the continuance of Barbary piracy and slavery: "England, which by a nod[16] could make all these thieves retire into their dens—England which possesses Malta and the Seven Islands, will never wash away the disgrace of having riveted the chains of Europe." And relating to the arguments about the link between the abolition of black slavery and white slavery, the *Quarterly* strongly argued that "it is not to be endured that the accredited agents of Spain and Portugal should presume to say that because England abolished the Negro slave trade, it is her duty to put an end to the slavery of the Whites—that she should embroil herself in hostilities and fight the battles of those grateful nations, in the North of Africa, that they may undisturbingly carry on the Black slave trade in the south!" (*Quarterly Review* 1816, 140, 141, 145).

In view of this evidence, it is my opinion that Smith's transnational campaign actually constructed a new British interest with regard to the corsairs of Algiers and the issue of white slavery there. His arguments presented a serious challenge to the new agenda that the British government wished to advance internationally: he exposed the atrocities of the Barbary corsairs exactly at a time when Britain portrayed itself as the world's most moral nation and adopted the identity of abolitionism. Furthermore, an expectation was created that Britain, the world's leading sea power, would employ this power in a cause that was now understood as a "European" one. This means that—contrary to the neorealist argument about the lack of specialization among states in international anarchy—the very possession of certain power capabilities can at times vest a state with a specialized duty in international politics.

The British government surely understood its absurd position with regard to the pirates and had to embrace Smith's call for an operation against the corsairs, if only to save face. For the other powers to accept the sincerity of the British effort against slavery, the latter had to demonstrate consistency in this matter. Showing moral consistency was the best means to buttress British Great Power authority. This was all the more important because the Algerians openly refused to abide by the British demand to abolish their Christian slave trade. Thus, from being allies the Barbary pirates became a burden for the British government. They had to be spectacularly punished in order to validate Britain's authority. This change of tide was evident even on the pages of the *Courier*—the news magazine that "had the closest connection with the government, and was indeed looked upon throughout Europe as its official organ. It certainly inserted news or opinions to which the government desired to give publicity" (Webster 1963, 26). Thus, on July 6, 1816, the *Courier* published "[r]ecitals of the deplorable situation, cruel treatment and horrid sufferings of the white slaves in Africa," furnished by none other than Admiral Sir Sidney Smith. When reporting about the parliamentary debate on Algiers, the *Courier* noted, "[A]t length the crisis of indignant Europe [has] resounded in the English Parliament; the voice of outraged humanity has prevailed over false political considerations and vengeance is about to reach the pirates of the coast of Africa. The time is passed, when Algiers, rich in the spoils of her Christians, could say in the avarice of her heart, 'I keep the sea under my laws, and the nations are my prey.' She is about to be attacked in her walls, like the bird of prey in her nest" (September 14, 1816).

Had Britain not acted decisively against the corsairs, the legitimacy of its call for the abolition of black slavery could have been seriously questioned. I suspect that the legitimacy of other British demands would have been undermined too, as the abolition of the slave trade occupied such a central place in Britain's diplomacy in Vienna. Skeptics already argued that Britain allowed its Barbary allies to continue their profits from slavery and piracy, serving as a British proxy against other nations, while Britain itself pressed other states to abolish the human traffic due to selfish reasons. We have already seen how the British were sensitive to their moral credibility and authority. Castlereagh, Britain's then chief international negotiator, especially treated the issue as a test of his country's sincerity and credibility. As Alastair I. Johnston argues, state agents (diplomats, decision makers, etc.) are very susceptible to criticism of moral integrity (2001, 506). Thus, in a letter to Exmouth following the Algiers operation, Castlereagh notes, "You have contributed to place the Character of the Country above all suspicion of mercenary policy, the great achievements of the War had not eradicated some lurking suspicion that we cherish'd Piracy as a commercial Ally; you have dispelled this cloud and I have no doubt the National Character in Europe will be Essentially Enobled by your Services" (quoted in Parkinson 1934, 467).

Britain's eagerness to show the world—and itself—that it had removed the stain on its moral character was manifested in its Parliament and press, which were monitored closely in Europe and by foreign governments. Following the success of Exmouth in Algiers, the British newspapers widely cited his official report that related how he and his men were "humble instruments in the hands of Divine Providence for bringing to reason a ferocious Government, and destroying for ever the insufferable system of Christian slavery. [The fleet] has poured the *vengeance of an insulted nation*, in chastising the cruelties of a ferocious Government, with a promptitude beyond example, and highly honourable to the national character, eager to resent oppression or cruelty" (*Times*, September 16, 1816; emphasis added). On February 3, 1817, the House of Commons even passed a special formal and unanimous Vote of Thanks to Exmouth and his men and also to the Dutch force that cooperated with them (*Parliamentary Debates* 1817, 36:177). The inclusion of foreigners in a Vote of Thanks—itself a solemn event—was unprecedented and indicated Britain's effort to publicize the expedition and highlight its cosmopolitan and humanitarian nature. The words of member of Parliament the Duke of Clarence on this occasion attest to this effort:

> it has often been asserted, by foreign states, that, in our maritime pursuits, we always fought and acted for ourselves alone. But all the nations of Europe could now judge, whether Great Britain, in sending out viscount Exmouth on this service, was not actuated by a pure feeling of humanity towards the rest of the world? By this act, Great Britain had proved, that she could and would exert herself to protect the rights of the seas against those who invade them unlawfully. (*Parliamentary Debates* 1816, 33:217)

We should remember that the debates of the British Parliament were thoroughly covered by the press in Europe, to the extent that the renowned French publicist Pradt noted, "Tant que nous aurons un Parlement en Angleterre, il y aura une tribune pour toute l'Europe" (As long as we will have a Parliament in England, there will be a platform for all Europe) (1815, 51). In addition to the parliamentary vote, Exmouth and his officers had many honors bestowed upon them and became popular celebrities for many months, as newspaper articles, operas, stage plays, and popular pamphlets described in detail their exploits in Barbary. This warm welcome strongly implies that the British public perceived the Algiers operation as a just cause, a moral war, and a face-saving operation. The attack on Algiers was also discussed in the series of international ambassadorial conferences hosted by the British between September and November 1816 on the abolition of the slave trade (Satow 1923, 45).

The attack on Algiers thus symbolized and validated Britain's delegitimization of all forms of piracy and the slave trade. At first, Britain simply attempted to threaten and cajole the pirates into releasing the Christian slaves (April–May 1816). We have seen that a direct attack on Algiers was perceived as a challenging mission. Probably the British government preferred first to use nonviolent measures, such as threats or bribes, to ward off the criticism against its forbearance of Barbary piracy while avoiding real risks. And, indeed, the Algerian dey sensed this and did not budge in front of the British show of force. However, the agreements that Exmouth negotiated with the piratical city-states only fostered more criticism against Britain, suggesting that it actually helped to perpetuate the system of slavery and ransoming. Exmouth returned to London, only to be immediately sent back to Algiers, but this time with orders to deliver the full blow. Appeasing international and domestic discontent about the results of the first expedition was crucial to the government's decision to seriously clamp down on Algiers in the second.

The British resolution to end Algiers's slave trade and the rigorous commands under which Exmouth operated in August are also evident from the following relation:

> After the British bombardment ended, when the *dey* released the Christian slaves, it came to the knowledge of Lord Exmouth that two Spaniards, the one a Merchant and the other the Vice Consul of that Nation, had not been released but were still held by the *dey* in very severe custody, on pretence that they were Prisoners for debt.
>
> The inquiries which his Lordship felt himself called upon to

make into these cases, satisfied him that the confinement of the Vice Consul was groundless and unjustifiable, and he therefore thought himself authorized to demand his release under the Articles of the Agreement for the deliverance of all Christian Prisoners.

It appear that the Merchant was confined for an alleged debt, on the score of a contract with the Algerine Government; but the circumstances under which the contract was stated to have been forced on the Individual, and the great severity of the confinement he suffered, determined his Lordship to make an effort on his favour also.

This his Lordship did, by requesting his release from the *dey*, offering himself to guarantee to the *dey* the payment of any sum of money which the merchant should be found to owe to his highness.

The *dey*, having rejected this demand and offer, his Lordship, still unwilling to have recourse to extremities, and the renewal of hostilities, proposed that the Spaniards should be released from irons, and the miserable dungeons in which they were confined; and that they should be placed in the custody of the Spanish Consul, or at least, that the Consul should be permitted to afford them such assistance and accommodation as was suitable to their rank in life.

These propositions the *dey* also positively refused; and Lord Exmouth then felt, that the private and pecuniary nature of the transactions for which these Persons were confined, must be considered as a pretence for the continuance of a cruel and oppressive system of Slavery, *the total and bona fide abolition of which his instructions directed him to insist upon.*

He, therefore, acquainted the *dey*, that His Highness having rejected all the fair and equitable conditions proposed to him on this point, his Lordship has determined to insist on the unconditional release of the two Spaniards. He therefore desired an answer, yes or no; and in the event of the latter, stated, that he would immediately recommence hostilities; and his Lordship made preparations for that purpose.

These measures had the desired effect, and the 2 Persons were released from a long and severe captivity; so that no Christian Prisoner remained at Algiers at his Lordship's departure. (*British and Foreign State Papers 1815–16,* 1838, 520–21; emphasis added)

This relation clearly demonstrates that Exmouth was instructed by his government to fully insist on the release of *all* the Christian captives—so as not to leave any doubt about British moral credibility and authority. The practice of Christian slavery and captivity in Algiers had to be abolished completely to block any future critique on Britain's moral authority. Otherwise, how can we explain Exmouth's willingness to resume hostilities on behalf of two persons only?

It is interesting to note in the context of the authority predicament that, after the cessation of hostilities, Exmouth also forced the dey to sign a declaration on the abolition of Christian slavery. I believe that this declaration, dated August 27, 1816, is highly revealing in the context of Great Power authority and the institutions of violence. The declaration states:

> His Highness, the *dey* of Algiers, in token of his sincere desire to maintain inviolable his friendly relations with Great Britain, and *to manifest his amicable disposition and high respect towards the powers of Europe,* declares that in the event of future Wars with any European Power, not any of the Prisoners shall be consigned to Slavery, but treated with all humanity as *Prisoners of War,* until regularly exchanged according to *European practice in like cases,* and that at the termination of hostilities, they shall be restored to their respective Countries without ransom; *and the practice of condemning Christian Prisoners of War to slavery is hereby formally and for ever denounced.* (*British and Foreign State Papers, 1815–16,* 1838, 517; emphasis added)

Not only were the British content with the Algerians releasing the last of the Spaniard prisoners, but they also made the *dey* declare that he respected the powers of Europe, for whom Britain acted as an enforcer and representative. In other words, the British tried to portray their punishment of Algiers as a *European* act of the Great Powers. The British schemes for an international league against the pirates later in that year also followed this line of policy. I suspect that the reason for this was the augmentation of British moral credibility and legitimacy in the face of the allegation that Britain connived with corsair slave trade and piracy. The declaration of the dey to treat prisoners of war according to European standards actually meant that Algiers was forced to denounce the practice of declaring war for the purpose of taking prisoners per se, and it pointed to the immense pressure the dey was under—he was willing to risk his life and comply with the British commands. Again, this attests to the British desire to bolster moral credibility in the eyes of European peers and nonpeers.

Also interesting in the context of authority is the professed self-restraint of Britain and the distinction between the dey and the civilian population of Algiers. During the eighteenth century, Europe began to distinguish between the Turkish ruling elite of Algiers—which was not native to Algiers and was recruited in the Ottoman Empire—and the Arab and Berber peoples who came under the rule of the Turks. Thus, after the bombardment, Exmouth sent a note to the dey: "As England does not war for the destruction of Cities, I am unwilling to visit your personal cruelties upon the inoffensive Inhabitants of the Country, and I therefore offer you the same terms of peace which I conveyed to you yesterday, in my Sovereign's name. Without the acceptance of these terms, you can have no Peace with England" (*British and Foreign State Papers, 1815–16*, 1838, 518). The message also carries a clear ethical content: Britain considers the dey to be responsible for the cruelties of the Christian slave trade and thus will not destroy the city of Algiers. The dey and his corsair associates—but not the inoffensive civilian population of Algiers—are at war with Britain. It is easy to see the similarity between this and the "personal" war of the United States against Saddam Hussein in 2003.

III. Conclusions

The Algerian corsair case discussed in this chapter showed that a Great Power's armed intervention against PATHs can result from the need to preserve moral authority, even if the PATHs do not cause any material harm to the Great Power itself. I agree with Kaufmann and Pape (1999) that the domestic reform movement was the crucial factor behind the British international campaign against the slave trade in general. But I find that Britain's interest to intervene against slavery in Algiers was mainly constructed by the need to avoid moral inconsistency in the broader context of the Atlantic abolition and the reconstruction of the European order in Vienna. Once abolition became a central British foreign policy goal, especially during and after the Congress of Vienna, it changed that country's interests toward Algiers. What really mattered for Britain was not the fate of the white slaves in Barbary. This problem was well known before 1816, and had the British wanted to do something about it, they would not have had to wait for Admiral Smith's campaign. Instead, the intervention was driven by the desire to refute allegations of moral inconsistency and double standards, as well as to legitimize British power and demands from the smaller states (namely, Spain and Portugal) and to win the moral approval of the Russians for these demands. As we have seen, Castlereagh understood that the question of white slavery was intrinsically connected to the legitimacy of Britain's call for abolition of the black slave trade. In 1799, Nelson's blood truly boiled that he could not chastise the pirates, but it was not until other states doubted British moral credibility in regard to the abolition of the slave trade that Britain became convinced there was a problem with its policy (or, rather, lack of policy) toward the Barbary corsairs. Social pressure to avoid incongruity in its practice was enough to push Britain into a significant armed intervention against Algiers. The British could have simply denied or ignored the accusations against them. But Britain was willing to pay in "blood and treasure" to ward off allegations of double standards and to avoid the loss of Russia's support for abolitionism.

From the position of being a useful ally during the eighteenth century, Algiers came to be considered by Britain as a "bird of prey" in 1816. This predatory status derived not from any change in the practice of the corsairs as such but from the incongruity of this "horrid war" with the new international moral order Britain strove to establish. The corsairs had not changed their practice for centuries. But the formalization of Great Power authority in Vienna forced Britain to reconsider its definition of the Barbary sea-raiding communities. Even though the corsairs did not harm British subjects, the harm they caused other people and states was now understood in Britain as undermining the British efforts to abolish the slave trade. The issue of Algiers's piracy and slave trade was framed within this context and was also seen as a deviance from the laws of war. The open insistence of the Algerians not to "depart from the laudable customs of their forefathers" amounted now to a direct challenge to Britain's international authority and could have compromised the British campaign to abolish the Atlantic slave trade. When the Great Powers institute new norms and notions of legitimacy in international politics, actors that until then had been tolerated might be severely punished for refusing to transform themselves along with the new norms. In other words, when the institutions of violence change, smaller actors who do not keep pace with this change, or even overtly resist it, become a stumbling block for authority. Merely by continuing to do what they have always done, such actors now undermine Great Power authority by revealing inconsistencies and inefficiencies in it. This is what happened to the Algerian corsair community in 1816. Given how important the international abolition of the slave trade was to Britain, the British could no longer accept the "right of depredation exercised by the barbarians" and had to act decisively to persuade Europe in this. In effect, the punishment of Algiers served a double purpose. First, it removed any international doubt about British moral authority. Second, this punishment and its wide publication were meant to augment British authority in the European international society by revealing Britain as a protector and enforcer of weaker states' rights. Thus, beyond delivering itself from the embrace of moral inconsistency, Britain exploited the punishment of the pirates to solidify its authority as a Great Power with special rights and responsibilities. This case also shows that punishment has the function of reassuring not only significant others of the legitimacy of the bearer of authority but also the authoritative actor itself. Punishment validates the righteousness of the punishing actor and allows it to congratulate itself on the law and order it provides and guarantees. In other words, punishment brings order and stable expectations into social reality by highlighting the fact that one is capable of exacting costs from those that deviate from social norms. Thus punishment increases the ontological security of the punisher.

"This Country Will Define Our Times, Not Be Defined by Them"

9/11 and the War on Terror

The time is out of joint:—O cursed spite,
That ever I was born to set it right!
—Shakespeare, *Hamlet*

Few were surprised when the United States launched an intensive military campaign against al Qaeda and the Taliban in Afghanistan after 9/11. Immediately following the terror attacks on New York and Washington, President George W. Bush stated that the bombings were an act of war. A "war on terror" was declared. Four weeks later, the United States and Britain started intensive targeting of Afghanistan from the air, and, with the support of the Afghan Northern Alliance opposition forces, they toppled the Taliban regime in that country. Several thousand al Qaeda and Taliban members were killed between October 7, 2001, and March 17, 2002 (called Operation Enduring Freedom). Although far from being the only component of the War on Terror, the military phase of this campaign was probably the most publicized and visible. Domestic and foreign audiences alike seemed to anticipate the U.S. response, assuming it inevitable. Furthermore, among the various measures taken to secure America (such as improved intelligence, international law enforcement cooperation, increased border controls, and financial measures curtailing terror funding and money laundering), the military response was prioritized by the Bush administration as not only necessary but the most urgent (Woodward 2002).

The aim of this chapter is to account for the purpose and intensity of the American military response against al Qaeda and the Taliban in Afghanistan. One could rightly question the need for explication in this case. After all, the harm caused by the terrorists was immense, and the threat of further terror attacks seemed very real. Al Qaeda terrorists and their hosts, the Taliban regime in Afghanistan, had to be destroyed in order to prevent this from happening. Also, one could plausibly argue that the U.S. government sought revenge in order to pacify a shocked and infuriated American domestic public. While this may be true, I believe that a systemic perspective will reveal important aspects that have not been sufficiently studied in this case. It could explain why this kind of harm (i.e., terrorism) was perceived by the United States to warrant military retribution and armed self-defense when other kinds of transnational harm have not (think the drug trade). In this regard, I contend that the War on Terror in Afghanistan was in essence a *disciplinary* effort to reestablish and reproduce the relations of authority that existed in world politics prior to 9/11. Furthermore, beyond mere retaliation and self-defense, this war was also meant to restore shaken concepts of *authority* in world politics and to set right a time out of joint. In this chapter I will therefore highlight the motives of discipline and authority in the War on Terror.

The hypothesis to which I am opposing my Great Power authority argument throughout this book is the one that contends that the intensity and type of a Great Power's response to PATHs are directly related to the degree of material harm caused by the transnational actors and that the response rationally matches the goal of reducing harm by the most effective means in this regard. In the case of the United States and its War on Terror in Afghanistan, I want to point out that, although the material harm suffered by the United States due to terror was immense, the response was not purely rational in the sense outlined previously and that this can be accounted for by the predatory threat al Qaeda posed to U.S. authority.

In the first section of this chapter, I outline some of the points that in my view indicate that the war in Afghanistan consisted of certain elements that went beyond the mere rational consideration of countering terrorism through military force. I focus on three arguments that represent conventional military logic and then demonstrate the problems with applying them to the War on Terror in Afghanistan. In the sections that follow this discussion, I show how the conduct of the war can be accounted for from the perspective of the challenge to America's Great Power authority.

I. The Military Phase of the War on Terror in Afghanistan

A. "Afghanistan Contained Many Attackable Terrorist Targets and Infrastructures That Had to Be Destroyed in Order to Prevent Future Terror Attacks"

If the purpose of unleashing American military force in Afghanistan was to destroy al Qaeda's infrastructure for projecting transnational terrorist violence, then we have to note that during the four weeks between 9/11 and the launching of Operation Enduring Freedom on October 7 the utility of using military power against al Qaeda and its Taliban host was questioned by senior Bush administration officials. The problem was that "actionable targets"—that is, fixed military assets—barely existed in Afghanistan (see Biddle 2003). Dual-use facilities and infrastructures were also few and in bad condition, ruined by two decades of war (the 1979–89 Soviet war and the Afghan civil war that has raged since the withdrawal of the Soviets). Defense Secretary Donald Rumsfeld and National Security Adviser Condoleezza Rice reportedly doubted whether bombing Afghanistan would prove to be an effective measure from a military point of view: "Afghanistan was in the fifteenth century. Wipe out the first target set and [the United States would] be left pounding sand." And "[t]o lose a pilot for these low-value fixed and mud-hut targets made no sense" (Woodward 2002, 153, 179). Richard Clarke, then national coordinator for counterterrorism, claims that, while discussing Afghanistan in the war cabinet after 9/11, Rumsfeld "complained that there were no decent targets for bombing in Afghanistan, and that we should consider bombing Iraq, which, he said, had better targets" (Clarke 2004, 31). Further compromising the utility of bombing Afghanistan were the apprehensions of the Bush war cabinet that al Qaeda would perpetrate further terror attacks in the United States in retaliation (Woodward 2002, 151, 162, 194, 291).

During the war itself, the United States and its Afghan tribal allies indeed killed thousands of Taliban and hundreds of al Qaeda members in Afghanistan,[1] but "most of the al Qaeda facilities and most of the foreign troops under their control in Afghanistan had to do with the civil war there. Most of the organization's capabilities to conduct far reaching terrorist acts resided and resides outside of Afghanistan, and thus fell beyond the scope of Operation Enduring Freedom" (Conetta 2002, 4). This fact would most likely have been well known to the Bush administration before the war. Bob Woodward reports that, lacking almost any "actionable" al Qaeda targets in Afghanistan, U.S. military and intelligence experts suggested focusing on bombing the "Arab Brigade"—one thousand elite al Qaeda fighters who mainly served as a disciplining force to the rank and file of the Taliban militia (2002, 123). Other al Qaeda troops and operatives were difficult to detect, as the training camps of the organization were deserted immediately after 9/11 and most of the al Qaeda troops dispersed.

With regard to al Qaeda's training camps in Afghanistan, prior to 9/11 their bombing was not considered to have a significant military value. High officials in the Clinton administration's Pentagon questioned the military utility of bombing the camps and other al Qaeda infrastructures in Afghanistan. The training camps were referred to as "jungle gyms" and "mud huts." *The 9/11 Commission Report* notes that the Pentagon "felt . . . that hitting inexpensive and rudimentary training camps with costly missiles would not do much good and might even help al Qaeda if the strikes failed to kill Bin Laden" (National Commission on the Terrorist Attacks 2004, 196). The training camps, of course, were the same rudimentary facilities after 9/11. Consequently, at the time the terrorists hit New York and Washington, the U.S. military "did not have an off-the-shelf plan to eliminate the al Qaeda threat in Afghanistan" (ibid., 332).

B. "Territorial Sanctuaries Like Afghanistan Are Essential for al Qaeda's Terrorist Enterprise"

Terrorists indeed require some territory in which to live, hide, practice, and coordinate their terrorism. But Carl Conetta's words in this regard are very important to consider here:

> The capacity of Al Qaeda to repair its lost capabilities for global terrorism rests on the fact that terrorist attacks like the 11 September crashes do not depend on the possession of massive, open air training facilities. Warehouses and small *ad hoc* sites will do. Moreover, large terrorist organizations have proved themselves able to operate for very long periods without state sanctuaries—as long as sympathetic communities exist. The Irish Republican

Army is an example. Thus, Al Qaeda may be able to recoup its lost capacity by adopting a more thoroughly clandestine and "stateless" approach to its operations, including recruitment and training. (2002, 5)

In this context, U.S. policymakers, counterterror experts, and military planners could not have been unaware of two important points: the "balloon effect" and the record of inefficiency in other such cases of intense military counterterror measures.

The balloon effect is the tendency of transnational harmful networks to relocate their bases from regions and countries in which they are militarily pressed to other locations. In the War on Drugs, for example, Latin American drug producers and traffickers moved back and forth between Colombia, Ecuador, Peru, Bolivia, Panama, and Mexico after the governments of these countries applied increasing military pressures on the drug industry due to U.S. demands to militarize the counterdrug effort. Drug traffickers shifted to relatively unpoliced regions in these countries to continue their business. Afghanistan and its bordering countries, such as Pakistan, Iran, and Uzbekistan, contain many unpoliced areas like these, and indeed many al Qaeda operatives slipped into these regions during the war. Pentagon officials such as Secretary Rumsfeld and Joint Chiefs of Staff Chairman Richard Myers in fact compared the War on Terror to the War on Drugs, claiming it to be a long-term effort against a persistent and elusive transnational threat. If the two "transnational wars" were believed to share some characteristics, then the balloon effect must have been considered a possible outcome in the context of the War on Terror. It may be plausible to argue that the solution to this problem would simply be to squeeze the "balloon" so strongly that it could not slip into unpoliced corners but would rather explode—as indeed was the aim of the Afghan campaign (to kill as many of the terrorists as possible). But even if this was the purpose of the intensive bombardment, we must remember that it began four weeks *after* 9/11, when many terrorists had already slipped into neighboring and unpoliced countries and regions. Furthermore, and I return to this point later in this section, al Qaeda was known to be a loose network made up of "sleeper cells" spreading into more than sixty countries. Obviously, the balloon effect had already occurred before the United States launched its military campaign.

The second point is that, in previous counterterror campaigns, harsh military response and denial of territorial sanctuaries not only failed to eliminate the threat of further terrorist attacks but sometimes exacerbated it. In fact, the United States was usually critical of other states' intense military measures against terrorists precisely because of their relative inefficiency and the resulting escalation of regional conflicts. Russian intense military campaigns in Chechnya in 1995–96, for example, and the consequent installation of a "friendly" regime actually spurred deadly terror attacks in Moscow and other major Russian cities in the summer of 1999 (causing more than three hundred deaths). Similarly, Israel's expulsion of the PLO from its Lebanese sanctuary in 1982 resulted in a much more serious terrorist threat: the birth of Hizb'allah, an organization hardened and consolidated through two decades of fighting with the occupying Israeli army in southern Lebanon. Israel also continued to suffer from Hamas suicide bombings—which began as an imitation of Hizb'allah's suicide bombings in Lebanon—even after it had reconquered large shares of the West Bank and Gaza and ended Palestinian Authority "terrorist sanctuaries" there.[2] In fact, many of the suicide bombings were planned and launched from Israeli-occupied regions. Like many other terrorist organizations, Hamas thrived on the support of local communities *and* on Israeli countermeasures, such as the demolition of houses of the families of suicide bombers.[3] In this context, certain communities in the Muslim world doubtless remained sympathetic to al Qaeda and, more important, to the terrorists' ideas.

These two inadequacies with the "state sanctuary" argument would have been well known to the United States in the period following 9/11, thus raising doubts about its validity. But beyond this, and in the context of al Qaeda's specific character, the United States knew that the state sanctuary in Afghanistan was less important to global terrorism than state and territorial sanctuaries in the cases of more territorially bound terrorists. Al Qaeda, after all, was said to be a loose and networked enterprise of global terrorism, lacking a permanent attachment to any specific territory. Indeed, much of al Qaeda's planning for 9/11 was done outside of Afghanistan. Khalid Sheik Muhammad (KSM), the mastermind of the attacks, was actually a freelance or a roaming terrorist entrepreneur who spent most of his time outside of Afghanistan, and it was he who persuaded an initially skeptic al Qaeda leadership to adopt the "planes plan" (National Commission on the Terrorist Attacks 2004, 145–54). In this sense, al Qaeda was understood as a franchise operation *before* 9/11. The details of KSM's role in the planning of 9/11 were revealed only after his capture in Pakistan in March 2003. But it was known before the commencement of the war in Afghanistan that four of the 9/11 hijackers—including the operation's commander, Muhammad

Atta, and the other three pilots—actually hatched terrorist plans in Hamburg, Germany, where they immersed themselves for years—without al Qaeda's involvement—in fundamentalist Islam and jihadist ideology. Also, it became public knowledge almost immediately after the 9/11 attacks that the hijackers took flying lessons in U.S. flight schools and not in al Qaeda's Afghan camps. It was also later revealed that bin Laden actually selected the four pilots very quickly, "before comprehensive testing in the training camps or in operations" (ibid., 166).

Indeed, American officials constantly declared the enemy a loose and "faceless" network spreading into many countries. Already prior to 9/11, American counterterror officials conceived of bin Laden's organization as a "loose amalgam of people with a shared ideology, but a very limited direction."[4] After 9/11, in his speech to the joint session of Congress on September 20, 2001, President Bush noted that al Qaeda is a "collection of loosely affiliated terrorist organizations" spreading into more than sixty states, the United States included (Bush, 9/20/2001). Even in the aftermath of the major military operations in Afghanistan, the threat ascribed by the United States to al Qaeda was not considerably diminished—despite the fact that the terror network was supposedly denied its state sanctuary. CIA director George Tenet, as well as other experts and scholars, continued to warn that the threat from al Qaeda was still very potent (see Stern 2003). In fact, the Department of Homeland Security's "Threat Advisory System" raised the threat level six times from "elevated" to "high" between September 2002 and August 2004. Although many within the United States criticized the color system of the threat advisory, no one seriously questioned the continuing threat of terrorism. And, finally, despite the toppling of the Taliban regime in Afghanistan, the country and its borders clearly remain largely unpoliced and ruled by tribal warlords, so that neither the United States nor the Afghan government has control over much more than the capital city of Kabul. One cannot even say with certainty that the sanctuary of al Qaeda has been completely destroyed in that country. Despite this, the sense that the war the United States waged in Afghanistan was inevitable remained sound. Why?

C. "The Intensity of the Bombing of al Qaeda and the Taliban Was Commensurate with the Latter's Military Counterattack Potential and Actual Combat Operations"

Operation Enduring Freedom involved intense aerial bombings, hardly commensurate with the military counterattack measures taken by the enemy against U.S. bombers. Stephen Biddle argues that Taliban and al Qaeda troops and vehicles that were located by U.S. bombers were easy prey for precision-guided weapons launched from great distances and heights. "The result was slaughter" (2003, 35). Paradoxically, the military effort exerted in Afghanistan exceeded that of Operation Allied Force—the 1999 NATO intervention in Kosovo—even though the enemy in the earlier intervention (Serbia) was much stronger militarily than the Taliban and al Qaeda and its counterattack measures put NATO's attacking forces at much higher risk than the resistance in Afghanistan. Nonetheless, in Kosovo NATO aircrafts flew fourteen thousand offensive sorties, whereas in Afghanistan coalition aircrafts embarked upon more than seventeen thousand offensive sorties. U.S. aircrafts performed 60 percent of total sorties in Kosovo and 92 percent in Afghanistan (Cordesman 2002, 32). And twenty-three thousand missiles and bombs were dropped over Serbia (a total of sixty-three hundred tons of munitions), while the bombardment of Afghanistan consumed twenty-four thousand missiles and bombs (more than twelve thousand tons of munitions).[5] But while Serbia had an army of almost one hundred thousand soldiers and an air force of one hundred jets and thirty armed helicopters on top of modern air defense systems, an operational navy, and large armored forces, the Taliban and al Qaeda lacked almost any fighting aircraft and their total men in arms were estimated at forty-five thousand, most of them in lightly armed bands.[6] In Kosovo NATO needed two weeks to gain "air superiority," and the U.S. Department of Defense noted that the Serbian air defense systems "were among the most capable that U.S. forces have ever faced in combat."[7] On the other hand, in Afghanistan control of the air was achieved after only three days.

Due to the relative lack of fixed military facilities, most of the bombing in Afghanistan was directed against lightly armed convoys and regrouping infantry forces of the Taliban and al Qaeda. Often, precision-guided weapons weighing up to one thousand pounds were used to target single enemy trucks or light-armored vehicles. Less than twenty-five thousand of the Taliban and al Qaeda were serious fighters, and their training was largely in light arms, artillery, and light infantry combat. They possessed no real "beyond line of sight target capabilities, no meaningful night vision capability, and no armored or mechanized units larger than battalion size. The largest operational element seems to have had less than seventy tanks" (Cordesman 2002, 16). The destruction of this level of force hardly seems to require such massive bombing as the one the United States inflicted. One might argue that the intensity of the

more, *particularly dangerous is terrorism the aim of which is the usurpation of state power.*"[57] Putin already introduced the concept of a threat to civilization immediately after 9/11, stating that "this was a strike against the whole of humanity, at least against the entire civilized world, of which Russia considers itself a part."[58] Putin also stated (on September 17) that the attacks were an act of violence that can be "compared in scale and cruelty to what the Nazis perpetrated." By this he invoked images of the Russian-American alliance of World War II, the evil common enemy faced by both states, the need for active cooperation against this threat, and the requirement of total victory and "unconditional surrender" (O'Loughlin, Tuathail, and Kolossov 2004, 7). Also, immediately after the attacks of 9/11, the G8 heads of state declared, "We, the leaders of the G8, condemn in the strongest terms the barbaric acts of terrorism carried out against the United States. . . . The perpetrators, and all who have harbored, assisted or supported them by any means, have launched an offensive against innocent persons and against the central values and interests of the international community."[59] Chinese president Jiang Zemin described terrorism as a "common scourge" for the international community and as a challenge to mankind.[60] Even Cuba's Fidel Castro strongly denounced terrorism and offered his condolences to the United States. These denunciations of mass destruction terrorism, in addition to the actual practice of states against terror, highlight the essence of systemic conservatism.

V. Conclusions

Prince Klemens von Metternich, the Austrian prime minister during the 1815 Congress of Vienna, is remembered in history as a person who did his utmost to stop and reverse time. Metternich's prime goal was to suppress the emerging forces of nationalism and revolution and to restore the ancien régime. In the War on Terror in Afghanistan, the United States—like Metternich (and Hamlet)—attempted to set right a time out of joint. The purpose of the war was not only revenge, self-defense, or even deterrence. The war embodied a strong effort to restore previous notions of authority (as legitimized power) and thus to realign the course of time, to relegate the unthinkable that suddenly materialized with 9/11 to the realm of fantasy once again. This desire, I believe, stood at the heart of the preventive national security strategy that the United States officially adopted in 2002. In a sense, the war against terrorism was actually a war against time. As former secretary of state George Shultz wrote in an e-mail from March 2004 distributed worldwide by the Foreign Policy Research Institute, "First and foremost, we must shore up the state system. The world has worked for three centuries with the sovereign state as the basic operating entity. . . . Increasingly, the state system has been eroding. Terrorists have exploited this weakness. . . . Our great task is restoring the vitality of the state system."

From the political and symbolic points of view, if not from the military-operational perspective, the Afghan war succeeded. The Great Powers and the international community supported the war, and even Pakistan—the Taliban's major international ally up to 9/11—denounced the terrorists and the Taliban. In effect, the international community—including Arab states such as Egypt, Jordan, Bahrain, Qatar, and the United Arab Emirates—shared the U.S. definition of the terrorists and their hosts as "enemies of civilization" and thus reaffirmed U.S. authority, legitimizing the American effort to put the heads of the terrorists "on sticks."

But the war in Afghanistan did not eliminate the terror threat nor its accompanying challenge to America's Great Power authority. No one knows if and when the terrorists will hit the U.S. homeland again, but the March 11, 2004, Madrid bombings and the July 7, 2005, London explosions, for which affiliated organizations of al Qaeda claimed responsibility, proved that al Qaeda is a persistent phenomenon or idea of transnational harm that continues to challenge U.S. authority. While Spain is not a major power, the Spanish government of Prime Minister Jose Maria Aznar was a key U.S. supporter in the war in Iraq. The Spanish and especially the British support were important to the United States in legitimating its use of preventive force, especially in light of the international opposition to this war prior to its outbreak. If the bombings in Madrid and London were indeed meant to "punish" Spain and Britain for their role in the American-led coalition against Iraq and Afghanistan, then the intent beyond the material damage to Spain and Britain themselves might be to undermine American authority over the allies. In fact, bin Laden warned Spain along with Britain, Poland, Australia, Japan, and Italy that al Qaeda would *revenge* against their participation in the Afghan and Iraqi wars.[61] In the future, allies might have doubts about joining an American-led coalition for fear of being "punished" by terrorists. In this respect I want to cite Bindert again:

> To punish someone is not just to harm them because of something they have done. It is to stake a claim to a certain kind of institu-

tional authority, even when the institution is only the family. To punish someone is to assert a right and accept an obligation to punish anyone similarly circumstanced and behaved. . . . to punish is to act as an officer or agent participating in a system for enforcing an authoritatively promulgated norm. (Bindert 2002, 321)

Beyond its material manifestation, then, a violent act also represents certain ideas: about what actors are entitled to do to each other, about who the actors are that possess the right to wield violence, and about what spheres violence can take place in. Between the early nineteenth century and the late twentieth century, nonstate extraterritorial wielders of violence posed no significant threat to the Great Powers in either the material or the authority sense. At the most, they were a nuisance. The Great Powers, busy constructing restraints on war in *inter*national relations, left many structural holes in the world system. Although realists often believe that material capabilities spur intentions, the presence of such unprotected holes and infrastructures enabled deep revisionist nonstate actors, such as al Qaeda, to transform intentions into destructive capabilities. This type of intensive destruction inevitably challenges authority because not only is the material damage (or, in other words, the deviation from the normative structure) so extreme, but the attacked hegemonic power cannot exact the full costs from the terrorists who claim a right to punish powerful states. Implicit in authority is the ability to exact costs for deviance, but the sovereignty-free nature of global terrorism today hinders the United States in this action. Furthermore, while the direct perpetrators or planners of terrorist attacks could be killed or captured, the idea of mass destruction terror is inescapable, and as a result the realms of possibility sanctioned by the contemporary institutions of violence have become fluid and unsound. In fact, al Qaeda proved that, in the realm of destruction, the powerful, although not in danger of being annihilated by the weak, are nonetheless much more dependent on international institutions for their well-being than in any other social, economic, or political sphere. This means that the War on Terror is in the long run indeed a battle for hearts and minds, but the question remains whether it is being waged in the right manner. I touch on this issue in the conclusion of this book.

Conclusions

The main conclusion of this book is that Great Power policy toward persistent agents of transnational harm depends largely on the extent and nature of the authority challenge the latter represent to the former. Great Powers are gatekeepers in the cartel of states. The greater the perceived threat of a PATH to this cartel, the harsher the Great Powers' treatment of it. From this perspective, punishment serves not only to deter or incapacitate but also to reassert the Great Power authority by secluding a challenger from the rest of society and thus demonstrating authority's commitment to the norms and institutions from which the challenger deviated. Punishment is meant to stop norm decay and even to initiate norm revival (Grossman and Minseong 2000). Punishment is thus propelled by strong normative and moral sentiments. As Emil Durkheim argued, "its effects are primarily to reaffirm the moral order" (quoted in Garland 1990, 47).

But beyond reaffirming a moral order, punishment is also meant to exclude competing ideologies and moralities. Thus, if a deviating agent also propagates a competing ideology to social norms and institutions, the punishment exacted by the bearers of authority will be harsher. In this context, predators are not merely deemed facilitators or propagators of harm, but they provoke a further sense of urgency due to the combined factors of their extreme deviation from the institutions of violence *and* the ontological doubts they raise as to the inevitability of the system of authority these institutions sanction. Parasites might cause or facilitate harm to a considerable extent and yet be tolerated because they pose a less acute threat to the institutions that sanction Great Power authority.

Parasites pose no competing ideology. Predators, however, threaten the very existence of the system of ideas and institutions that enable and constitute social power. They threaten the hegemonic or dominant ideology that Marxists talk about.

In the punishment of a parasite, the aim can range from incapacitation to socialization into the existing structure of authority (or "correction"). In punishing a predator, on the other hand, the punisher is defending a structure of authority from a perceived hostile pretender to social power; punishment in this case has a system-maintaining function. Parasites are framed as an issue of control or management. Management, according to Philip Selznick, is about maximizing given ends. Counter-harm policy against parasites depends on calculations of expediency and cost-effectiveness. Thus, parasites are usually managed with law enforcement agencies or semimilitary organizations (e.g., the coast guard and its role in the War on Drugs). Beyond the operational and utilitarian reasons for these approaches to the problem of parasitic harm, however, I believe there is also a constitutive reason: as the state evolved over the last five hundred years, the military came to be the most visible symbol of state power and identity. The military, in fact, enabled state authority, preserving it from inside and outside challengers (Tilly 1990). Military issues are traditionally regarded as relating to security and "high politics." During the last centuries, the armed forces, at least in "developed" states, have been used primarily in defending the sovereignty of the state from external enemies who openly seek to harm or compromise its authority through the intensive use of designated means of destruction. The whole ethos of the armed forces is based on engaging such enemies. In this sense, parasites are often seen as enemies not worthy of the use of the armed forces. There is no glory in fighting them because they do not represent an outright evil, nor do they constitute a challenge to the state's authority. Because the attitude of the parasite toward the normative order of the state and the states system is perceived as ambivalent, it is not seen to be seeking its destruction. In some cases, in fact, engaging the armed forces against parasites is considered by state rulers and men at arms to be degrading, corrupting, or inappropriate.

Predators, on the other hand, are an issue of governance. Governance, according to Selznick, deals with broader political aspects of the preservation and reproduction of a social system.[1] Predators, unlike parasites, are perceived as wishing to destroy the normative order and to replace it with their own political vision. Containment, international law enforcement, and even limited military operations are somehow equivalent to varying degrees and forms of "crime control" on the domestic level. On the other hand, severe punishment through intensive military intervention, such as that inflicted on al Qaeda and the Taliban in Afghanistan, is meant to symbolize that the authoritative power—and not its challengers—is in control. Such punishment signifies to the world and to the agents of harm that the latter are "enemies of all mankind" who stand against the ultimate values of international society. Thus, the specific extent and nature of the perceived challenge to authority constitute the definition of a harmful practice and, consequently, inform the policy response of the Great Power toward PATHs.

Great Power authority as discussed in this book is first and foremost based on the legitimization of coercive power. This legitimization is enabled through the Great Powers' authorship of institutions of violence *and* by their abiding by them. The institutionalization of violence constructs an order in world politics in which actors acknowledge some rights and needs of each other and treat each other not solely based on instrumental considerations but also as moral persons. By defining legitimate and illegitimate ends, extents, justifications, targets, and actorhood in the sphere of transborder organized violence, some symmetry of ideas and expectations emerges among states. Beyond mere material capability, power also represents social conventions. In this sense, certain forms of power serve as a normative framework that somehow holds competing interests together. A hierarchy is thus enabled, and the Great Powers emerge as bearers of authority in that they possess more legitimized power than other actors.

The empirical discussion of the Congress of Vienna and the War on Terror demonstrated that Great Power authority can move on a continuum: on one end is "legalized hegemony" as Simpson (2004) perceives it (i.e., open mutual empowerment among the Great Powers to actively govern world politics and a recognition of this claim by the smaller actors), and on the other end are the minimal definitions of *illegitimate* resistance to power (e.g., the categorization of terrorism during the Cold War). When Great Powers wield or wish to wield legalized hegemony, they are expected by the smaller states in the system to also bear some responsibility for the preservation of the rights and needs of weaker actors (Cronin 2001). Thus, the smaller powers in Vienna demanded that Britain end the scandal of the Barbary pirates, which at that time harmed only the civilians of small states. Britain, from its position as legalized hegemon, wanted to obtain universal abolition of the Atlantic slave trade. But the fact that the British turned a blind eye to the slave trade and the depredations of the Barbary pirates compromised the moral authority of the demand they made upon the colonial powers to cease their slave trade. The latter argued that in order for them to consent to the British demands, Britain, "the mistress of the seas," first had to end the outrage of the Barbary pirates and redeem the European slaves whose states were too weak to protect them from the pirates. As discussed in this book, authority is highly dependent on communal consent. The British realized this and therefore punished the pirates, who further exacerbated the threat to British authority by openly refusing to cease their violent practice. But this punishment was not intended to annihilate the pirate communities altogether, just to "correct" and impose a new moral order on them. The pirates were not seen to propagate an ideology in competition with Britain's. While the British believed slavery was evil in itself, there is no evidence that the Barbary corsair communities viewed European slavery as a moral value to be preserved as such. Rather, their attitude toward slavery and captivity was instrumental. They did not question or challenge the ideological, moralistic, and normative elements of the British antislavery effort—or at least the British did not document any such defiance. Even when reporting that the pirates refused to abandon the "laudable ways" of their forefathers, the *Times* related this refusal to the corsairs' way of making a living and not directly to an ideology they had: "Lord Exmouth himself went on shore to prescribe to the Dey . . . the condition that the Algerines should treat the sailors and passengers who may fall into their hands not as slaves but as prisoners of war. *It was as if one should require a people who had only one branch of industry to renounce it"* (May 31, 1816; emphasis added). In addition, the religious aspects of Barbary sea predation, which were strong only in the early sixteenth century, had mostly disappeared by the late eighteenth and early nineteenth centuries. In 1768, for example, when fifteen hundred Spanish nationals were redeemed from Algiers by the Mercedarian friars, it was agreed that eighteen hundred Algerians held captive in Spain would be an integral part of the deal on top of the cash paid for the Spaniards. The Algerian negotiators nonetheless stated from the outset that they preferred silver to Algerian captives; the Algerian dey told the friars that he "did not want Moors but money" (Friedman 1980, 632). By the time Britain ended Barbary slavery, therefore, the North Africans were seen not as savages to be destroyed but as barbarians who had to be disciplined by the British.

In the case of the American War on Terror, on the other hand, al Qaeda and the Taliban were framed as enemies of civilization—savage murderers who want to not merely end lives but destroy a way of life through a combination of mass destruction terror and repressive ideology. Thus, what was mainly at stake in this war was U.S. authority—in the sense that authority defines illegitimate ways to resist power. Indeed, one might wonder why, if this was the case, the United States avoided military intervention in the cases of terrorists that attacked other states prior to 9/11. Russia, Britain, France, Israel, Sri Lanka, India, and many other states were victims of terrorism (including suicide bombings) long before al Qaeda hit the United States in September 2001. But unlike the demands of the smaller European powers in 1815, which urged Britain to put an end to Barbary piracy through military intervention, no state in the 1980s and 1990s demanded such action from the United States. At the most, states desired that the United States not interfere with their counterterror campaigns, or they wanted only the political backing and legitimization of the United States for these campaigns.[2] And because before 9/11 the United States perceived terrorism mainly as a parasitic phenomenon to be dealt with through law enforcement, it is doubtful that America would have militarily intervened even if requested to do so by a smaller state. Moreover, while for the British the abolition of slavery was a prime national interest and a defining element in their national identity and international authority, the abolition of terrorism played no such role in U.S. foreign policy prior to 9/11 (see National Commission on the Terrorist Attacks Upon the United States 2004). Therefore, unlike the British, the Americans were not faced with an international demand to lead a military campaign to abolish terrorism (if this is operationally possible at all) because the United States did not consider the threat to be predatory. Furthermore, and most important, no terrorist group dared to challenge American authority the way al Qaeda did. We have seen that previous anti-American terrorists very rarely openly defied the authority of the United States. Thus they exhibited ambivalence toward the international normative order that the United States pursued. This ambivalence garnered the hope that such terrorists and their sponsoring states could be contained or deterred. Indeed, the "correction" of Qaddafi's Libya in August 2003 (Hurd 2005) suggests that parasitic actors can be reintegrated into society given the right combination of sanctions and rewards. Al Qaeda, on the other hand, is perceived as "an enemy of ruthless ambition unconstrained by law or morality"[3] that has in many respects clearly declared and actually demonstrated its defiance of the current normative order, calling for its replacement by an opposing vision of political authority (Mendelsohn 2005). As such, it positioned itself beyond any likelihood of reintegration. But in spite of the operational limits of its ability to exact costs from the terrorists—which the United States knew very well—the need for severe punishment seemed inevitable. This reflects David Garland's notion of the "tragic quality of punishment": on the one hand it is deemed necessary, and on the other hand it is destined to a degree of futility (1990, 80).

From the U.S. perspective, then, the attacks of 9/11 threatened to start a cascade of norm decay, and therefore the terrorists had to be severely punished. The depredations of the Barbary corsairs on Spain in the sixteenth and seventeenth centuries on the other hand were not framed as predatory resistance to Great Power authority (a concept that is almost irrelevant for that time), and hence the response of Spain to this practice of intensive transnational harm depended on extrinsic considerations not directly related to the harm of the corsairs per se. The depredations of the corsairs were framed within a larger threat environment, in which states—and especially the dominant military powers—barely considered each other capable of authority. Few norms or institutions existed to regulate and restrain violence. And when states fought, self-defense and the protection of their civilian populations were not the major issues at stake. Violent harm and high bellicosity were routine in that international system. In the same way as we today perceive civil strife and daily occurrences of intensive violence in failed states to be almost inevitable, sixteenth- and early seventeenth-century state rulers and societies perceived violence to be a part of everyday life. The Barbary corsairs were known to be an integral part of this system. In addition, in spite of the fact that they were mainly Muslims, the corsairs did not concentrate on advancing a competing ideology to Spain's Catholicism. In fact, as we have seen, they abused this state ideology of Spain in order to maximize their financial revenues. Therefore, Spain and the other major European powers in the early modern period did not feel such an urgent need to enter into the "degradation ceremony" (Garfinkel 1956) that both al Qaeda and the United States sought to impose on each other in 2001–2.

The punishment of terrorists and their allies in Afghanistan was followed by the 2003 Iraqi war. But somehow, paradoxically, the causes behind the international coalition against al Qaeda and the Taliban regime of Afghanistan were also responsible for the United States' inability to reach consensus with many other states and Great Powers over the Iraqi crisis. Namely, al Qaeda's threat to the international institutions of violence, which led to systemic conservatism, was much the same as the U.S. threat in the Iraqi war. This was largely because the American move was not widely perceived as a legitimate preemptive war (recall the mass demonstrations worldwide before the war) but was seen as an illegitimate *preventive* or aggressive one seeking regime change. I believe that the international opposition to the Iraqi war was the result, at least partially, of the fear that the U.S. strategy of preventive war could threaten the institutions of violence in a manner similar to al Qaeda. Systemic conservatism was therefore invoked against the United States.

While the attacks of 9/11 demonstrated the difficulty that Great Powers face in deterring deviant nonstate actors such as al Qaeda and exacting costs from them for their deviance, the Iraqi war strained the institutions of violence because of the hegemon's own deviation from them. Both the Afghan and Iraqi wars contained an element of disciplinary punishment. Such punishment functions to restore authority. But it can also lead to an *authority dilemma*. In the first case (Afghanistan), punishment to a certain extent augmented American Great Power authority by preserving the distinction between legitimate and illegitimate violence and by demonstrating that the United States could exact costs for deviance. In the second case (Iraq), punishment may have exacerbated the threat: post-Saddam Iraq actually seems to have become a magnet for terrorists and a legitimizing cause for further terrorism, much as Afghanistan was during the war with the USSR.

The Iraqi war strained the institutions of violence because of the hegemon's own policy. In effect, the strategy of preventive war represented punishment for a perceived future challenge rather than for concrete or impending bellicose actions. Prior to the Iraqi war, Bush noted, "We fight for lawful change against chaotic violence."[4] In this context, rogue states and terrorists were framed as agents of chaotic violence because, argued the "National Security Strategy," they "hate the United States and everything for which it stands." This hatred alone—the strategy reasoned—might translate into aggressive actions. But in "adapting" the concept of preemptive war after 9/11 (Bush 2002a, 15), the United States actually declared contemporary international order obsolete.

Now, hegemons and other Great Powers author new rules in international politics, as this book indeed argues. This is an important aspect of the leadership role of Great Powers (Jervis 2003). However, if Great Powers want these norms to become authoritative standards of behavior they cannot impose them through mere force, completely disregarding the previous norms that they themselves instituted or inherited from history. "[T]he art of political change," David Garland argues, "[is] one of articulating a new morality while claiming to ground it in the values which everyone holds" (1990, 54). Indeed, the United States worked hard to do this before and during the war in Iraq, but it was far from successful in convincing other states and societies of the validity of the charges against Iraq (Kaufmann 2004). In spite of this, the United States went ahead, with a "coalition of the willing." Military victory was achieved quickly, but it was paid for by loss of authority. The issue of punishing for a yet unrealized future challenge was crucial here: whereas states were supportive of or at least more willing to tolerate American use of force for the purpose of stopping humanitarian crises in the Balkans during the 1990s, even though such interventions violated previous norms of state sovereignty, punishing Iraq for a violation it has not yet committed roused much more alarm in the international system. As no clear-cut evidence existed as to Iraq's actual plans to build weapons of mass destruction and to use them, many states and societies perceived the war as motivated either by unsubstantiated American fears or by a desire for regime change and expansionist plans. This opposition to the U.S. preventive war doctrine emerged precisely because almost all the other Great Powers and many smaller states saw the doctrine as an effort to relegitimize norms that were already denounced in history. During the last centuries, important differences were constructed between preemptive and preventive wars: "whereas a preventive war involves the deliberate and premeditated initiation of hostilities at the most propitious time, a pre-emptive attack involves an action in which the attempt is made to seize the initiative from an adversary who has either already resorted to force or is certain to initiate hostilities in the immediate future" (Tucker 1960, 142–43). Preventive war thus is perceived to belong to the violent and chaotic past.

Having broken the rules of the game, the hegemon has in effect justified and legitimized such violation of the institutions of violence by other states and nonstate actors. This potentially blurs the distinction between the weak and powerful, especially in the context of the current technological realities, which allow even militarily weak actors to inflict massive damages on the Great Powers. Establishing the precedent of preventive war might also encourage other states to follow suit. All this could eventually lead to decay from a Lockean anarchy back into a Hobbesian one. This latter world is full of surprises and uncertainties— and those who are most prone to be surprised in the current technological and ideological reality are the Great Powers themselves.

Hatred toward America might be considered by the United States as a threat in and of itself, but others do not necessarily perceive it as such. Throughout this book I have tried to demonstrate that institutional power is significantly linked to hard power in that it preserves normative macrostructures that define certain *legitimate* methods, targets, capabilities, and employment of resistance to power. America strives to preserve these distinctions in the War on Terror. The deep meaning of this effort is to delegitimize terror, as the "National Security Strategy" itself admits. However, the preventive war doctrine might actually compromise the delegitimization of terror, since many people and states construe preventive war as a manifestation of unrestrained hegemony. But this is a hegemony that, because of many of its fundamental characteristics (open society, rule of law, interdependent economy, etc.), is highly vulnerable to terror. These characteristics of America combined with the extrainstitutional nature of terror warfare mean that there is absolutely no certainty that preventive war would indeed prevent the next act of mass destruction terror. As noted in chapter 5, the real threat is bin Ladenism, not just bin Laden or Saddam Hussein themselves. The rise of terrorism against the United States in Iraq is indicative in this sense. And here we find the terrible authority dilemma that the United States faces as a result of 9/11. On the one hand, "enemies of civilization" might attack the United States under any circumstances, no matter what the United States does or does not do. On the other hand, new and dangerous enemies might emerge in response to or as a result of illegitimate *American* practice. There are no easy solutions to this dilemma, if any at all. Still, in my view the United States should strive to clearly distinguish itself from its enemies. America is morally just in its War on Terror, but in order to retain its moral superiority it must acknowledge that only a law that equally binds the powerful and the weak can establish legitimacy for hegemony. If anything can be learned from bin Laden it is the fact that it is not merely the possession of superior military and economic capabilities that gives the Great Powers their great power but other actors' acceptance—even if only passive—of their authority in world politics. Society is to a great extent a product of man's necessity, and society is no less important in world politics than in domestic politics. In this context, moral consistency and just conduct were never more important to the preservation of Great Power authority.

Notes

Introduction

1. On the concept of transnational harm see Linklater 2002. See also Feinberg 1984. Feinberg considers harm to represent setback to vital interests.

2. See, for example, Waltz 1979; Gilpin 1981; Miller 1995; Mearsheimer 2001; and to some extent also Wendt 1999.

3. The term *weak state* in this context does not refer necessarily to states that are weak in military terms but to those that lack legitimacy from their societies. See Migdal 1988; Ayoob 1995.

4. State weakness (in the sense of a lack of legitimacy) in the globalized world might also generate PATH threats by creating grievances and resentment in local groups that eventually erupt against the Great Powers. Thus, the authoritarian and nonrepresentative nature of states such as Egypt, Saudi Arabia, or Pakistan is considered by many to lead to Islamic fundamentalism and anti-American terror. Moreover, the recent terror attacks in Madrid (March 2004) and London (July 2005) also could indicate that state weakening (as opposed to state weakness per se) is not limited to the Third World. In Britain, Spain, France, and other Western European states, growing segments of society (namely, communities of Muslim immigrants) feel estranged and rejected by the state, and these feelings are germane to the turn of specific individuals from these communities to terror or to their affiliation with al Qaeda.

5. Simpson (2004, 50) notes that the investigation of political inequality is "the professional concern of international relations scholars, or those who wish to investigate the sociology of international treaty-making. These are fascinating projects, but they are not mine."

6. An interesting case in the context of the emergence of private authority in international politics is Transparency International (TI). This transnational organization annually ranks more than one hundred states according to their perceived degree of corruption as part of a worldwide campaign against corruption. As such, TI might be said to be a private authority on international politics: its

index is often cited, and its anticorruption campaign receives significant media attention. However, the goal of the anticorruption campaign is to reform the state and not to replace it. Corruption is portrayed by TI as a malady of the ideal state, and the mission of the anticorruption coalition is to cure this malady and to help restore good governance. Therefore, this is private authority that actually works to strengthen the state, not replace it. On TI's anticorruption campaign, see Wang and Rosenau 2001.

7. On PMCs, see Lynch and Walsh 2000; Mandel 2002; Singer 2002. See especially Zarate 1998, where the author argues that in fact PMCs reinforce the international system of sovereign states by strengthening weak and failed states (153).

8. Similarly, another PMC closed its operations due to state disapproval. The following announcement appears on the Web page of Sandline International, a PMC that was involved in actual fighting in Sierra Leone in the 1990s: "On 16 April 2004 Sandline International announced the closure of the company's operations. The general lack of governmental support for Private Military Companies willing to help end armed conflicts in places like Africa, in the absence of effective international intervention, is the reason for this decision. Without such support the ability of Sandline to make a positive difference in countries where there is widespread brutality and genocidal behaviour is materially diminished." See http://www.sandline.com/ (accessed August 29, 2004).

9. *Right* not necessarily in the sense of *just* but rather in the sense of a taken-for-granted entitlement.

10. On rights as a system of entitlements and obligations, see McDermott 2001. On property rights and the role of the state in this institution, see Burch 1998.

11. See Orviska and Hudson 2003, 87. See also Paternoster and Simpson 1996; McAdams 2000; and Dau-Schmidt 1990. Frey (1997) argues that people are motivated not just by a concern to maximize their own well-being but by a sense of civic duty. But see for an opposite argument Krawiec 2000; Bhide and Stevenson 1990; and Khanna 2003.

12. For the best contribution in this context, see Mendelsohn 2005.

13. *Quarterly Review* 25 (1816): 142.

14. Thus I believe that drug trafficking cannot be conceived of as "harmless wrongdoing." See Feinberg 1990.

15. While certain U.S. agencies of the armed forces and the national security apparatus engage in antidrug operations, their role stops short of actual combat engagement with drug traffickers, as opposed to the active participation of Colombian and Mexican armed forces in action against drug groups in their countries.

16. See the discussion in chapter 2 for the meaning of Foucauldian disciplinary acts.

Chapter 1

1. Note that even Waltz implied special responsibilities for the Great Powers: "in any realm populated by units that are functionally similar but of different

capability, those of greatest capability take on special responsibilities" (Waltz 1979, 198).

2. In this regard, Hurd's understanding of the Security Council is very interesting. He notes that "the Security Council is at its heart a political pact among the Great Powers to keep the peace among themselves. . . . The fact that the veto works negatively, in permitting Great Powers to kill resolutions with which they disagree, means that it biases the Council in the direction of inaction. But inaction, as the UN founders knew, can be very useful. The inaction implied by the veto guarantees that the Council will be paralyzed at precisely those moments of the greatest tension between the Great Powers. . . . When the Great Powers disagree, the Council will not be able to act, and the drafters of the UN Charter believed that in such cases it should *not* act since to act would be to invite disaster for the whole organization. The veto is the convenient institutional mechanism by which the Council gets out of the way when the Great Powers clash. This is not a 'flaw' in the design of the Council—this is the *sine qua non* of the Council" (I. Hurd 2004, 70, 71).

3. However, "[s]ecularization [after Westphalia] remained situated within a broader Christian context. . . . Secular political authority, then, was imagined and enacted within an unquestioned Christian framework" (E. Hurd 2004, 241).

4. On the legitimization of spheres of influence during the Cold War, see Lipson 1991, 496; Nye 1987, 393.

5. During this Anglo-American crisis, U.S. Secretary of State Richard Olney stated in a note to the British government, "Today the United States is practically sovereign on this continent and its fiat is law upon the subjects to which it confines its interposition" (Langley 1976, 161, cited in Gent 2003, 11). The British did not accept this statement, but neither did they reject it. Furthermore, "by 1903 Britain's Prime Minister, Arthur Balfour, openly proclaimed his support for American regional hegemony, claiming that: '. . . the Monroe Doctrine has no enemies in this country that I know of. We welcome any increase of the influence of the United States of America upon the great Western hemisphere'" (Lobell 2001, 181).

6. On Great Power recognition, see Ringmar 2002.

7. The 2003 war on Iraq and the American occupation of this country might seem to falsify the effect of the territorial integrity norm. However, from the outset the professed goal of the United States was not to annul Iraqi sovereignty but to "reconstruct" it and enforce democratization. The United States maintained all along that it was about to restore Iraqi sovereignty. Even if mere "cheap talk," this issue raises the question of why the United States—the hegemon of the international system—described its intentions and actions toward Iraq in the language of sovereignty and why, from the outset, it seemed to have to justify its moves against Iraq. Obviously, no other power would have militarily intervened on Iraq's behalf in any case. Furthermore, the American efforts to legitimize the Iraqi war through various ways—such as the UN Security Council, the "National Security Strategy of the United States," and the multinational coalition ("the coalition of the willing")—seem to point to the fact that even the world's single superpower cannot have its own way all of the time.

8. I am greatly thankful to Alexander Wendt for turning my attention to this line of thought.

9. It is very interesting to note in this context that the famous idiom "might is right," which comes from Thucydides' *Melian Dialogue,* was most likely never spoken by the Athenians to the Melians. The Athenians' refusal to justify themselves in moral and normative terms is so unlikely (and we know that in ancient Greece such justifications were built into international relations; see Reus-Smit 1999) that their overt terms could be seen as Thucydides' attempts to emphasize beyond any doubt the lesson of imperial hubris and overexpansion that he wants to teach in the ensuing chapter on the Sicilian campaign. Note that he admits in the first chapter of his book, "With reference to the speeches in this history . . . some I heard myself, others I got from various sources; it was difficult in all cases to carry them word for word in one's memory, *so my habit has been to make the speakers say what was in my opinion demanded of them by the various occasions*" (1943, 44; emphasis added).

10. Hurd's work is quite exceptional in this regard.

11. Neoliberals, on their part, also consider international politics as anarchic but nonetheless mitigated by international regimes and interdependence. See Milner 1993. Milner assumes that what is lacking in an anarchy is a structure of authority defined as a legitimized power.

12. For various definitions or understandings of the concept of Great Powers that highlight material capabilities of violence, see Levy 1983, 10–19. See also Kennedy 1987; Layne 1993; Miller and Kagan 1997.

13. For similar understandings of sovereignty as a communitarian value, see Wendt 1999, 292; Philpott 2001, 13; Biersteker and Weber 1996, 2; Wight 1977, 23; Barkin and Cronin 1994, 110.

14. See Gong 1984; Bowden 2004.

15. A major problem with Krasner's hypocrisy theme is that he implicitly considers "Westphalian" sovereignty as a transhistorical norm, when in fact in Westphalia states merely agreed not to interfere in each other's religious matters. Consequently, the religious reasons for war were removed from the list of legitimate interests that could motivate a state to use transborder force. As said previously, Westphalia did not annul the Right of Conquest, nor did it delegitimize reasons other than religious ones for war or, more generally, foreign coercive intervention. The Right of Conquest and the legitimate or appropriate reasons for transborder violence and intervention (that entail coercive interference with one's sovereignty) were transformed during the centuries after Westphalia. Hence, the perception of sovereignty per se as organized hypocrisy is historically problematic.

16. In reality, it is very difficult to conceive of slavery in its extreme sense of lack of minimal recognition of slaves by masters. Thus, even American Old South slavery was a system of paternalistic authority because the slaveholders had some obligations toward the slaves. "Theoretically, modern slavery rested, as had ancient slavery, on the idea of a slave as *instrumentum vocale*—a chattel, a possession, a thing, a mere extension of his master's will. But the vacuousness of such pretensions had been exposed long before the growth of the New World slave societies." Slavery in the Old South consisted of paternalism, which "was accepted by both masters and slaves. . . . Paternalism defined the involuntary labor of the slaves as a legitimate return to their masters for protection and direc-

tion. But the masters' need to see their slaves as acquiescent human beings constituted a moral victory for the slaves themselves. Paternalism's insistence upon mutual obligations—duties, responsibilities, and ultimately even rights—implicitly recognized the slaves' humanity" (Genovese 1976, 4–5).

17. Similarly, Krasner (1999, 10) argues that "If authority is effective, force or compulsion would never have to be exercised. Authority would be coterminous with control. But control can be achieved simply through the use of brute force with no mutual recognition of authority at all."

18. "[P]ower and influence are often derived from the role of a protector of certain rules and core values. The notion of a Great Power . . . [is] a case in point" (Kratochvil 1989, 50).

19. In a sense, this might explain the theoretical difficulty of understanding the phenomenon of global terrorism. IR theory, and especially constructivism, has occupied itself with norm emergence and not with norm decay.

20. In its War on Terror in Afghanistan in 2001–2, the United States allied with Afghan opposition forces and local warlords in order to topple the Taliban regime and to destroy al Qaeda in that country. This could be said to represent a major deviance from the principles mentioned in the previous discussion of actorhood. Yet while the local Afghan forces joined the United States also due to the fact that the CIA was paying them millions of dollars to fight for America, the United States did not publicly admit that it hired Afghan mercenary units. Instead, the United States depicted the participation of the local Afghan forces in the war as one of national liberation from foreign elements such as al Qaeda's Arab forces and from the despotic and cruel Taliban regime. See Woodward 2002, 165.

21. This line of argument is similar to Norbert Elias's conception of the "civilizing process" as the constitutive cause of self-restraint: "The monopoly organization of physical force [of the state] does not usually constrain the individual by a direct threat. A strongly predictable compulsion or pressure mediated in a variety of ways is constantly exerted on the individual. This operates to a considerable extent through the medium of his own reflection. . . . in other words, it imposes on people a greater or lesser degree of self-control" (Elias 1982, 239).

Chapter 2

1. These points are only distinguished for illustrative purposes, and the range of counter-PATH measures could be inclusive.

2. Because they are corporate actors, states have longer and more detailed historical memory, knowledge of international institutions, and developed mechanisms and bureaucracies to interact in world politics.

3. See Wendt 1999, chap. 6, for why states can reasonably know each other's strategic intentions.

4. The slave trade and its abolition could be regarded as belonging to the realm of the institutions of violence because slavery is based on coercion and slaves were taken in Africa during intertribal wars or specially designated raids.

5. Of course, one can object that the whole strategy of mutually assured destruction was based on the targeting of civilians. But the superpowers defined

this policy as a constraint and not a choice, and during this time they vowed not to implement it.

6. This again highlights the fact that Hobbesian cultures cannot be internalized to the third degree, because enemies see *nothing* common among themselves. Their whole identity is built on negating the other.

7. I mean *hegemonic* in the Gramscian sense.

8. On free riding in international security, see Olson and Zeckhauser 1966; Christensen and Snyder 1990.

9. For a critique of hegemonic stability theory and its dealing with the issue of free riders, see Grunberg 1990.

10. Corruption represents an illegal manipulation of authority by advancing or protecting interests through nonviolent means.

11. Thus, "traditional" terrorism (i.e., limited terrorism for specific political purposes) such as that practiced in the 1970s and 1980s was defined by most states as a criminal offence because it was not seen as an attempt to destroy a system.

12. See, in this regard, Mearsheimer and Walt 2003, where the authors argue that Saddam Hussein is effectively a parasitic actor that can be contained.

13. This argument is based on the logic of Trevaskes 2003.

14. On the distinction between authority and its administration, see Edmundson 1998.

15. See Appeal No. 4714/04: Yigal Amir vs. the Prison Service, September 8, 2004 (in Hebrew). The Association for Civil Rights in Israel protested against this decision.

16. The Rosenbergs pleaded not guilty up until their very last moments. They even appealed for executive clemency, but the fact that they refused to confess largely contributed to the decline of their appeal. See Radosh and Milton 1997. "Confession" is actually an implicit recognition of the state's right to pass moral judgment and hence of its superior authority. It is interesting to note that an alternative to confessing is to plead insanity. This too implicitly sends a message of recognition of authority, because it means that one has to be insane to disobey state authority by committing a crime.

17. Revenge is defined by Jon Elster as "the attempt, at some cost or risk to oneself, to impose suffering upon those who have made one suffer, because they have made one suffer" (1990, 862).

18. In this sense, insiders to authority states are self-policing, in Robert Axelrod's terms. There is no need to punish them for not punishing a norm violator, because they will punish the deviant on their own initiative (they observe what he calls "metanorms"). See Axelrod 1986, 1102–3.

19. I thank Barak Mendelsohn for this insight.

20. This in spite of the fact that the actual elimination of PATHs is much more difficult than that of states, and often it fails because their transnational nature makes them more elusive.

Chapter 3

1. It is not an easy task to pinpoint the exact end of the Spanish Golden Age. However, the second decade of the seventeenth century might serve as a useful

reference point in this regard, especially due to the self-perception in Spain itself of decline.

2. There is no conclusive evidence as to the exact share of corsairing in the Barbary regencies' budgets, as records of such budgets are rare. However, even in 1768, when the profitability of corsairing declined due to the growing naval strength of the major European powers, corsair-related revenues represented more than half of the income of Algiers. Moreover, for the Barbary regencies, the income from corsairing was not easily replaceable. By the late eighteenth century and early nineteenth century, with the decline of corsairing, the Algerian government tried to impose taxes on its population to make up for the lost income. The result was popular discontent and several unsuccessful uprisings. See Friedman 1980, 630–31.

3. In seventy-two organized redemption efforts during seventy-seven years in the 1600s, a total of 15,573 Spanish nationals were redeemed. There are no definitive numbers as to the sixteenth century and also as to the total Spanish nationals enslaved in Barbary. Note that a great many Spanish captives were not redeemed, remaining slaves for life, and many others died while waiting to be ransomed. See Davis 2003, 19.

4. For a favorable depiction of Barbary slavery, see Fisher 1957, 102–6.

5. See Christofforo Surian, Venetian secretary in the Netherlands, to the Doge and Senate, February 20, 1618, in Hinds 1909, 147.

6. For a general discussion of this back-and-forth crossing between piracy and privateering, as well as brigandage and mercenarism, see Thomson 1994.

7. The most acknowledged maritime authorities of the time were unanimous that only combined and continuous naval operations and blockades by the European maritime powers would eliminate the shared threat. See Sir William Monson's counsel concerning the pirates in Morgan 1731, 632–35.

8. The States General of the Low Countries to the Doge of Venice, December 21, 1617, in Hinds 1909, 90.

9. The Senate to the Resident Surian at the Hague, February 9, 1618, in Hinds 1909, 138.

10. Piero Contarini, Venetian ambassador in Spain, to the Doge and the Senate, in Hinds 1909, 509.

11. See letters of Christofforo Surian and Girolamo Lando, Venetian ambassadors in the Netherlands and England, to the Doge and Senate, February 20, 1618, and June 3, 1622, in Hinds 1909, 147; and Hinds 1911, 337, respectively.

12. Dynastic rights of inheritance can be said to be a normative constraint on territorial expansion in this period. Yet, monarchs often raised fraudulent inheritance pretensions too as a pretext for war. On the other hand, rulers were also willing to barter claims for "equivalents"—other benefits to which they had no legal right. See Black 1998, 66.

13. Venetian ambassador in England, to the Doge and Senate, June 3. In Hinds 1911, 334.

14. Ibid., 335.

15. Fisher mentions that, in 1619, Biscayan corsairs were said to have taken sixteen hundred prizes in the Mediterranean and the Atlantic. See Fisher 1957, 176, 180.

16. Interestingly, and indicatively in my view, Tenenti characterizes the Maltese privateers as a "company of international adventurers" (1967, 35).

Chapter 4

1. In their eighteenth-century peace treaties with Algiers, the British always insisted that once a British man-of-war arrived in the port of Algiers, any Christian slave who managed to escape and take refuge on board the British ship would be redeemed without any payment of ransom. But they did not demand the abolition of Christian slavery as such.

2. Citing the British deputy consul in the duchy of Oldenburg, to British foreign secretary Canning, August 18, 1823 (see Harding 2000, 42).

3. Two notable antislavery naval expeditions during that campaign were the Niger expedition of 1841–42 and the attack against Brazil in 1850. But these operations involved only small vessels. The Niger expedition comprised three small steamers, carrying 157 men altogether. The 1850 operation against Brazil was executed by a force of one frigate and five sloops. See Temperley 1998 and Lloyd 1968. On the British effort against Atlantic slavery as a costly moral action, see Kaufmann and Pape 1999.

4. See *British and Foreign State Papers, 1815–16*, 1838, 513, 515.

5. The composition of the British fleet was as follows: one first-rate ship of the line; one second-rate ship of the line; three third-rate ships of the line; three fourth-rate frigates; two fifth-rate frigates; five brig-sloops; four bombs; five gunboats; eight rocket boats; sixteen gunboat yawls; ten mortar boats; and sixteen gunboat barges. In addition, five more auxiliary/transport ships were dispatched. See Clowes 1901, 227.

6. See *House of Commons Parliamentary Papers* 1817 (410) IV 249 mf. 18.22.

7. Compare this to the Spanish bombardment of Algiers in 1783, which lasted nine days but consumed only four thousand bombs and a similar number of round shots. See Wolf 1979, 305.

8. Since the navy did not detail the costs of specific battles, my estimation is based on a summary of various data from the *Parliamentary Papers,* the budget appendices of the *Parliamentary Debates* (Hansard), and secondary sources. To confirm my estimation, I presented it to Professor Andrew Lambert, from King's College at London. Professor Lambert is a renowned authority regarding the nineteenth-century British navy, and he agreed that my estimation sounds reasonable. I also consulted the staff of the National Maritime Museum at Greenwich, and they concurred with my assessment.

9. See *Parliamentary Debates,* vol. 36, 1816, appendix, i–ii, xix–xx, xxiii–xxxiv.

10. British expansionist aspirations in North Africa were not manifested until the 1880s. The *Morning Chronicle,* reflecting the opinion of the British government, welcomed in 1830 (July 23, 24) France's expedition and even praised the natural aptitude of the French for colonizing. See also the account of Lord Cowley, the British ambassador to France, in "Dispatch from the Earl of Aberdeen to

Her Majesty's Ambassador at Paris, January 28, 1842," in *House of Commons Parliamentary Papers* 1842 (94) XLV 25 mf. 46.314.

11. In fact, such allegations had been raised against British abolitionists since the late eighteenth century. Thus, for example, the French publicist Venture de Paradis wrote: "Would it not be also relevant to say that at a period when there is so much untimely interest in the freedom of the Negroes, no-one has yet been concerned to ensure the freedom of the whites?" (quoted in Thomson 1987, 132).

12. See "Declaration of the Eight Powers on the Abolition of the Slave Trade, of the 8th February 1815," in *House of Commons Parliamentary Papers,* vol. 32, 200–201.

13. In fact, most African slaves were not obtained in wars but were kidnapped in designated slave-taking expeditions. See Patterson 1982, 119.

14. See Thomson 1987, 123, where she cites d'Arvieux's view on Algiers. He believes that Algiers can be considered "without fear of error as the most unworthy rabble in Africa and as a lair of thieves." For a late-seventeenth-century similar view, see Baker 1989, 59, where the author talks about the practice of "Christian stealing."

15. The letter, from September 30, 1816, is indexed in the Vane (1851) volume under the title "On the Result of the Deliberations Relative to the Slave Trade and the Barbary States."

16. In this context, it is interesting to cite Plutarch, who says that "even a nod from a person who is esteemed is of more force than a thousand arguments or studied sentences from others" (quoted in Lasswell and Kaplan 1950, 135).

Chapter 5

The quote given in the chapter title is from President George W. Bush, address to the joint session of Congress, September 20, 2001; hereafter cited in the text as Bush, 9/20/2001. Available at http://www.whitehouse.gov/news/releases/2001/09/20010920–8.html (accessed January 20, 2005).

1. The exact number of al Qaeda and Taliban fighters who were killed by the Americans during the war is unknown, but Northern Alliance commanders reported that the United States overestimated the number of enemies killed. See PBS's Frontline, "Campaign against Terror," available at http://www.pbs.org/wgbh/ pages/frontline/shows/campaign/etc/epilogue.html (accessed February 3, 2005).

2. Military operations against terrorists should not be overruled in principle. In fact, "surgical" strikes against "ticking bombs" have proven to be a highly efficient counterterror method in Israel's experience with terrorism. Israel's counterterror intensive military efforts—as well as targeted killings and assassinations of terrorist leaders—are interpreted by many in the country as being responsible for the decline in Palestinian suicide bombings, the so-called strategic weapon of the Palestinians. Statistically, however, suicide bombings were reduced considerably after the construction of walls and fences around much of the West Bank and Gaza Strip, which prevent the penetration of the bombers into Israel per se. In addition, indications are that Palestinian militants are looking for ways to

transcend the wall (e.g., missiles and mortar bombs) or to literally undermine it (e.g., booby-trapped tunnels). Furthermore, while the killing of terrorist leaders might have had a deterrent effect on the surviving ones, an unintended consequence of this strategy has been a fragmentation of the terrorist groups into gangs and local militias, on which almost no prior intelligence exists. In the long run, this could become a much more serious threat to Israel.

3. In February 2005 a committee of the Israeli army recommended stopping the destruction of houses of terrorists' families because the hatred generated by the demolition outweighed the deterrent effect. See Amos Har'el, "The IDF Will Stop Demolishing Terrorists' Houses in the Territories," *Ha'aretz* (in Hebrew), February 18, 2005.

4. See Benjamin Weiser, "The Terror Verdict: The Organization," *New York Times,* May 31, 2001, sec. A, col. 2.

5. For data on Kosovo, see PBS's Frontline, "War in Europe," available at http://www.pbs.org/wgbh/pages/frontline/shows/kosovo/etc/facts.html (accessed February 1, 2005). For data on Afghanistan, see "Operation Enduring Freedom," available at the Global Security Web site, http://www.globalsecurity.org/military/ops/enduring-freedom-ops.htm (accessed February 1, 2005).

6. For a comparison of the military power of Serbia and Afghanistan, see *The Military Balance 2000–2001,* 107–8 (Serbia) and 166 (Afghanistan).

7. See U.S. Department of Defense, *Kosovo/Operation Allied Force after Action Report to Congress* (Washington, DC, January 2000), 133.

8. This calculation is based on data from Cordesman 2002, 30.

9. See U.S. Department of Defense News Briefing, Secretary Rumsfeld and General Pace, November 6, 2001, available at http://www.defenselink.mil/transcripts/2001/t11062001_t1106sd.html (accessed February 10, 2005).

10. See Thomas Shanker and Eric Schmitt, "Taliban Defeated, Pentagon Asserts, but War Goes On," *New York Times,* December 11, 2001.

11. George W. Bush, Presidential Address to the Nation, October 7, 2001, available at http://www.whitehouse.gov/news/releases/2001/10/20011007–8.html (accessed January 26, 2006).

12. In Foucault 1977, chap. 1.

13. Interesting in this context is political scientist Robert Keohane's comparison of fear in the Cold War and fear in the age of terror: "Those of us who grew up in the United States during the Cold War experienced such [terrorizing] fear only in our imaginations, although nuclear threats and wars such as those in Korea and Vietnam gave our imaginations plenty to work with. The generations that have come of age in the United States since the mid-to-late 1980s—essentially, those people under 35—have been able to take the basics of liberalism for granted, as if the United States were insulated from the despair of much of the world's population" (2002, 41). One of the problems that the *9/11 Commission Report* highlights in its critique of the U.S. government's framing of the terror threat prior to 9/11 is the "lack of imagination."

14. U.S. Department of State 1986, 8.

15. For a similar argument, see Ringmar 2002. On détente as a process of mutual empowerment, see Suri 2003.

16. This is a paraphrase of George W. Bush's argument that Western Euro-

pean powers holding nuclear weapons during the Cold War were "responsible allies." See "Remarks by the President to Students and Faculty at National Defense University," available at http://www.whitehouse.gov/news/releases/2001/05/20010501–10.html (accessed February 17, 2005).

17. The Geneva communiqué of November 1985, quoted in Nye 1987, 385–86.

18. But see Lebow and Stein 1994.

19. See "Statement by Director of Central Intelligence George J. Tenet Before the Senate Foreign Relations Committee on the Worldwide Threat in 2000: Global Realities of Our National Security," March 21, 2000, available at http://www.cia.gov/cia/public_affairs/speeches/2000/dci_speech_032100.html (accessed February 16, 2005).

20. On the legal status of peacekeeping forces, see Dinstein 2001, 266–68.

21. There are unconfirmed reports that Reagan also ordered the CIA to back a Lebanese Christian faction's car bombing in Beirut, attempting to kill the leader of the Hizb'allah group. The bomb killed eighty and wounded more than two hundred civilians. The United States denied involvement.

22. Interview with Robert Oakley, a former State Department coordinator for counterterrorism in the 1980s, on PBS's Frontline, "Target America," available at http://www.pbs.org/wgbh/pages/frontline/shows/target/interviews/oakley.html (accessed June 17, 2004).

23. Also, Hizb'allah has never claimed responsibility for the Western hostages crisis of the 1980s in Lebanon, during which eighty-seven foreign nationals, mainly Westerners, were kidnapped by elements associated with Hizb'allah. Although the United States argued that Hizb'allah was responsible, the organization consistently denied any responsibility for the kidnappings. See Ranstorp 1997.

24. Foreign Broadcast Information Service [FBIS], FBIS-NES-88-248, December 27, 1988.

25. FBIS-NES-88-001, January 3, 1989.

26. The full text of the Lockerbie verdict is available at http://www.guardian.co.uk/Lockerbie/0,2759,431005,00.html (accessed June 20, 2004).

27. A minicrisis did develop between the United States and Libya, though, when on January 5, 1989, U.S. jets shot down two Libyan MIG-23s over international water, 110 kilometers from the Libyan coast, as the USS *John F. Kennedy* was holding maneuvers in the central Mediterranean. The cause for the crisis was American allegations that Libya was developing a chemical weapons program.

28. See President Ronald Reagan, "Address to the Nation on the US Air Strike Against Libya, April 14, 1986." Available at the Reagan Presidential Library Web site, http://www.reagan.utexas.edu/resource/speeches/1986/41486g.htm (accessed April 15, 2004).

29. FBIS-MEA-86-003, January 6, 1986, Q4.

30. FBIS-MEA-86-069, April 10, 1986.

31. FBIS-MEA-86-057, 4.

32. FBIS-MEA-86-074, 17 April 1986, Q2.

33. See Rahimullah Yusufzai, "Wrath of God: Osama bin Laden Lashes Out against the West," *Time Asia,* January 11, 1999, available at http://www.time.com/time/asia/asia/magazine/1999/990111/osama3.html (accessed January 20, 2005).

34. See David Bamber, "Bin Laden: Yes, I Did It," *Sunday Telegraph* (London), November 11, 2001. See also Peter Maas, "When al Qaeda Calls," *New York Times,* February 2, 2003, sec. 6, p. 48, col. 1.

35. Giles Tremlett, "Al-Qaida Leaders Say Nuclear Power Stations Were Original Targets. Reporter Meets Contender for Next Bin Laden," *Guardian,* September 9, 2002.

36. Bin Laden's al Jazeerah interview from October 7, 2001. Note that the statement was likely taped at least a day prior to the first American strikes on Afghanistan. The statement is taped during daylight hours; however, the attacks began when it was already late evening and dark in Afghanistan. Transcript of bin Laden's interview with al Jazeera is available at http://www.cnn.com/2002/WORLD/asiapcf/south/02/05/binladen.transcript/index.html (accessed May 25, 2004).

37. See "Text: Bin Laden Discusses Attacks on Tape," *Washington Post,* December 13, 2001.

38. "President Bush's Remarks at the White House Ceremony to Honor the Victims of the September 11 Terrorist Attacks," March 11, 2002 (emphasis added), available at http://vietnam.usembassy.gov/wwwhcat14.html (accessed April 3, 2005).

39. Bin Laden interview with ABC reporter John Miller, May 1998. Available at http://www.pbs.org/wgbh/pages/frontline/shows/binladen/who/interview.html (accessed February 20, 2005).

40. See, for example, bin Laden's Sermon for the Feast of the Sacrifice, March 2003, available at the Middle East Media Research Institute Web site, http://www.memri.org/bin/articles.cgi?Page=subjects&Area=jihad&ID=SP47603 (accessed June 4, 2004). Even before 9/11, bin Laden talked about American power as a "legend." In a CNN interview in January 1999 he said, "I am confident that Muslims will be able to end the legend of the so-called superpower that is America" (quoted in Parachini 2001, 397).

41. See "Text: Bin Laden Discusses Attacks on Tape," *Washington Post,* December 13, 2001.

42. "President Bush and Italian Prime Minister Discuss War Effort," available at http://www.whitehouse.gov/news/releases/2001/10/20011015–3.html (accessed January 25, 2005).

43. Soviet forces in Afghanistan never exceeded 104,000 men, and throughout the years of the war 13,833 Soviet soldiers died. See Shaw and Spencer 2003.

44. Bin Laden quoted by Simon Reeve and Giles Foden, "A New Breed of Terror," *Guardian,* September 12, 2001.

45. See PBS's Frontline, "Campaign against Terror: Interview with Condoleezza Rice," available at http://www.pbs.org/wgbh/pages/frontline/shows/campaign/interviews/rice.html (accessed February 3, 2005).

46. "President Bush's Remarks," March 11, 2002.

47. Thus, when Cofer Black, director of the CIA Counterterrorist Center, was visiting Moscow in late September 2001 to coordinate with the Russians the American attack on Afghanistan, a Russian intelligence official reportedly warned him that Afghanistan was "ambush heaven" and that the Americans, like the Soviets, were going to suffer there tremendously. "We're going to put their

heads on sticks. We're going to rock their world," responded Black (Woodward 2002, 103).

48. Biddle (2003, 39) even denotes the Taliban and al Qaeda prisoners who participated in the "uprising" as "renegades." The *Merriam-Webster Dictionary* on-line defines *renegade* as "an individual who rejects lawful or conventional behavior."

49. This was due to the high-flying altitude of the American bombers or because the planes were remote from the scene of the bombing itself: American planes released precision-guided weapons from a distance of up to eight kilometers from the target, which was marked in laser signatures by U.S. special forces teams operating on the ground.

50. President Bush's address to the nation, October 7, 2001.

51. See John F. Burns, "After the Attacks: In Pakistan," *New York Times,* September 15, 2001, sec. A, col. 1.

52. See Michael Gordon and Eric Schmitt, "A Nation Challenged: Tactics," *New York Times,* October 9, 2001, sec. A, col. 3.

53. On Soviet war crimes in Afghanistan, see Reuveny and Prakash 1999, 702.

54. Michael R. Gordon, "A Nation Challenged: Military Analysis," *New York Times,* October 21, 2001, sec. 1A, col. 5.

55. See "White House's Campaign Against Terrorism: A Coalition Update," available at http://www.whitehouse.gov/march11/coalition/coalitionupdate .html#2 (accessed July 31, 2004).

56. On the alleged penetration of al Qaeda to China, see *People's Daily,* November 16, 2001; see also Chung 2002.

57. See speech by Russian president Vladimir Putin at the Russian Rectors Conference, Moscow, December 6, 2002, available at http://www.ln.mid.ru/ Bl.nsf/arh/3977216E424B078D43256C8A005EFA97?OpenDocument (accessed July 26, 2004); emphasis added.

58. See interview of Russian president Vladimir Putin with German ARD Television Company, September 19, 2001, available at http://www.ln.mid.ru/ Bl.nsf/arh/5C4D35E784EBC9B543256AD2003D61FF?OpenDocument (accessed July 28, 2004).

59. See G8 Heads of State and Government Statement, September 21, 2001, available at http://www.g7utoronto.ca/g7/terrorism/sept.192001html (accessed January 15, 2003).

60. See *People's Daily,* October 1, 2001.

61. See "Al-Jazeera Airs Purported bin Laden Audiotapes. Voice Calls for Suicide Attacks against Americans, Their Allies," October 19, 2003, available at http://www.cnn.com/2003/WORLD/meast/10/18/binladen.tape/ (accessed on July 28, 2004).

Conclusions

1. On Selznick's distinction between governance and management, see Garland 1990, 58–59.

2. The last point—legitimization—is clearly indicative of the authority of the United States and other Great Powers: smaller states often seek the political

approval of the Great Powers in their regional conflicts not simply due to fear of sanctions or hope of positive rewards but also as a way to enhance their self-esteem and to marginalize the claims of their rivals and opponents.

3. "President Bush's Remarks at the White House Ceremony to Honor the Victims of the September 11 Terrorist Attacks," March 11, 2002 (emphasis added), available at http://vietnam.usembassy.gov/wwwhcat14.html (accessed April 3, 2005).

4. See Bush's words on November 3, 2002: "Bush: 'America Will Not Forget,'" available at http://archives.cnn.com/2002/US/03/11/gen.bush.speech/ (accessed April 13, 2005).

Bibliography

Abun-Nasr, Jamil M. 1987. *A History of the Maghrib in the Islamic Period*. Cambridge: Cambridge University Press.

Adler, Emanuel, and Michael Barnett, eds. 1998. *Security Communities*. New York: Cambridge University Press.

Adler, Emanuel, and Beverly Crawford, eds. 1991. *Progress in Postwar International Relations*. New York: Columbia University Press.

Allison, A. 1861. *Lives of Lord Castlereagh and Sir Charles Stewart, the Second and Third Marquesses of Londonderry*. London: Blackwood.

Allison, Graham T., Owen R. Cote, Richard A. Falkenrath, and Steven E. Miller. 1996. *Avoiding Nuclear Anarchy: Containing the Threat of Loose Russian Nuclear Weapons and Fissile Material*. Cambridge, MA: MIT Press.

Amoraga, Francisco Requena. 1999. *El corso turco–berberisco en la Gobernacion de Orihuela (Siglo XVI y XVII)*. Elche: Patronage Historico Artistico Cultural D'Elig.

Anderson, Garry, and Adam Gifford. 1991. "Privateering and the Private Production of Naval Power." *Cato Journal* 11 (1): 99–122.

Anderson, M. S. 1956. "Great Britain and the Barbary States in the Eighteenth Century." *Bulletin of the Institute of Historical Research* 29:87–107.

———. 1995. *Europe in the Eighteenth Century, 1713–1783*. New York: Longman.

Anderson, Olive. 1960. "The Establishment of British Supremacy at Sea and the Exchange of Naval Prisoners of War, 1689–1783." *English Historical Review* 75 (294): 77–89.

Andrews, Kenneth R. 1984. *Trade, Plunder, and Settlement: Maritime Enterprise and the Genesis of the British Empire, 1480–1630*. Cambridge: Cambridge University Press.

Arenal, Mercedes García, and Miguel Angel Bunes. 1992. *Los españoles y el Norte de Africa, Siglos XV–XVIII*. Madrid: Mapfre.

Arendt, Hannah. 1958. "What Was Authority?" In *Authority*, ed. C. J. Friedrich, 81–112. Cambridge, MA: Harvard University Press.

Arreguín-Toft, Ivan. 2001. "How the Weak Win Wars: A Theory of Asymmetric Conflict." *International Security* 26 (1): 93–128.

Asch, Ronald G. 2000. "'Wo der soldat hinkombt, da ist alles sein': Military Violence and Atrocities in the Thirty Years War Re-examined." *German History* 18 (3): 291–309.

Avant, Deborah, and James Lebovic. 2000. "U.S. Military Attitudes toward Post-Cold War Missions." *Armed Forces and Society* 27 (1): 37–56.

Axelrod, Robert. 1984. *The Evolution of Cooperation.* New York: Basic Books.

———. 1986. "An Evolutionary Approach to Norms." *American Political Science Review* 80 (4): 1095–111.

Ayoob, Mohammed. 1995. *The Third World Security Predicament: State Making, Regional Conflict, and the International System.* Boulder, CO: Lynne Rienner.

Badey, Thomas J. 1998. "Defining International Terrorism: A Pragmatic Approach." *Terrorism and Political Violence* 10 (1): 90–107.

Baker, Sherston, ed. 1908. *Hallecks International Law, or Rules Regulating the Intercourse of States in Peace and War.* Vol. 2. London: Kegan Paul.

Baker, Thomas. 1989. *Piracy and Diplomacy in Seventeenth Century North Africa: The Journal of Thomas Baker, English Consul in Triploi, 1677–1685.* Ed. with an introduction by C. R. Pennel. Cranbury, NJ: Associated University Presses.

Ballis, William. 1973. *The Legal Position of War: Changes in Its Practice and Theory from Plato to Vattel.* New York: Garland.

Barkin, J. Samuel, and Bruce Cronin. 1994. "The State and the Nation: Changing Norms and the Rules of Sovereignty in International Relations." *International Organization* 48 (1): 107–30.

Barrow, John. 1848. *The Life and Correspondence of Admiral Sir William Sidney Smith.* Vol. 2. London: Richard Bentley.

Bartelson, Jens. 1995. *A Genealogy of Sovereignty.* Cambridge: Cambridge University Press.

Bartlett, C. J. 1963. *Great Britain and Sea Power, 1815–1853.* Oxford: Clarendon Press.

Baumeister, Roy F., and Laura Smart. 1996. "Relation of Threatened Egotism to Violence and Aggression: The Dark Side of High Self-Esteem." *Psychological Review* 103 (1): 5–33.

Baumgold, Deborah. 1993. "Pacifying Politics: Resistance, Violence, and Accountability in Seventeenth Century Contract Theory." *Political Theory* 21 (1): 6–27.

Bennett, Norman R. 1960. "Christian and Negro Slavery in Eighteenth Century North Africa." *Journal of African History* 1 (1): 65–82.

Bernard, Chester I. 1968. *The Functions of the Executive.* Cambridge, MA: Harvard University Press.

Bhide, Amar, and Howard H. Stevenson. 1990. "Why Be Honest If Honesty Doesn't Pay." *Harvard Business Review* 68 (5): 121–29.

Biddle, Stephen. 2003. "Afghanistan and the Future of Warfare." *Foreign Affairs* 82 (2): 31–46.

Biersteker, T. J., and C. Weber, eds. 1996. *State Sovereignty as a Social Construct.* Cambridge: Cambridge University Press.

Bindert, Guyora. 2002. "Punishment Theory: Moral or Political?" *Buffalo Criminal Law Review* 5 (2): 321–71.

Black, J. B. 1959. *The Reign of Elizabeth, 1558–1603.* Oxford: Clarendon Press.

Black, Jeremy. 1998. *Why Wars Happen.* New York: New York University Press.

Blumer, Herbert. 1969. *Symbolic Interactionism: Perspective and Method.* Englewood Cliffs, NJ: Prentice Hall.

Bowden, Brett. 2004. "In the Name of Progress and Peace: The 'Standard of Civilization' and the Universalizing Project." *Alternatives* 29 (1): 43–68.

Braudel, Fernand. 1973. *The Mediterranean and the Mediterranean World in the Age of Philip II.* Vol. 2. New York: Harper and Row.

British and Foreign State Papers, 1815–16. 1838. London: James Ridgeway.

Brown, Chris. 2002. *Sovereignty, Rights and Justice: International Political Theory Today.* Cambridge: Polity Press.

Brown, David K. 1990. *Before the Ironclad: Development of Ship Design, Propulsion, and Armament in the Royal Navy, 1815–60.* London: Conway.

Browning, Peter. 2002. *The Changing Nature of Warfare: The Developments of Land Warfare from 1792 to 1945.* Cambridge: Cambridge University Press.

Brummett, Palmira. 1999. "The Ottoman Empire, Venice, and the Question of Enduring Rivalries." In *Great Power Rivalries,* ed. William R. Thompson, 225–53. Columbia: University of South Carolina Press.

Bukovansky, Mlada. 2002. *Legitimacy and Power Politics: The American and French Revolutions in International Political Culture.* Princeton: Princeton University Press.

Bull, Hedley. 1977. *The Anarchical Society: A Study of Order in International Politics.* London: Macmillan.

Burch, Kurt. 1998. *"Property" and the Making of the International System.* Boulder, CO, and London: Lynne Rienner.

Burt, Ronald S. 1992. *Structural Holes: The Social Structure of Competition.* Cambridge, MA: Harvard University Press.

Bush, George W. 2002a. *National Security Strategy of the United States.* September. Washington, DC: The White House.

———. 2002b. *National Security Strategy for the United States on Weapons of Mass Destruction.* December. Washington, DC: The White House.

Butterfield, H. 1953. "Acton and the Massacre of St Bartholomew." *Cambridge Historical Journal* 11 (1): 27–47.

Buzan, Barry. 2004. *From International to World Society? English School Theory and the Social Structure of Globalisation.* Cambridge: Cambridge University Press.

Campbell, David. 1998. *Writing Security: United States Foreign Policy and the Politics of Identity.* Minneapolis: University of Minnesota Press.

Carnahan, Burrus M. 1998. "Lincoln, Lieber, and the Laws of War: The Origins and Limits of the Principle of Military Necessity." *American Journal of International Law* 92 (2): 213–31.

Carroll, Stuart. 2003. "The Peace in the Feud in Sixteenth and Seventeenth Century France." *Past and Present* 178:74–115.

Carter, Charles H. 1964. *The Secret Diplomacy of the Habsburgs, 1598–1625.* New York: Columbia University Press.

Chapman, Tim. 1998. *The Congress of Vienna: Origins, Processes, and Results.* New York: Routledge.

Christensen, Thomas J., and Jack Snyder. 1990. "Chain Gangs and Passed Bucks: Predicting Alliance Patterns in Multipolarity." *International Organization* 44 (2): 137–68.

Chung, Chien-peng. 2002. "China's 'War on Terror': September 11 and Uighur Separatism." *Foreign Affairs* 81 (4): 8–12.

Clark, G. N. 1944. "The Barbary Corsairs in the Seventeenth Century." *Cambridge Historical Journal* 8 (1): 22–35.

Clark, Ian. 1989. *The Hierarchy of States: Reform and Resistance in the International Order.* Cambridge: Cambridge University Press.

Clark, Sir George. 1958. *War and Society in the Seventeenth Century.* Cambridge: Cambridge University Press.

Clarke, Richard. 2004. *Against All Enemies: Inside America's War on Terror.* New York: Free Press.

Claude, Inis L., Jr. 1966. "Collective Legitimization as the Political Function of the United Nations." *International Organization* 20 (3): 367–79.

Clissold, Stephen. 1977. *The Barbary Slaves.* London: Paul Elek.

Clowes, W. L. 1898. *The Royal Navy: A History from the Earliest Times to the Present.* Vol. 2. London: Sampson, Low, Marston.

———. 1901. *The Royal Navy.* Vol. 5. London: Sampson, Low, Marston.

Colbert, Evelyn S. 1948. *Retaliation in International Law.* New York: Columbia University King's Crown Press.

Coles, Paul. 1968. *The Ottoman Impact on Europe.* London: Thames and Hudson.

Colley, Linda. 2002. *Captives: Britain, Empire, and the World, 1600–1850.* New York: Anchor Books.

Conetta, Carl. 2002. "Strange Victory: A Critical Appraisal of Operation Enduring Freedom and the Afghanistan War." Project on Defense Alternatives Research Monograph No. 6.

Conquergood, Dwight. 2002. "Lethal Theatre: Performance, Punishment, and the Death Penalty." *Theatre Journal* 54:339–67.

Cooper, H. H. A. 2001. "Terrorism: The Problem of Definition Revisited." *American Behavioral Scientist* 44 (6): 881–93.

Cooper, J. P. 1971. "Sea Power." In *The New Cambridge Modern History.* Vol. 4, *The Decline of Spain and the Thirty Years War, 1609–1648/59,* ed. J. P. Cooper, 226–38. Cambridge: Cambridge University Press.

Corbett, Julian S. 1917. *England in the Mediterranean: A Study of the Rise and Influence of British Power within the Straits.* London: Longmans, Green.

Cordesman, Anthony H. 2002. *The Air War Lessons of Afghanistan: Change and Continuity.* Washington, DC: Center for Strategic and International Studies.

Cordovez, Diego, and Selig S. Harrison. 1995. *Out of Afghanistan: The Inside Story of the Soviet Withdrawal.* New York: Oxford University Press.

Cowdrey, H. E. J. 1970. "The Peace and the Truce of God in the Eleventh Century." *Past and Present* 46:42–67.

Crawford, Neta C. 2000. "The Passion of World Politics: Propositions on Emotion and Emotional Relationships." *International Security* 24 (4): 116–56.

Crocker, William. 1816. *The Cruelties of the Algerine Pirates*. London: W. Hone.

Cronin, Bruce. 2001. "The Paradox of Hegemony: America's Ambiguous Relationship with the United Nations." *European Journal of International Relations* 7 (1): 103–30.

Dannreuther, Roland. 1998. *The Soviet Union and the PLO*. New York: St. Martin's Press.

Dau-Schmidt, Kenneth G. 1990. "An Economic Analysis of the Criminal Law as a Preference-Shaping Policy." *Duke Law Journal* 1 (1): 1–38.

David, Steven R. 1989. "Why the Third World Still Matters." *International Security* 14 (1): 50–85.

Davies, Trevor R. 1964. *The Golden Century of Spain, 1501–1621*. London: Macmillan.

Davis, Paul K., and Brian M. Jenkins. 2002. *Deterrence and Influence in Counterterrorism: A Component in the War on al Qaeda*. Santa Monica, CA: RAND.

Davis, Robert C. 2001. "Counting European Slaves on the Barbary Coast." *Past and Present* 172 (1): 87–124.

———. 2003. *Christian Slaves, Muslim Masters: White Slavery in the Mediterranean, the Barbary Coast, and Italy, 1500–1800*. London: Palgrave Macmillan.

de Gomara, Francisco Lopez. 1989. *Cronica de los muy nombrados Oruch y Jaradin Barbarroja*. Madrid: Ediciones Polifemo.

de Grazia, Sebastian. 1959. "What Authority Is Not." *American Political Science Review* 53 (2): 321–31.

de Groot, Alexander H. 1978. *The Ottoman Empire and the Dutch Republic: A History of the Earliest Diplomatic Relations, 1610–1630*. Leiden and Istanbul: Nederlands Historisch-Archaelogisch Institut.

———. 1985. "Ottoman North Africa and the Dutch Republic in the Seventeenth and Eighteenth Centuries." *Revue de l'Occident Musulman et de la Méditerranée* 39:131–47.

de Ibarra Bunes, M. A. 1998. "Felipe II y el Mediterráneo: la frontera olvidada y la frontera presente de la Monarquía Católica." In *Felipe II (1527–1598). Europa y la Monarquía Católica. Actas del Congreso Internacional: Felipe II (1527–1598). Europa dividida, la Monarquía Católica de Felipe II* (U.A.M., 20–23 de abril de 1998), vol. 1-1, ed. M. J. Martinez, 97–110. Madrid: Editorial Parteluz.

de Souza, Philip. 1999. *Piracy in the Graeco-Roman World*. Cambridge: Cambridge University Press.

Debord, Guy. 1995. *Society of the Spectacle*. New York: Zone Books.

Des Pres, Terrence. 1991. *Writing into the World*. New York: Viking.

Deudney, Daniel. 2000. "Geopolitics as Theory: Historical Security Materialism." *European Journal of International Relations* 6 (1): 77–107.

Diebert, Ronald, and Janice Stein. 2002. "Hacking Networks of Terror." *Dialogue-IO* 1 (1): 1–14.

Dingott Alkopher, Tal. 2004. "Wars by Right: Wars as a Social and Historical

Construct of Constitutive Rights." Paper presented at the annual meeting of the International Studies Association, Montreal, March 17–20.

Dinstein, Yoram. 2001. *War, Aggression, and Self-Defence*. 3d ed. Cambridge: Cambridge University Press.

Donagan, Barbara. 1994. "Atrocity, War Crime, and Treason in the English Civil War." *American Historical Review* 99 (4): 1137–166.

Donnelly, Jack. 2000. *Realism and International Relations*. Cambridge: Cambridge University Press, 2000.

Doran, Michael. 2002. "The Pragmatic Fanaticism of al Qaeda: An Anatomy of Extremism in Middle Eastern Politics." *Political Science Quarterly* 117 (2): 177–90.

Drescher, Simon. 1986. *Capitalism and Antislavery: British Mobilization in Comparative Perspective*. Basingstoke and London: MacMillan Press.

Drew, Jerry Ira. 2002. "Entrepreneurial Warriors: Privateers in Trade and War." PhD diss., University of Pennsylvania.

Earle, Peter. 1970. *Corsairs of Malta and Barbary*. London: Sidgwick and Jackson.

Edmundson, William A. 1998. "Legitimate Authority without Political Obligation." *Law and Philosophy* 17 (1): 43–60.

Edwards, S. 1968. *Barbary General: The Life of William Eaton*. Englewood Cliffs, NJ: Prentice-Hall.

Elias, Norbert. 1982. *The Civilizing Process*. Vol. 2, *Power and Civility*. Trans. Edmond Jephcott. New York: Pantheon Books.

Elliott, John H. 1977. "Self-Perception and Decline in Early Seventeenth Century Spain." *Past and Present* 74:41–61.

———. 1983. "A Question of Reputation? Spanish Foreign Policy in the Seventeenth Century." *Journal of Modern History* 55 (3): 475–83.

———. 1986. *The Count-Duke of Olivares: The Statesman in an Age of Decline*. New Haven: Yale University Press.

———. 1989. *Spain and Its World, 1500–1700*. New Haven: Yale University Press.

Elster, Jon. 1990. "Norms of Revenge." *Ethics* 100 (4): 862–85.

Feijoo, Ramiro. 2003. *Corsarios Berberiscos*. Barcelona: Belacqva/Carroggio.

Feinberg, Joel. 1984. *The Moral Limits of the Criminal Law*. Vol. 1, *Harm to Others*. Oxford: Oxford University Press.

———. 1990. *Harmless Wrongdoing*. New York: Oxford University Press.

Ferguson, Yale H., and Richard W. Mansbach. 2005. "War and Innocent Victims: The Paradox of Westphalia." Paper presented at the annual meeting of the International Studies Association, Honolulu, Hawaii, March 2–5.

Fernandez, Enrique. 2000. "*Los tratos de Argel*: obra testimonial, denuncia política y literatura terapéutica." *Cervantes: Bulletin of the Cervantes Society of America* 20 (1): 7–26.

Finnemore, Martha, and Kathryn Sikkink. 1998. "International Norm Dynamics and Political Change." *International Organization* 52 (4): 887–917.

Fisher, Godfrey. 1957. *Barbary Legend: War, Trade and Piracy in North Africa, 1415–1830*. Oxford: Oxford University Press.

Floristan, Imizcoz J. M. 1988. *Fuentes para la política oriental de los Austrias*. La *documentación griega del Archivo de Simancas (1571–1621)*. Vol. 2. León: Universidad de León.

Foreign Relations of the United States. 1801.

Foucault, Michel. 1977. *Discipline and Punish: The Birth of Prison*. New York: Pantheon Books.

Franck, Thomas M. 1990. *The Power of Legitimacy among Nations*. New York: Oxford University Press.

Fraser, Antonia. 1996. *The Gunpowder Plot: Terror and Faith in 1605*. London: Weidenfeld and Nicolson.

Frey, Bruno S. 1997. *Not Just for the Money: An Economic Theory of Personal Motivation*. Cheltenham: Edward Elgar.

Friedman, Ellen G. 1975. "The Exercise of Religion by Spanish Captives in North Africa." *Sixteenth Century Journal* 6 (1): 19–34.

———. 1980. "Christian Captives at 'Hard Labor' in Algiers, 16th–18th Centuries." *International Journal of African Historical Studies* 13 (4): 616–32.

———. 1983. *Spanish Captives in North Africa in the Early Modern Age*. Madison: University of Wisconsin Press.

Friedrich, Carl J. 1958. "Authority, Reason, and Discretion." In *Authority*, ed. C. J. Friedrich, 28–48. Cambridge, MA: Harvard University Press.

Fuchs, Barbara. 2001. *Mimesis and Empire: The New World, Islam, and European Identities*. Princeton: Princeton University Press.

Fursenko, Aleksandr, and Timothy Naftali. 1998. *One Hell of a Gamble: The Secret History of the Cuban Missile Crisis*. New York: W. W. Norton.

Gaddis, John L. 1987. *The Long Peace*. Oxford: Oxford University Press.

GAO (United States General Accounting Office). 1999. *Drug Control: Assets DoD Contributes to Reducing the Illegal Drug Supply Have Declined*. Report to Congressional Requesters, December. GAO/NSIAD-00-9. Washington, DC: GAO.

Garcés, Maria A. 2002. *Cervantes in Algiers: A Captive's Tale*. Nashville: Vanderbilt University Press.

Garfinkel, Harold. 1956. "Conditions of Successful Degradation Ceremonies." *American Journal of Sociology* 61 (5): 420–24.

Garland, David. 1990. *Punishment and Modern Society: A Study in Social Theory*. Oxford: Clarendon Press.

Garst, Daniel. 1989. "Thucydides and Neorealism." *International Studies Quarterly* 33:3–27.

Gat, Azar. 1989. *The Origins of Military Thought: From the Enlightenment to Clausewitz*. Oxford: Clarendon Press.

Genovese, Eugene D. 1976. *Roll, Jordan, Roll: The World the Slaves Made*. New York: Vintage Books.

Gent, Stephen E. 2003. "Instability, Intervention, and Inter-Power Politics." Working Paper, University of Rochester. Available at http://troi.cc.rochester .edu/~gent/instability.pdf. Accessed July 22, 2005.

Gentili, Alberico. 1921. *Hispanicae Advocationis Libri Dvo*. Trans. F. F. Abbott. New York: Oxford University Press.

Gewirth, Allan. 1988. "Rights and Duties." *Mind* 97 (387): 441–45.

Gholz, Eugene, Daryl G. Press, and Harvey M. Sapolsky. 1997. "Come Home

America: The Strategy of Restraint in the Face of Temptation." *International Security* 21 (4): 5–48.

Gibbons, Donald. 1968. *Society, Crime, and Criminal Careers: An Introduction to Criminology*. Englewood Cliffs, NJ: Prentice-Hall.

Giddens, Anthony. 1985. *The Nation State and Violence. Volume Two of a Contemporary Critique of Historical Materialism*. Cambridge: Polity Press.

Gilpin, Robert. 1981. *War and Change*. New York: Cambridge University Press.

Glete, Jan. 2000. *Warfare at Sea, 1500–1650: Maritime Conflicts and the Transformation of Europe*. London: Routledge.

———. 2002. *War and the State in Early Modern Europe: Spain, the Dutch Republic, and Sweden as Fiscal-Military States, 1500–1660*. London: Routledge.

Golan, Galia. 1976. *The Soviet Union and the Palestine Liberation Organization: An Uneasy Alliance*. New York: Praeger.

———. 1988. *The Soviet Union and National Liberation Movements in the Third World*. Boston: Unwin Hyman.

Goldgeiger, James M., and Michael McFaul. 1992. "A Tale of Two Worlds: Core and Periphery in the Post–Cold War Era." *International Organization* 46 (2): 467–91.

Gong, Gerrit W. 1984. *The Standard of Civilization in International Society*. Oxford: Clarendon Press.

Goodman, David. 1997. *Spanish Naval Power, 1589–1665: Reconstruction and Defeat*. Cambridge: Cambridge University Press.

Gosse, Philip. 1932. *The History of Piracy*. Glorieta, NM: Rio Grande Press.

Grossman, Herschel, and Kim Minseong. 2000. "Predators, Moral Decay, and Moral Revivals." *European Journal of Political Economy* 16 (2): 173–87.

Grunberg, Isabelle. 1990. "Exploring the 'Myth' of Hegemonic Stability." *International Organization* 44 (4): 431–77.

Gunn, Steven. 2001. "War, Religion, and the State." In *Early Modern Europe: An Oxford History*, ed. Euan Cameron, 102–33. Oxford: Oxford University Press.

Habermas, Jürgen. 1984. *The Theory of Communicative Action*. Vol. 1, *Reason and the Rationalization of Society*. Boston: Beacon Press.

Hair, P. E. H., ed. 1990. *To Defend Your Empire and the Faith: Advice on Global Strategy Offered c.1590 to Philip, King of Spain and Portugal, by Manoel de Andrada Castel Blanco*. Liverpool: Liverpool University Press.

Hale, J. R. 1968. "Armies, Navies, and the Art of War." In *The New Cambridge Modern History*. Vol. 3, *The Counter-Reformation and Price Revolution, 1559–1610*, ed. R. B. Wernham, 171–208. Cambridge: Cambridge University Press.

———. 1985. *War and Society in Renaissance Europe*. New York: St. Martin's Press.

Hall, Rodney Bruce. 1997. "Moral Authority as a Power Resource." *International Organization* 51 (4): 591–622.

Hall, Rodney Bruce, and Thomas J. Biersteker. 2002. "The Emergence of Private Authority in the International System." In *The Emergence of Private Author-*

ity in Global Governance, ed. B. Hall and T. Biersteker, 3–22. Cambridge: Cambridge University Press.

Halliday, Fred. 1999. "Soviet Foreign Policymaking and the Afghanistan War: From 'Second Mongolia' to 'Bleeding Wound'." *Review of International Studies* 25 (4): 675–91.

Handel, Michael. 1981. *Weak States in the International System.* London: Frank Cass.

Harding, Nicholas. 2000. "North African Piracy, the Hanoverian Carrying Trade, and the British State, 1728–1828." *Historical Journal* 43 (1): 25–47.

Hathaway, Andrew D., and Michael F. Atkinson. 2001. "Tolerable Differences Revisited: Crossroads in Theory on the Social Construction of Deviance." *Deviant Behavior: An Interdisciplinary Journal* 22:353–77.

Hebb, David D. 1994. *Piracy and the English Government, 1616–1642.* Aldershot: Scholar Press.

Heers, Jacques. 2003. *The Barbary Corsairs: Warfare in the Mediterranean, 1480–1580.* London: Greenhill Books.

Herz, John. 1962. *International Politics in the Atomic Age.* New York: Columbia University Press.

Hess, Andrew. 1968. "The Moriscos: An Ottoman Fifth Column in Sixteenth Century Spain." *American Historical Review* 74 (1): 1–25.

———. 1977. "The Forgotten Frontier: The Ottoman North African Provinces during the Eighteenth Century." In *Studies in Eighteenth Century Islamic History,* ed. Thomas Naff and Roger Owen, 74–88. Carbondale: Southern Illinois University Press.

———. 1978. *The Forgotten Frontier: A History of the Sixteenth Century Ibero-African Frontier.* Chicago: University of Chicago Press.

Hicks, F. C. 1908. "The Equality of States and the Hague Conferences." *American Journal of International Law* 2 (3): 530–61.

Hillgarth, J. N. 2000. *The Mirror of Spain, 1500–1700: The Formation of a Myth.* Ann Arbor: University of Michigan Press.

Hinds, Allen B., ed. 1909. *Calendar of State Papers and Manuscripts Relating to English Affairs Existing in the Archives and Collections of Venice and in the Other Libraries of Northern Italy.* Vol. 15, 1617–1619. Hereford: Hereford Times Press.

———. 1911. *Calendar of State Papers and Manuscripts Relating to English Affairs Existing in the Archives and Collections of Venice and in the Other Libraries of Northern Italy.* Vol. 17, 1621–1623. Hereford: Hereford Times Press.

Hinsley, F. H. 1986. *Sovereignty.* 2d ed. Cambridge: Cambridge University Press.

Hoffman, Aaron M. 2004. "Taking Credit for Their Work: When Groups Announce Responsibility for Acts of Terror, 1968–1977." Paper presented at the annual meeting of the International Studies Association, Montreal, Canada, March 17.

Hoffman, Bruce. 1997. "Why Terrorist Don't Claim Credit." *Terrorism and Political Violence* 9 (1): 1–6.

———. 1998. *Inside Terrorism.* New York: Columbia University Press.

Hoffman, Paul E. 1980. *The Spanish Crown and the Defence of the Caribbean,*

1535–1585: Precedent, Patrimonialism and Royal Parsimony. Baton Rouge: Louisiana State University Press.

Hollis, Martin, and Steven Lukes, eds. 1982. *Rationality and Relativism.* Oxford: Blackwell.

Holsti, K. J. 1991. *Peace and War: Armed Conflicts and International Order, 1648–1989.* New York: Cambridge University Press.

———. 1996. *The State, War, and the State of War.* Cambridge: Cambridge University Press.

———. 2004. *Taming the Sovereigns: Institutional Change in International Politics.* Cambridge: Cambridge University Press.

Howard, Edward. 1839. *Memoirs of Admiral Sir Sidney Smith, K.C.B., &c.* London: R. Bentley.

Howard, Michael. 1976. *War in European History.* Oxford: Oxford University Press.

Hunter, I., and D. Saunders, eds. 2002. *Natural Law and Civil Sovereignty: Moral Right and State Authority in Early Modern Political Thought.* New York: Polgrave-Macmillan.

Huntington, Samuel P. 1957. "Conservatism as an Ideology." *American Political Science Review* 51 (2): 454–73.

Hurd, Elizabeth Shakman. 2004. "The Political Authority of Secularism in International Relations." *European Journal of International Relations* 10 (2): 235–62.

Hurd, Ian. 1999. "Legitimacy and Authority in International Politics." *International Organization* 53 (2): 379–408.

———. 2002. "Legitimacy, Power, and the Symbolic Life of the Security Council." *Global Governance* 8 (1): 35–51.

———. 2004. "Of Words and Wars: The Security Council's Hard Life among the Great Powers." *Seton Hall Journal of Diplomacy and International Relations* 5 (1): 69–75.

———. 2005. "The Strategic Use of Liberal Internationalism: Libya and the UN Sanctions, 1999–2003." *International Organization* 59 (3): 495–526.

Huth, Paul. 1997. "Reputations and Deterrence: A Theoretical and Empirical Assessment." *Security Studies* 7 (1): 72–99.

Ikenberry, G. John. 2001. *After Victory: Institutions, Strategic Restraint, and the Rebuilding of Order after Major Wars.* Princeton: Princeton University Press.

Irwin, Ray W. 1970. *The Diplomatic Relations of the Unites States with the Barbary Powers, 1776–1816.* New York: Russell and Russell.

Israel, Jonathan I. 1977. "A Conflict of Empires: Spain and the Netherlands, 1618–1648." *Past and Present* 76:34–74.

———. 1982. *The Dutch Republic and the Hispanic World, 1606–1661.* Oxford: Clarendon Press.

Jackson, Robert. 2000. *The Global Covenant: Human Conduct in a World of States.* Oxford: Oxford University Press.

James, William D. [1827] 1902. *The Naval History of Great Britain From the Declaration of War by France in 1793 to the Accession of George IV.* Vol. 6. London: Macmillan.

Jervis, Robert. 2001. "Was the Cold War a Security Dilemma?" *Journal of Cold War Studies* 3 (1): 36–60.

———. 2003. "Understanding the Bush Doctrine." *Political Science Quarterly* 118 (3): 365–88.

Joaquinet, A. 2002. *Nuestros Piratas*. Madrid: Editorial Noray.

Johnson, James Turner. 2000. "Maintaining the Protection of Noncombatants." *Journal of Peace Research* 37 (4): 421–48.

Johnston, Alastair I. 2001. "Treating International Institutions as Social Environments." *International Studies Quarterly* 45 (4): 487–515.

Julien, C. A. 1970. *History of North Africa*. London: Routledge and Kegan Paul.

Kaldor, Mary. 2003. "American Power: From 'Compellance' to Cosmopolitanism?" *International Affairs* 79 (1): 1–22.

Kantorowicz, Ernst Hartwig. 1970. *The King's Two Bodies: A Study in Mediaeval Political Theology*. Princeton: Princeton University Press.

Katzenstein, Peter J., ed. 1996. *The Culture of National Security: Norms and Identity in World Politics*. New York: Colombia University Press.

Kaufmann, Chaim. 2004. "Threat Inflation and the Failure of the Marketplace of Ideas: The Selling of the Iraq War." *International Security* 29 (1): 5–48.

Kaufmann, Chaim, and Robert Pape. 1999. "Explaining Costly International Moral Action: Britain's Sixty-Year Campaign against the Atlantic Slave Trade." *International Organization* 53 (4): 631–68.

Keal, Paul. 1983. *Unspoken Rules and Superpower Dominance*. New York: St. Martin's Press.

Kelsey, Harry. 1998. *Sir Francis Drake: The Queen's Pirate*. New Haven and London: Yale University Press.

Kennedy, Paul M. 1987. *The Rise and Fall of the Great Powers: Economic Change and Military Conflict from 1500 to 2000*. New York: Random House.

Kennedy, Robert. 1999. "Is One's Terrorist Another's Freedom Fighter? Western and Islamic Approaches to Just War." *Terrorism and Political Violence* 11 (1): 1–21.

Keohane, Robert O. 2002. "The Globalization of Informal Violence, Theories of World Politics, and the 'Liberalism of Fear'." *Dialogue-IO* 1 (1): 29–43.

Khalil, Elias L. 2000. "Symbolic Products: Prestige, Pride and Identity Goods." *Theory and Decision* 49:53–77.

Khanna, Vikramaditya S. 2003. "A Political Theory of Corporate Crime Legislation." Columbia Law School, Center for Law and Economic Studies, Working Paper No. 220.

Kielstra, Paul M. 2000. *The Politics of Slave Trade Suppression in Britain and France, 1814–48: Diplomacy, Morality, and Economics*. London: Macmillan Press.

Kiernan, V. G. 1980. *State and Society in Europe, 1550–1650*. New York: St. Martin's Press.

Klein, Robert A. 1974. *Sovereign Equality among States: The History of an Idea*. Toronto: University of Toronto Press.

Klein, Susan R. 1999. "Redrawing the Criminal-Civil Boundary." *Buffalo Criminal Law Review* 2 (2): 679–722.

Kocs, Stephen A. 1994. "Explaining the Strategic Behavior of States: International Law as System Structure." *International Studies Quarterly* 38:535–56.

Korman, Sharon. 1996. *The Right of Conquest: The Acquisition of Territory by Force in International Law and Practice.* Oxford: Clarendon Press.

Krasner, Stephen D. 1985. *Structural Conflict: The Third World against Global Liberalism.* Berkeley: University of California Press.

———. 1992. "Sovereignty, Regimes, and Human Rights." In *Regime Theory and International Relations,* ed. Volker Rittberger, 139–67. Oxford: Oxford University Press.

———. 1999. *Sovereignty: Organized Hypocrisy.* Princeton: Princeton University Press.

Kratochvil, Friedrich V. 1989. *Rules, Norms, and Decisions: On the Conditions of Practical and Legal Reasoning in International Relations and Domestic Affairs.* Cambridge: Cambridge University Press.

Krawiec, Kimberly D. 2000. "Accounting for Greed: Unraveling the Rogue Trader Mystery." *Oregon Law Review* 79 (2): 301–38.

Kuperman, Alan J. 1999. "The Stinger Missile and U.S. Intervention in Afghanistan." *Political Science Quarterly* 114 (2): 219–63.

Lafeber, Walter. 2002. "The Bush Doctrine." *Diplomatic History* 26 (4): 543–58.

Lake, David A. 2003. "The New Sovereignty in International Relations." *International Studies Review* 5:303–23.

Lake, David, and Patrick M. Morgan, eds. 1997. *Regional Orders: Building Security in a New World.* University Park: Pennsylvania State University Press.

Lana, Enrique Otero. 1999. *Los corsarios espanoles durante la decadencia de los Austrias. El corso espanol del Atlantico peninsular en el siglo XVII (1621–1697).* Madrid: El Ministerio de la Defensa.

Lane, Kris. 1998. *Pillaging the Empire: Piracy in the Americas, 1500–1750.* Armonk, NY, and London: M. E. Sharpe.

Lane-Poole, Stanley. 1890. *The Barbary Corsairs.* London: T. Fisher Unwin.

Langley, Lester D. 1976. *Struggle for the American Mediterranean: United States—European Rivalry in the Gulf-Caribbean, 1776–1904.* Athens: University of Georgia Press.

Laqueur, Walter. 1987. *The Age of Terrorism.* Rev. ed. Boston: Little Brown.

Lasswell, Harold D., and Abraham Kaplan. 1950. *Power and Society: A Framework for Political Inquiry.* New Haven: Yale University Press.

Latham, Andrew. 2002. "Warfare Transformed: A Braudelian Perspective on the 'Revolution in Military Affairs'." *European Journal of International Relations* 8 (2): 231–66.

Launder, I. Bauer. 1921. *La Marina Española en el siglo XVI: Don Francisco de Benavides Cuatralvo de las Galeras de España.* Madrid: Real Academia de la Historia.

Layne, Christopher. 1993. "The Unipolar Illusion: Why New Great Powers Will Arise." *International Security* 17 (4): 5–51.

Le Gall, Michel. 1997. "Forging the Nation-State: Some Issues in the Historiography of Modern Libya." In *The Maghrib in Question: Essays in History and Historiography,* ed. Michel Le Gall and Kenneth Perkins, 95–108. Austin: University of Texas Press.

Lea, Henry Charles. 1907. *A History of the Inquisition of Spain.* Vol. 3. New York: Macmillan.

Lebow, Richard Ned, and Janice Stein. 1994. *We All Lost the Cold War.* Princeton: Princeton University Press.

Lee, Jong-Sup, and Uk Heo. 2001. "The US-South Korea Alliance: Free Riding or Bargaining?" *Asian Survey* 41 (5): 822–45.

Lee, Rensselaer W. 1999. *Smuggling Armageddon: The Nuclear Black Market in the Former Soviet Union and Europe.* New York: St. Martin's Griffin.

Lee-Wiess, Gillian. 2002. "Back from Barbary: Captivity, Redemption and French Identify in the Seventeenth and Eighteenth Century Mediterranean." PhD diss., Department of History, Stanford University.

Levie, Howard S. 1978. *Prisoners of War in International Armed Conflict.* Newport, RI: Naval War College Press.

Levy, Jack S. 1983. *War in the Modern Great Power System.* University Press of Kentucky.

Lewis, Bernard. 1982. *The Muslim Discovery of Europe.* New York: W. W. Norton.

Lewis, M. A. 1960. *A Social History of the Navy, 1793–1815.* London: Allen and Unwin.

Linklater, Andrew. 2002. "Towards a Critical Historical Sociology of Transnational Harm." In *Historical Sociology of International Relations,* ed. Stephen Hobden and John A. Hobson, 162–80. Cambridge: Cambridge University Press.

Lipschutz, Ronnie D. 2000. *After Authority: War, Peace, and Global Politics in the 21st Century.* Albany: State University of New York Press.

Lipson, Charles. 1991. "Why Are Some International Agreements Informal?" *International Organization* 45 (4): 495–538.

Lloyd, C. 1968. *The Navy and the Slave Trade: The Suppression of the African Slave Trade in the Nineteenth Century.* London: Frank Cass.

Lobell, Steven. 2001. "Britain's Paradox: Cooperation or Punishment Prior to World War I." *Review of International Studies* 27 (2): 169–86.

Lovett, A. W. 1986. *Early Habsburg Spain, 1517–1598.* Oxford: Oxford University Press.

Löwenheim, Oded. 2002. "Transnational Organized Crime: The Case against Inflating the Threat." *International Journal* 57 (4): 513–36.

———. 2003. "Do Ourselves Credit and Render a Lasting Service to Mankind: The British Attack on the Algerian Pirates in 1816 as an Armed Humanitarian Intervention." *International Studies Quarterly* 47 (1): 23–48.

Löwenheim, Oded, and Jeremy Paltiel. 2004. "Defining Sovereignty." Paper presented at the annual meeting of the International Studies Association, Montreal, March.

Lundestad, Geir. 1999. " 'Empire by Invitation' in the American Century." *Diplomatic History* 23 (2): 189–217.

———. 2003. *The United States and Western Europe since 1945: From "Empire" by Invitation to Transatlantic Drift.* Oxford: Oxford University Press.

Lupovici, Amir. 2004. "Let's Talk! The Synthesis of Rational Choice Explanations and Normative Explanations: A Case for Deterrence Strategy as a Rational Norm." University of Jerusalem. Manuscript.

Lynch, John. 1992. *The Hispanic World in Crisis and Change, 1598–1700.* Oxford: Blackwell.

Lynch, Tony, and A. J. Walsh. 2000. "The Good Mercenary?" *Journal of Political Philosophy* 8 (2): 133–53.

Lynn, J. A. 1993. "How War Fed War: The Tax of Violence and Contributions during the *Grand Siècle*." *Journal of Modern History* 65 (2): 286–310.

Mack, Andrew. 1975. "Why Big Nations Lose Small Wars: The Politics of Asymmetric Conflicts." *World Politics* 27 (2): 175–200.

Mackay, Ruth. 1999. *The Limits of Royal Authority: Resistance and Obedience in Seventeenth-Century Castile.* Princeton: Princeton University Press.

Malamud-Goti, Jaime. 1992. *Smoke and Mirrors: The Paradox of the Drug Wars.* Boulder, CO: Westview Press.

Malone, Michael, William Miller, and Joseph Robben. 1986. "From Presence to American Intervention." *Survival* 28 (5): 422–30.

Maltby, William S. 1971. *The Black Legend in England: The Development of Anti-Spanish Sentiment, 1558–1660.* Durham, NC: Duke University Press.

Mandel, Robert. 2002. *Armies without States: The Privatization of Security.* Boulder, CO: Lynne Rienner.

Markey, Daniel S. 1999. "Prestige and the Origins of War: Returning to Realism's Roots." *Security Studies* 8 (4): 126–73.

Matar, Nabil. 1997. "Wives, Captives, Husbands, and Turks: The First Women Petitioners in Caroline England." *Explorations in Renaissance Culture* 23:111–28.

———. 1999. *Turks, Moors, and Englishmen in the Age of Discovery.* New York: Columbia University Press.

———. 2001. "Introduction: England and Mediterranean Captivity, 1577–1704." In *Piracy, Slavery, and Redemption: Barbary Captivity Narratives from Early Modern England,* ed. Daniel J. Vitkus, 1–52. New York: Columbia University Press.

Mathieson, William L. 1929. *Great Britain and the Slave Trade, 1839–1865.* London: Longman.

McAdams, Richard. 2000. "An Attitudinal Theory of Expressive Law." *Oregon Law Review* 79 (2): 339–90.

McDermott, Daniel. 2001. "The Permissibility of Punishment." *Law and Philosophy* 20:403–32.

———. 2002. "Debts to Society." *Journal of Political Philosophy* 10 (4): 439–64.

Mearsheimer, John. 1990. "Why We Will Soon Miss the Cold War." *Atlantic Monthly,* August, 35–50.

———. 2001. *The Tragedy of Great Power Politics.* New York: W. W. Norton.

Mearsheimer, John, and Stephen Walt. 2003. "An Unnecessary War." *Foreign Policy* 134:50–60.

Mendelsohn, Barak. 2005. "Sovereignty under Attack: The International Society Meets the Al Qaeda Network." *Review of International Studies* 31:45–68.

Mercer, Jonathan. 1997. "Reputation and Rational Deterrence Theory." *Security Studies* 7 (1): 100–113.

————. 2005. "Rationality and Psychology in International Studies." *International Organization* 59 (1): 77–106.

Merriman, Roger Bigelow. 1962. *The Rise of the Spanish Empire in the Old World and in the New.* Vol. 3. New York: Cooper Square.

Michaelsen, Scott, and Scott C. Shershow. 2004. "Beyond and Before the Law at Guanta'namo." *Peace Review* 16 (3): 293–303.

Migdal, Joel S. 1988. *Strong Societies and Weak States: State-Society Relations and State Capabilities in the Third World.* Princeton: Princeton University Press.

Mill, John Stuart. 1955. *On Liberty.* Chicago: H. Regnery.

Miller, Benjamin. 1995. *When Opponents Cooperate: Great Power Conflict and Cooperation in World Politics.* Ann Arbor: University of Michigan Press.

————. 1998. "The Logic of US Intervention in the Post Cold War Era." *Contemporary Security Policy* 19 (3): 71–109.

Miller, Benjamin, and Korina Kagan. 1997. "The Great Powers and Regional Conflicts: Eastern Europe and the Balkans from the Post-Napoleonic Era to the Post–Cold War Era." *International Studies Quarterly* 41:51–85.

Milner, Helen. 1993. "The Assumption of Anarchy in International Relations Theory: A Critique." In *Neorealism and Neoliberalism: The Contemporary Debate,* ed. David A. Baldwin, 143–69. New York: Columbia University Press.

Minow, Martha. 1998. *Between Vengeance and Forgiveness: Facing History after Genocide and Mass Violence.* Boston: Beacon Press.

Mitchell, B. R. 1988. *British Historical Statistics.* Cambridge: Cambridge University Press.

Mitzen, Jennifer. 2004. "Ontological Security in World Politics and Implications for the Study of European Security." Paper prepared for CIDEL Workshop, Oslo, October 22–23. Available at http://www.arena.uio.no/cidel/Work shopOsloSecurity/Mitzen.pdf.

Molloy, Charles. 1682. *De Jure Maritimo et Navali: Or, A Treatise of Affairs Maritime and of Commerce.* London: Printed for John Bellinger and John Walthoe.

Moravcsik, Andrew. 1997. "Taking Preferences Seriously: A Liberal Theory of International Politics." *International Organization* 51 (4): 513–53.

Morgan, J. 1731. *A Complete History of Algiers . . . From the Earliest Times.* London: J. Bettenham.

Mori, Jennifer. 2000. *Britain in the Age of the French Revolution.* London: Longman.

Morrow, James D. 2001. "The Institutional Features of the Prisoners of War Treaties." *International Organization* 55 (4): 971–91.

Mueller, John E. 1989. *Retreat from Doomsday: The Obsolescence of Major War.* New York: Basic Books.

————. 2004. *The Remnants of War.* Ithaca: Cornell University Press.

Mullins, Kerry, and Aaron Wildavsky. 1992. "The Procedural Presidency of George Bush." *Political Science Quarterly* 107 (1): 31–62.

Murray, David R. 1980. *Odious Commerce: Britain, Spain, and the Abolition of the Cuban Slave Trade.* Cambridge: Cambridge University Press.

Nadal, Gonçal López. 2001. "Corsairing as a Commercial System: The Edges of Legitimate Trade." In *Bandits at Sea: A Pirates Reader,* ed. C. R. Pennel, 125–36. New York: New York University Press.

———. 2004. "El Corsarismo en el Mediterráneo." Paper presented at the annual meeting of Maritime History, Institute of Naval History and Culture, Madrid, March 23–25.

Nadelmann, Ethan A. 1990. "Global Prohibition Regimes: The Evolution of Norms in International Society." *International Organization* 44 (4): 479–526.

National Commission on the Terrorist Attacks Upon the United States. 2004. *The 9/11 Commission Report.* Washington, DC: Government Printing Office.

Nau, Henry R. 2001. "Why 'The Rise and Fall of the Great Powers' Was Wrong." *Review of International Studies* 27:579–92.

Nelson, Bernard H. 1942. "The Slave Trade as a Factor in British Foreign Policy, 1815–1862." *Journal of Negro History* 27 (2): 192–209.

Nicholson, Harold. 1970. *The Congress of Vienna: A Study in Allied Unity: 1812–1822.* London: Methuen.

North, Douglass. 1991. "Institutions." *Journal of Economic Perspectives* 5 (1): 97–112.

Nussbaum, Arthur. 1954. *A Concise History of the Law of Nations.* New York: Macmillan.

Nye, Joseph S. 1987. "Nuclear Learning and US-Soviet Security Regimes." *International Organization* 41 (3): 371–402.

———. 2002. *The Paradox of American Power: Why the World's Only Superpower Can't Get It Alone.* Oxford: Oxford University Press.

O'Loughlin, John, Gearóid Ó Tuathail, and Vladimir Kolossov. 2004. "A 'Risky Westward Turn'? Putin's 9-11 Script and Ordinary Russians." *Europe-Asia Studies* 56 (1): 3–34.

Olson, Mancur, and Richard Zeckhauser. 1966. "An Economic Theory of Alliances." *Review of Economics and Statistics* 48 (3): 266–79.

O'Neill, Barry. 1999. *Honor, Symbols, and War.* Ann Arbor: University of Michigan Press.

Onuf, Nicholas, and Frank F. Klink. 1989. "Anarchy, Authority, Rule." *International Studies Quarterly* 33:149–73.

Orviska, Marta, and John Hudson. 2003. "Tax Evasions, Civic Duty, and the Law Abiding Citizen." *European Journal of Political Economy* 19 (1): 83–102.

Osgood, Robert E., and Robert W. Tucker. 1967. *Force, Order, and Justice.* Baltimore: Johns Hopkins University Press.

Osiander, Andreas. 1994. *The States System of Europe, 1640–1990: Peacemaking and the Conditions of International Stability.* Oxford: Clarendon Press.

———. 2001. "Sovereignty, International Relations, and the Westphalian Myth." *International Organization* 55 (2): 251–87.

Osler, Edward. 1835. *The Life of Admiral Viscount Exmouth.* London: Smith, Elder.

Parachini, John V. 2001. "Comparing Motives and Outcomes of Mass Casualty Terrorism Involving Conventional and Unconventional Weapons." *Studies in Conflict and Terrorism* 24 (5): 389–406.

Parker, Geoffrey. 1972. *The Army of Flanders and the Spanish Road, 1567–1659:*

The Logistics of Spanish Victory and Defeat in the Low Countries' Wars. Cambridge: Cambridge University Press.

———. 1988. *The Geopolitics of Domination.* London: Routledge.

———. 1994. "The Making of Strategy in Habsburg Spain: Philip II's 'Bid for Mastery,' 1556–1598." In *The Making of Strategy: Rulers, States and War,* ed. Murray Williamson, Macgregor Knox, and Alvin Bernstein, 115–50. Cambridge: Cambridge University Press.

———. 1997. "The War for Bohemia." In *The Thirty Years War,* 2d ed., ed. G. Parker, 43–55. London: Routledge.

———. 1998. *The Grand Strategy of Philip II.* New Haven: Yale University Press.

———. 2000. *The World Is Not Enough: The Imperial Vision of Philip II of Spain.* Waco, TX: Baylor University Press.

Parkinson, C. Northcote. 1934. *Edward Pellew: Viscount Exmouth, Admiral of the Red.* London: Methuen.

Parry, J. H. 1966. *The Spanish Seaborne Empire.* London: Hutchinson.

Passas, Nikos. 2001. "Globalization and Transnational Crime: Effects of Criminogenic Asymmetries." In *Combating Transnational Crime: Concepts, Activities and Responses,* ed. Phil Williams and Dimitri Vlassis, 22–56. London: Frank Cass.

Paternoster, Raymond, and Sally Simpson. 1996. "Sanction Threats and Appeals to Morality: Testing a Rational Choice Model of Corporate Crime." *Law and Society Review* 30 (3): 549–83.

Patterson, Orlando. 1982. *Slavery and Social Death: A Comparative Study.* Cambridge, MA: Harvard University Press.

Payne, Stanley G. 1973. *A History of Spain and Portugal.* Vol. 1. Madison: University of Wisconsin Press.

Pedersen, Vibeke Schou. 2003. "In Search of Monsters to Destroy? The Liberal American Security Paradox and a Republican Way Out." *International Relations* 17 (2): 213–32.

Pennell, C. R. 1994. "The Geography of Piracy: Northern Morocco in the Mid-Nineteenth Century." *Journal of Historical Geography* 20 (3): 272–82.

Perkins, R., and K. J. D. Douglas-Morris. 1982. *Gunfire in Barbary: Admiral Lord Exmouth's Battle with the Corsairs of Algiers in 1816.* Homewell, UK: Kenneth Mason.

Philpott, Daniel. 2001. *Revolutions in Sovereignty: How Ideas Shaped Modern International Relations.* Princeton: Princeton University Press.

Pike, Ruth. 1983. *Penal Servitude in Early Modern Spain.* Madison: University of Wisconsin Press.

Playfair, Robert L. 1884. *The Scourge of Christendom: Annals of the British Relations with Algiers Prior to the French Conquest.* London: Smith, Elder.

Pradt, M. 1815. *Du Congres de Vienne.* Paris: Deterville.

Press-Barnathan, Galia. 2004. "The War against Iraq and International Order: From Bull to Bush." *International Studies Review* 6 (2): 195–212.

Preto, P. 2001. "I Turchi fra Otranto (1489) e Tunisi (1535): la lotta per il controllo del Mediterraneo Occidentale." In *De la unión de coronas al imperio de Carlos V,* ed. C. E. Belenguer, 3:473–84. Madrid: Sociedad Estatal Para la Commemoracion de los.

Price, Richard. 1997. *The Chemical Weapons Taboo*. Ithaca: Cornell University Press.

Radosh, Ronald, and Joyce Milton. 1997. *The Rosenberg File*. 2d ed. New Haven: Yale University Press.

Ranstorp, Magnus. 1997. *Hizb'allah in Lebanon: The Politics of the Western Hostage Crisis*. New York: St. Martin's Press.

———. 1998. "Interpreting the Broader Context and Meaning of Bin Laden's *Fatwa*." *Studies in Conflict and Terrorism* 21 (4): 321–30.

Rawls, John. 1971. *A Theory of Justice*. Cambridge, MA: Belknap Press of Harvard University Press.

Raz, J. 1984. "On the Nature of Rights." *Mind* 93 (370): 194–214.

Reeve, Simon. 1999. *The New Jackals: Ramzi Yousef, Osama bin Laden, and the Future of Terror*. Boston: Northeastern University Press.

Reich, Jerome. 1968. "The Slave Trade at the Congress of Vienna—A Study in English Public Opinion." *Journal of Negro History* 53 (2): 129–43.

Reus-Smit, Christian. 1999. *The Moral Purpose of the State: Culture, Social Identity, and Institutional Rationality in International Relations*. Princeton: Princeton University Press.

Reuveny, Rafael, and Aseem Prakash. 1999. "The Afghanistan War and the Breakdown of the Soviet Union." *Review of International Studies* 25:693–708.

Ringmar, Eric. 2002. "The Recognition Game: Soviet Russia against the West." *Cooperation and Conflict* 37 (2): 115–36.

Ritchie, Robert C. 1997. "Government Measures against Piracy and Privateering in the Atlantic Area, 1750–1850." In *Pirates and Privateers: New Perspectives on the War on Trade in the Eighteen and Nineteenth Centuries,* ed. D. Starkey, E. S. Van Eyck Van Heslinga, and J. A. De Moor, 10–28. Exeter: University of Exeter Press.

Roberts, Adam. 1994. "The Laws of War in the 1990–91 Gulf Conflict." *International Security* 18 (3): 134–81.

Rodriguez-Salgado, M. J. 1988. *The Changing Face of Empire: Charles V, Philip II, and Habsburg Authority, 1551–1559*. Cambridge: Cambridge University Press.

Rosecrance, Richard. 1986. *The Rise of the Trading State: Commerce and Conquest in the Modern World*. New York: Basic Books.

———. 1999. *The Rise of the Virtual State: Wealth and Power in the Coming Century*. New York: Basic Books.

Rubin, Alfred P. 1998. *The Law of Piracy*. 2d ed. Irvington-on-Hudson, NY: Transnational.

Ruff, Julius R. 2001. *Violence in Early Modern Europe, 1500–1800*. Cambridge: Cambridge University Press.

Ruggie, John G. 1993. "Territoriality and Beyond: Problematizing Modernity in International Relations." *International Organization* 47 (1): 139–74.

———. 1998. "What Makes the World Hang Together? Neo-Utilitarianism and the Social Constructivist Challenge." *International Organization* 52 (4): 855–85.

Rule, John C. 1999. "The Enduring Rivalry of France and Spain ca. 1462–1700."

In *Great Power Rivalries,* ed. William R. Thompson, 31–59. Columbia: University of South Carolina Press.

Ryden, D. B. 2000. "Does Decline Make Sense? The West Indian Economy and the Abolition of the British Slave Trade." *Journal of Interdisciplinary History* 31 (3): 347–74.

Saad-Ghorayeb, Amal. 2002. *Hizbu'llah: Politics and Religion.* London: Pluto Press.

Satow, Ernest. 1923. "Peacemaking, Old and New." *Cambridge Historical Journal* 1 (1): 23–60.

Schabas, William. 2002. *The Abolition of the Death Penalty in International Law.* 3d ed. Cambridge: Cambridge University Press.

Schmitt, Carl. 2004. "Theory of the Partisan: Intermediate Commentary on the Concept of the Political." *Telos* 27:11–79.

Schroeder, Paul W. 1992. "Did the Vienna Settlement Rest on a Balance of Power?" *American Historical Review* 97 (3): 683–706.

———. 1994. *The Transformation of European Politics, 1763–1848.* Oxford: Clarendon Press.

Schweller, Randall. 1994. "Bandwagoning for Profit: Bringing the Revisionist State Back In." *International Security* 19 (1): 72–108.

Senior, C. M. 1976. *A Nation of Pirates: English Piracy in Its Heyday.* Newton Abbot: Charles and David.

Shaler, William. 1823. *Sketches of Algiers, Political, Historical, and Civil, containing an account of the Geography, Population, Government, Revenues, Commerce, Agriculture, Arts, Civil Institutions and Recent Political History of the Country.* Boston: Cummings, Hilliard.

Shaw, Geoff, and David Spencer. 2003. "Fighting in Afghanistan: Lessons from the Soviet Intervention, 1979–89." *Defense and Security Analysis* 19 (2): 177–88.

Sheptycki, James. 2003. "Against Transnational Organized Crime." In *Critical Reflections on Transnational Organized Crime, Money Laundering, and Corruption,* ed. Margaret Beare, 120–44. Toronto: University of Toronto Press.

Sherry, Frank. 1986. *Raiders and Rebels: The Golden Age of Piracy.* New York: Hearst Marine Books.

Simon, Jeffrey. 1994. *The Terrorist Trap: America's Experience with Terrorism.* Indianapolis: Indiana University Press.

Simpson, Gerry. 2004. *Great Powers and Outlaw States: Unequal Sovereigns in the International Legal Order.* Cambridge: Cambridge University Press.

Singer, P. W. 2002. "Corporate Warriors: The Rise of the Privatized Military Industry and Its Ramifications for International Security." *International Security* 26 (3): 186–220.

Sklair, Leslie. 2002. "The Transnational Capitalist Class and Global Politics: Deconstructing the Corporate-State Connection." *International Political Science Review* 23 (2): 159–74.

Smith, Steve. 2004. "Singing Our World into Existence: International Relations Theory and September 11. Presidential Address to the International Studies Association, February 27, 2003, Portland, OR." *International Studies Quarterly* 48:499–515.

Smith, Tony. 2000. "New Bottles for New Wine: A Pericentric Framework for the Study of the Cold War." *Diplomatic History* 24 (4): 567–91.

Snyder, Jack. 2002. "Anarchy and Culture: Insights from the Anthropology of War." *International Organization* 56 (1): 7–45.

Sola, Emilio, and José F. de la Peña. 1996. *Cervantes y la Berbería*. Madrid: Fondo de Cultura Económica.

Sorel, Albert. 1964. *Europe under the Old Regime*. New York: Harper Torchbooks.

Sorel, Georges. 1961. *Reflections on Violence*. Trans. T. E. Hulme and J. Roth. London: Macmillan.

Spiel, Hilde, ed. 1965. *The Congress of Vienna: An Eyewitness Account*. Philadelphia: Chilton.

Spiro, Herbert J. 1958. "Authority, Values, and Policy." In *Authority,* ed. C. J. Friedrich, 49–57. Cambridge, MA: Harvard University Press.

Spruyt, Hendrik. 1994. *The Sovereign State and Its Competitors: An Analysis of Systems Change*. Princeton: Princeton University Press.

Stanik, Joseph T. 2003. *El Dorado Canyon: Reagan's Undeclared War With Qaddafi*. Annapolis, MD: Naval Institute Press.

Starkey, D., E. S. Van Eyck Van Heslinga, and J. A. De Moor, eds. 1997. *Pirates and Privateers: New Perspectives on the War on Trade in the Eighteenth and Nineteenth Centuries*. Exeter: University of Exeter Press.

Steele, Brent J. 2005. "Ontological Security and the Power of Self-Identity: British Neutrality and the American Civil War." *Review of International Studies,* 31 (3): 519–40.

Steinberg, Blema S. 1991. "Shame and Humiliation in the Cuban Missile Crisis: A Psychoanalytic Perspective." *Political Psychology* 12 (4): 653–90.

Stern, Jessica. 1999. *The Ultimate Terrorists*. London: Harvard University Press.

———. 2003. "The Protean Enemy." *Foreign Affairs* 82 (4): 27–40.

Storrs, Christopher. 1998. "The Army of Lombardy and the Resilience of Spanish Power in Italy in the Reign of Carlos II (1665–1700) (Part II)." *War in History* 5 (1): 1–22.

Stradling, Robert. 1992. *The Armada of Flanders: Spanish Maritime Policy and European War, 1568–1668*. Cambridge: Cambridge University Press.

Sturdy, David J. 2002. *Fractured Europe: 1600–1721*. Oxford: Blackwell.

Suri, Jeremi. 2003. *Power and Protest: Global Revolution and the Rise of Détente*. Cambridge, MA: Harvard University Press.

Swart, K. W. 1971. "The Black Legend during the Eighty Years War." In *Britain and the Netherlands: Metropolis, Dominion and Province,* ed. J. S. Bromley and E. H. Kossmann. The Hague: Nijhoff.

Tallett, Frank. 1992. *War and Society in Early Modern Europe, 1495–1715*. London: Routledge.

Tannenwald, Nina. 1999. "The Nuclear Taboo: The United States and the Normative Basis of Nuclear Non-Use." *International Organization* 53 (3): 433–68.

———. 2005. "Stigmatizing the Bomb: Origins of the Nuclear Taboo." *International Security* 29 (4): 5–49.

Taylor, Bruce. 1997. "The Enemy Within and Without: An Anatomy of Fear on the

Spanish Mediterranean Littoral." In *Fear in Early Modern Society,* ed. W. G. Naphy and P. Roberts, 78–99. Manchester: Manchester University Press.

Temperley, Howard. 1998. "Abolition and Anti-Slavery: Britain." In *A Historical Guide to World Slavery,* ed. S. Drescher and S. L. Engerman, 10–15. Oxford: Oxford University Press.

Temprano, Emilio. 1989. *El Mar Maldito: Cautivos y Corsarios En El Siglo De Oro.* Madrid: Mondadori.

Tenenti, Alberto. 1967. *Piracy and the Decline of Venice, 1580–1615.* Berkeley and Los Angeles: University of California Press.

Teschke, Benno. 2002. "Theorizing the Westphalian System of States: International Relations from Absolutism to Capitalism." *European Journal of International Relations* 8 (1): 5–48.

Thielemann, Eiko R. 2001. "'Balance of Efforts' across Borders: From Burden-Shifting to Burden-Sharing in the European Union?" Paper presented at the annual meeting of the International Studies Association, Chicago, February 21–24.

Thompson, I. A. A. 1976. *War and Government in Habsburg Spain, 1560–1620.* London: University of London Athlone Press.

Thomson, Ann. 1987. *Barbary and Enlightenment: European Attitudes towards the Maghreb in the 18th Century.* Leiden: E. J. Brill.

Thomson, Janice E. 1994. *Mercenaries, Pirates, and Sovereigns: State-Building and Extraterritorial Violence in Early Modern Europe.* Princeton: Princeton University Press.

———. 1995. "State Sovereignty in International Relations: Bridging the Gap between Theory and Empirical Research." *International Studies Quarterly* 39 (2): 213–33.

Thucydides. 1943. *The History of the Peloponnesian War.* Vol. 89. London: Oxford University Press.

Tilly, Charles. 1990. *Coercion, Capital, and European States, AD 990–1990.* Oxford: Basil Blackwell.

Trevaskes, Susan. 2003. "Public Sentencing Rallies in China: The Symbolizing of Punishment and Justice in a Socialist State." *Crime, Law, and Social Change* 39:359–82.

Trevor-Roper, H. R. 1971. "Spain and Europe, 1598–1621." In *The New Cambridge Modern History.* Vol. 4, *The Decline of Spain and the Thirty Years War, 1609–1648/59,* ed. J. P. Copper, 260–82. Cambridge: Cambridge University Press.

Tuck, Richard. 1998. *The Rights of War and Peace: Political Thought and International Order from Grotius to Kant.* Oxford: Oxford University Press.

Tucker, Robert. 1960. *The Just War: A Study in Contemporary American Doctrine.* Baltimore: Johns Hopkins University Press.

U.S. Congress. 1832. *American State Papers.* 7th Cong., 1st sess. Vol. 2, *Foreign Relations.* Washington, DC: Gales and Seaton.

U.S. Congress. 2002. U.S. House Permanent Select Committee on Intelligence and the U.S. Senate Select Committee on Intelligence. *Report of the Joint Inquiry into the Terrorist Attacks of September 11, 2001.* 107th Cong., 2d sess. H. Rept. No. 107-792. December.

U.S. Department of State. 1986. *Patterns of Global Terrorism*. Washington, DC.

van Royen, P. C. 1990. "The First Phase of the Dutch *Straatvaart* (1591–1605): Fact and Fiction." *International Journal of Maritime History* 2 (2): 69–102.

Vane, Charles, ed. 1851. *Memoirs and Correspondence of Viscount Castlereagh, Second Marquess of Londonderry*. Vol. 11. London: H. Colburn.

Veale, F. J. P. 1993. *Advance to Barbarism: The Development of Total Warfare from Sarajevo to Hiroshima*. London: Institute for Historical Review.

Volkov, Vadim. 2002. *Violent Entrepreneurs: The Use of Force in the Making of Russian Capitalism*. Ithaca: Cornell University Press.

Walt, Stephen S. 1989. "The Renaissance of Security Studies." *International Studies Quarterly* 35:211–39.

Waltz, Kenneth. 1979. *Theory of International Politics*. Reading, MA: Addison Wesley.

Walvin, James. 1999. *The Slave Trade*. London: Sutton.

Walzer, Michael. 1984. *Spheres of Justice: A Defense of Pluralism and Equality*. New York: Basic Books.

Wang, Hongying, and James N. Rosenau. 2001. "Transparency International and Corruption as an Issue of Global Governance." *Global Governance* 7 (1): 25–49.

Ward, A. W., and G. P. Gooch, eds. 1922. *The Cambridge History of British Foreign Policy, 1783–1919*. Vol. 1. Cambridge: Cambridge University Press.

Ward, Thomas. 2000. "Norms and Security: The Case of International Assassinations." *International Security* 25 (1): 105–33.

Watkin, Kenneth. 2004. "Controlling the Use of Force: A Role for Human Rights in Contemporary Armed Conflict." *American Journal of International Law* 98 (1): 1–34.

Waxman, Matthew C. 1997. "Strategic Terror: Philip II and Sixteenth-Century Warfare." *War in History* 4 (3): 339–47.

Weber, Max. 1966. *The Sociology of Religion*. London: Methuen.

———. 1968. *On Charisma and Institution Building: Selected Papers*. Chicago: University of Chicago Press.

———. 1978. *Economy and Society*. Berkeley: University of California Press.

Weber, Wolfang. 1995. "What a Ruler Should Not Do: Theoretical Limits of Royal Power in European Theories of Absolutism, 1500–1700." *Sixteenth Century Journal* 26 (4): 897–915.

Webster, C. K. 1963. *The Foreign Policy of Castlereagh, 1815–22*. London: Bell.

———, ed. 1921. *British Diplomacy, 1813–1815: Select Documents Dealing with the Reconstruction of Europe*. London: Bell.

Weiner, Sharon K. 2002. "Preventing Nuclear Entrepreneurship in Russia's Nuclear Cities." *International Security* 27 (2): 126–58.

Welch, David. 1993. *Justice and the Genesis of War*. Cambridge: Cambridge University Press.

Weldes, Jutta. 1999. *Constructing National Interests: The United States and the Cuban Missile Crisis*. Minneapolis: University of Minnesota Press.

Wendt, Alexander. 1992. "Anarchy Is What States Make of It: The Social Construction of Power Politics." *International Organization* 46 (2): 391–425.

———. 1999. *Social Theory of International Politics*. Cambridge: Cambridge University Press.

———. 2003. "Why a World State Is Inevitable." *European Journal of International Relations* 9 (4): 491–542.

———. 2004. "The State as Person in International Theory." *Review of International Studies* 30:289–316.

Wendt, Alexander, and Daniel Friedheim. 1996. "Hierarchy under Anarchy: Informal Empire and the East German State." In *State Sovereignty as a Social Construct*, ed. T. J. Biersteker and C. Weber, 240–77. Cambridge: Cambridge University Press.

Wenzel, Michael. 2000. "Justice and Identity: The Significance of Inclusion for Perception of Entitlement and the Justice Motive." *Personality and Social Psychology Bulletin* 26 (2): 157–76.

Wheeler, Nicholas J., and Timothy Dune. 1996. "Hedley Bull's Pluralism of the Intellect and Solidarism of the Will." *International Affairs* 72 (1): 91–107.

Wight, Martin. 1977. *System of States*. Leicester: Leicester University Press.

Williams, Phil. 2001. "Transnational Criminal Networks." In *Networks and Netwars: The Future of Terror, Crime, and Militancy,* ed. J. Arquila and D. Ronfeldt, 61–97. Santa Monica, CA: RAND.

———. 2002. "Transnational Organized Crime and the State." In *The Emergence of Private Authority in Global Governance,* ed. B. Hall and T. Biersteker, 161–82. Cambridge: Cambridge University Press.

Williamson, Jeffrey G. 1984. "Why Was British Growth So Slow during the Industrial Revolution?" *Journal of Economic History* 44 (3): 687–712.

Wolf, John B. 1979. *The Barbary Coast: Algiers under the Turks, 1500 to 1830*. New York: W. W. Norton.

Wolfers, Arnold. 1962. *Discord and Collaboration: Essays on International Politics*. Baltimore: Johns Hopkins University Press.

Woodward, Bob. 2002. *Bush at War*. New York: Simon and Schuster.

Woodward, G. Thomas. 2004. "The Costs of State-Sponsored Terrorism: The Example of the Barbary Pirates." *National Tax Journal* 37 (3): 599–612.

Zacher, Mark W. 2001. "The Territorial Integrity Norm: International Boundaries and the Use of Force." *International Organization* 55 (2): 215–50.

Zanini, Michele, and Sean J. A. Edwards. 2001. "The Networking of Terror in the Information Age." In *Networks and Netwars: The Future of Terror, Crime, and Militancy,* ed. John Arquilla and David Ronfeldt, 29–60. Santa Monica, CA: RAND.

Zarate, Juan Carlos. 1998. "The Emergence of a New Dog of War: Private International Security Companies, International Law and the New World Disorder." *Stanford Journal of International Law* 34:75–162.

Žižek, Slavoj. 2002. "Welcome to the Desert of the Real!" *South Atlantic Quarterly* 101 (2): 385–91.

Index

- Great Powers
  - Phillipines
  - Consu
  - Endogeneity
  - AI qreck
    - Parasi Predator
    - Pre-git
      Parasite
    - Predator

- Inaction
  - Rwanda
  - Uganda
  - Somalia
  - Drug Cartels
  - Voldemort
  - Human Trafficking